Foreign Affairs Litigation in United States Courts

Sokol Colloquium

VOLUME 6

The titles published in this series are listed at brill.com/soco

Foreign Affairs Litigation in United States Courts

Edited by

John Norton Moore

MARTINUS
NIJHOFF
PUBLISHERS

LEIDEN • BOSTON
2013

Library of Congress Cataloging-in-Publication Data

Foreign affairs litigation in United States courts / edited by John Norton Moore.
p. cm. — (Sokol Colloquium ; Volume 6)
ISBN 978-90-04-25727-6 (hardback : alk. paper) — ISBN 978-90-04-25728-3 (e-book) 1. United States—Foreign relations—Law and legislation. 2. Immunities of foreign states—United States. 3. Jurisdiction—United States. 4. Aliens—United States. I. Moore, John Norton, 1937– editor of compilation.

KF4651.F675 2013
342.73'0412—dc23

2013027419

This publication has been typeset in the multilingual "Brill" typeface. With over 5,100 characters covering Latin, IPA, Greek, and Cyrillic, this typeface is especially suitable for use in the humanities. For more information, please see www.brill.com/brill-typeface.

ISSN 1873-6572
ISBN 978-90-04-25727-6 (hardback)
ISBN 978-90-04-25728-3 (e-book)

This book is printed on acid-free paper.

FSC www.fsc.org MIX Paper from responsible sources FSC® C109576

Printed by Printforce, the Netherlands

CONTENTS

FOREWORD

Paul G. Mahoney[1]

I am pleased to open the 25th Sokol Colloquium on Private International Law. A 25th anniversary is of course an auspicious occasion and the University of Virginia School of Law is proud of the Sokol Colloquium's contributions to our intellectual life. The colloquium is part of the Gustave Sokol Program on Private International Law, established in 1976 under a grant from the Gustave Sokol Fund. Colloquia bring together distinguished scholars, government officials and practioners from the United States and abroad to discuss a specific topic of private international law. This year, as in past years, the colloquium is co-sponsored by the John Bassett Moore Society of International Law and the *Virginia Journal of International Law.*

Virginia prides itself on a rich international law tradition that encompasses our founder Thomas Jefferson, Woodrow Wilson, Hardy Dillard, a former dean of this law school who served on the International Court of Justice, and the many State Department Counselors on International Law who have come from our faculty. The Sokol Colloquium is a proud part of this international law tradition.

The topic of this year's Sokol Colloquium is "Foreign Affairs Litigation in United States Courts."

Central to the notion of the rule of law is the citizen's ability to vindicate rights through a system of litigation. Law functions as a core check on the arbitrary exercise of power both in international and national life.

Yet foreign affairs litigation in national courts is more controversial than litigation raising similarly complex issues but lacking an international component. The plaintiffs or defendants in such actions are often sovereign nations or present or former government officials, raising difficult issues of sovereign immunity, the act of state doctrine, cross-border enforcement of judgments, and the relative

---

[1] Paul G. Mahoney is the Dean of the School of Law at the University of Virginia. The 25th Sokol Colloquium took place on April 19, 2012.

authority of the judicial and executive branches with respect to foreign relations, to name a few.

This Colloquium will address many of these issues, focused on those with particular contemporary relevance. Panel I will focus on Foreign Sovereign Immunity and the Foreign Sovereign Immunities Act, particularly as that Act was amended in the 2008 Defense Authorization Act. It will also address the immunities of foreign officials and discuss a recent decision of the International Court of Justice urging a limitation of exceptions to sovereign immunities in suits in national courts.

We are particularly honored to have a keynote address from Chief Judge Royce Lamberth of the Federal District Court for the District of Columbia, the most active District Court for foreign affairs litigation. Judge Lamberth will speak on "The Role of the Courts in Foreign Affairs," a topic on which he is as experienced and thoughtful as anyone in the nation.

The second panel will focus on human rights litigation in national courts, particularly contemporary issues concerning the Alien Tort Claims Act. Of particular and continuing concern is the question of the parameters of corporate liability under the Alien Tort Claims Act.

Next, we will address an issue of great interest but less hard law; that of "Foreign Affairs Takings Actions in The Court of Federal Claims." A core question here is whether, when an otherwise judicially cognizable action is extinguished through government exercise of the foreign affairs power, such as a negotiated claims settlement agreement, or even a bilateral treaty barring suit in United States courts, whether, and under what circumstances, a takings actions will lie in the Court of Federal Claims.

Finally, first in a keynote address by Chairman Timothy Feighery of the Foreign Claims Settlement Commission, and then in additional papers, we will review that Commission's role and jurisprudence.

In addition to our keynote speakers we are privileged to have the participation of top national scholars, practitioners, and government officials dealing with these issues. On behalf of the Law School and the Sokol Colloquium I thank each of you for giving your time to this important discussion.

INTRODUCTION

John Norton Moore[1]

Foreign Affairs Litigation in United States Courts is increasingly important for the international law practitioner. This book is an indispensable resource for those engaged in such litigation. It examines in turn the topics of foreign sovereign immunity and the FSIA; human rights litigation; foreign affairs takings actions in the Court of Federal Claims; the Foreign Claims Settlement Commission; and the Hague Convention on Choice of Court Agreements.

Under each heading, the chapters are prepared by some of the nation's top authorities in foreign affairs litigation. The opening essay by Judge Royce C. Lamberth on "The Role of Courts in Foreign Affairs" is by itself worth the price of the book. But the book then goes on to discuss important issues and trends in foreign affairs litigation including the use of the FSIA against state sponsors of terror, adjudicating acts of state, the recent International Court of Justice decision pushing back against the expansion of suits against sovereign states in national courts, and recent issues in the Alien Tort Claims Act, and acts of state litigation. Of particular importance, this volume is also one of the few sources to examine foreign affairs takings actions in the Court of Federal Claims, and to discuss the work of the Foreign Claims Settlement Commission. The book concludes with a rare review of the Hague Convention on Choice of Court Agreements.

Litigation is an important component of the rule of law. In turn, the rule of law is a core of good governance. We know today, far better than earlier generations, of the central role played by the rule of law in facilitating human rights,

[1] John Norton Moore is the Walter L. Brown Professor of Law at the University of Virginia School of Law, Director of the Center for Oceans Law and Policy, and Director of the Center for National Security Law at Virginia. Formerly he served as Counselor on International Law to the Department of State, United States Ambassador to the United Nations Conference on the Law of the Sea, and Chairman of the Board of the United States Institute of Peace. John Norton Moore was one of the drafters of the original Foreign Sovereign Immunities Act during his time as Counselor on International Law.

reducing violent conflict, enhancing economic growth, and supporting a host of other human aspirations. The rule of law, in all its dimensions of free elections, separation of powers, stable contract and property rights, fairness in criminal process, and more, serves as a crucial check on power. This function of law, as a core check on power, is as true in international life as it is in national life. One might assume, then, that foreign affairs litigation in national courts would be no more remarkable than litigation about a host of complex national law matters. For a variety of reasons, however, that is not the case. Most centrally, as Dean Mahoney has stated in his opening remarks, in one way or another the plaintiffs or defendants in many such actions are sovereign nations or present or former government officials—raising issues of state immunities, act of state, enforcement of judgments, the relations between the courts and executive exercise of the foreign relations power, and a host of other characteristic features of litigation involving foreign relations. As such, there has been an ongoing struggle to define the appropriate balance in application of what under national law are frequently straight-forward tort, contract and property type judicial actions to litigation settings charged with foreign affairs implications.

The Twenty-Fifth Sokol Colloquium (2012) addressed many of these issues, focusing on those with particular contemporary relevance. This proceedings volume documents the presentations and is organized around the panels of the Colloquium. The first chapter addresses Foreign Sovereign Immunity and the Foreign Sovereign Immunities Act, particularly as that Act was amended in the 2008 Defense Authorization Act. It also looks at the question of what are the immunities of foreign officials now that the Supreme Court has surprised the bar by ruling that foreign officials are not covered by the Foreign Sovereign Immunities Act. Further, it looks at a recent decision of the International Court of Justice considering the international law parameters of sovereign immunity. Sadly, the International Court has embraced the familiar old thinking of "the King can do no wrong" as opposed to more progressive thought about the rule of law.

We are honored to include the keynote address of the Honorable Chief Judge Royce C. Lamberth of the Federal District Court for the District of Columbia. This Court is among the most important in foreign affairs litigation in the United States. One of the most experienced and thoughtful judges to address these issues, Chief Judge Lamberth explores "The Role of the Courts in Foreign Affairs." Few but Chief Judge Lamberth could meaningfully address such a weighty topic.

The second chapter turns to the always important human rights litigation in national courts, particularly contemporary issues concerning the Alien Tort Claims Act. Of particular and continuing concern is the question of the limitations of corporate liability under the Alien Tort Claims Act. On the one hand it would not seem helpful to hold corporations liable for the actions of foreign governments simply because the corporation is doing business in those nations. Yet, if the corporation significantly participates in or facilitates serious human rights abuses, should they not be held accountable? This whole area of the law is made more complex by the focus of the Alien Tort Claims Act as requiring a tort under "international law" and the requirements of our federal system concerning proper sources for related "causes of action." Issues in the scope of the Alien Tort Claims Act are currently before the Supreme Court in the *Kiobel Case* which has been set for re-argument. The issues before the Court will certainly include the extra-territorial applicability of the Alien Tort Statute, as to which the Court has specifically requested additional briefing, but may also include corporate liability, liability for aiding and abetting, universal civil jurisdiction or exhaustion of remedies.

The third chapter addresses a matter of great and increasing interest but less hard law; that of "Foreign Affairs Takings Actions in the Court of Federal Claims." A core question here is whether, when an otherwise judicially cognizable action is wiped out through government exercise of the foreign affairs power, whether, and under what circumstances, a takings actions will lie in the Court of Federal Claims. As early as 1886 it was held in the famous *French Spoliation* case that when the United States agreed to dispose of claims of its nationals by setting them off against French claims on the United States that "the citizen whose property is thus sacrificed for the safety and welfare of his country... has a right of compensation." [*Gray v. U.S.*, 21 Ct. Cl. 340, 392–93 (1886)]. More recently, Justice Powell's concurring opinion in the 1981 case of *Dames & Moore v. Regan*, growing out of the Iranian Hostage Crises, summarized the views of his colleagues on the Supreme Court as:

> *I agree with the Court's opinion with respect to the suspension and settlement of claims against Iran and its instrumentalities.... The Court holds that parties whose valid claims are not adjudicated or not fully paid may bring a "taking" claim against the United States in the Court of Claims, the jurisdiction of which this Court acknowledges. The Government must pay just compensation when it furthers the Nation's foreign policy goals by using as "bargaining chips" claims lawfully held by a relatively few persons and subject to the jurisdiction of our courts. The extraordinary powers of the President and Congress upon which our decision rests cannot, in the circumstances of this case, displace the Just Compensation Clause of the Constitution.* [453 U.S. 654, 690, at 691 (1981)].

There have been few cases in the Court of Claims, or other courts, fleshing out the parameters of just how the Fifth Amendment's guarantee that private property shall not be taken for a public use without just compensation applies to the taking of the claims of Americans for foreign policy purposes. The third chapter addresses these vexing issues.

In the fourth chapter, first in a keynote address by the Honorable Timothy J. Feighery, the Chairman of the Foreign Claims Settlement Commission, and then in papers focused on the work of the Commission, we review the role and jurisprudence of the little-known but important Commission charged with resolving foreign claims for those claims matters referred to the Commission in the course of United States foreign relations. Sadly the important work of the Commission has not received the attention it should. I hope the chapters in this volume will help to change that.

Finally, a paper by David Stewart on the Hague Convention on Choice of Court Agreements rounds out the volume by examining the 2005 Hague Convention on Choice of Court Agreements. This Convention provides an alternative to the expanding cost and complexities of commercial arbitration by providing an alternative dispute resolution forum in national courts. The contribution by David Stewart is the definitive work on this subject and is a must-read for attorneys with transnational commercial dealings.

This book is a unique reference source on an important component of international law practice. It serves an important need in addressing this increasingly central area of practice.

The University of Virginia School of Law is grateful for the generous donation from Gustave Sokol which has made this outstanding Sokol series possible. Special thanks are also due to Professors John K. Setear and Pierre-Hugues Verdier who helped organize this Sokol Colloquium, and Ms. Judy Ellis who assisted in the administration of the Colloquium and the editing of these proceedings.

FOREIGN SOVEREIGN IMMUNITY AND THE FSIA

THE ROLE OF COURTS IN FOREIGN AFFAIRS

Royce C. Lamberth[1]

I. Introduction

A large part of my judicial career has involved consideration of the role of courts in foreign affairs. Because Title 28 provides that many suits against foreign states be venued in the United States District Court for the District of Columbia, over time our Court has seen more than its fair share of suits with important foreign policy implications.[2] In fact, my law clerk tells me that since the passage of the state-sponsored terrorism exception in 1996,[3] I have published more than seventy opinions on various provisions of the Foreign Sovereign Immunities Act (FSIA). That same law clerk was also born just before I was appointed to the bench in 1987.

First, this paper will provide a historical overview of FSIA litigation in my Court.[4] This overview will focus on the development of the state-sponsored

[1] Chief Judge, United States District Court for the District of Columbia. This Article is drawn from a speech given by Chief Judge Lamberth during the Sokol Colloquium at the University of Virginia School of Law on April 19, 2012. Citations and minor modifications have been added. The Judge would like to thank Professor John Norton Moore and his colleagues at the Center for National Security Law and the University of Virginia School of Law for inviting him to participate in this important colloquium. For excellent research assistance in preparing this speech, the Judge would like to express his appreciation to J. Matthew Williams, J.D., 2010 Pepperdine University School of Law; Editor-in-Chief, *Pepperdine Law Review*, 2009–2010; Law Clerk, Justice Michael J. Gableman, Supreme Court of Wisconsin, 2010–2011; Law Clerk, Chief Judge Royce C. Lamberth, U.S. District Court for the District of Columbia, 2011–2012.

[2] *See* 28 U.S.C. § 1391(f) ("A civil action against a foreign state ... may be brought ... (4) in the United States District Court for the District of Columbia if the action is brought against a foreign state or political subdivision thereof.").

[3] Antiterrorism and Effective Death Penalty Act of 1996 ("AEDPA"), Pub. L. No. 103–132 § 221, 110 Stat. 1214 (codified at 28 U.S.C. § 1605(a)(7)).

[4] *See infra* Part II.

John Norton Moore (ed.) Foreign Affairs Litigation in United States Courts, pp. 3–20
 ISBN 978-90-04-25727-6

terrorism exception to sovereign immunity.[5] Second, the paper will highlight a number of issues my Court has encountered in cases involving Iraq, Libya, Sudan, Syria, Russia, and Exxon Mobile.[6] Third and in conclusion, it will comment on the effectiveness of private civil suits against state sponsors of terror and the foreign affairs implications of these suits.[7]

II. Overview of the FSIA Terrorism Exception

I will begin with a brief overview of the FSIA, specifically the state-sponsored terrorism exception. If you would like a more detailed overview of the FSIA state-sponsored terrorism exception, I commend to you my 140-page opinion *In re Islamic Republic of Iran Terrorism Litigation*.[8] I will provide enough background to lead into my later points, while hopefully sparing you the burdensome details contained in that lengthy opinion.

In 1976, Congress passed the FSIA affirming the general rule of foreign state immunity from suit in our Courts but enumerating certain exceptions to this general rule.[9] Congress subsequently added the state sponsor of terrorism exception in 1996 as part of the Antiterrorism and Effective Death Penalty Act (AEDPA).[10] The original terrorism exception eliminated sovereign immunity for acts of torture, extrajudicial killing, aircraft sabotage, hostage taking, and where the state provided material support or resources for these activities.[11] The original terrorism exception, § 1605(a)(7), was clear in its waiver of sovereign immunity, but was less clear as to whether it created an independent federal cause of action against foreign states.[12]

To remedy this ambiguity, only five months after Congress passed the original terrorism exception, it felt it necessary to clarify it. Congress passed the so-called "Flatow Amendment."[13] This amendment was named for Alisa Michelle Flatow, a 20-year old Brandeis University student from New Jersey who was mortally wounded in a suicide bombing on the Gaza strip in April 1995. Alisa Flatow's case—which was one of the first cases in the country involving the terrorism

5 The state-sponsored terrorism exception is at 28 U.S.C. § 1605A.

6 *See infra* Part III.

7 *See infra* Part IV.

8 659 F. Supp. 2d 31 (D.D.C. 2009).

9 Pub. L. No. 94–583, 90 Stat. 2891 (1976).

10 Pub. L. No. 103–132 § 221, 110 Stat. 1214 (1996) (codified at 28 U.S.C. § 1605(a)(7)).

11 28 U.S.C. § 1605(a)(7) (2000).

12 *See id.*

13 Flatow Amendment, Pub. L. No. 104–208, § 589, 110 Stat. 30091, 3009–172 (1997) (codified at 28 U.S.C. § 1605 note).

exception—was assigned to me.[14] In a 1998 opinion, I decided that the state-sponsorship exception, as supplemented by the Flatow Amendment, both conferred subject matter jurisdiction on federal courts[15] and created a federal cause of action against foreign state sponsors of terror.[16] Additionally, I found that punitive damages equal to three times Iran's estimated annual expenditures on terrorism were warranted.[17] At the time, I noted Congress's hope that subjecting foreign state sponsors of terror to massive civil liability would deter such terrorist acts.[18] The idea was that we would sue the terrorists out of business—perhaps a naïve thought.

I was forced to bring expectations back down to earth only one year later. In 1999, I authored two separate *Flatow* opinions involving attachment of Iranian assets.[19] I held that the Foreign Sovereign Immunities Act neither allowed the attachment of Iran's diplomatic properties located in the United States[20] nor did it allow the attachment of Iranian assets held in the U.S. Treasury.[21] Because these two asset categories contained nearly all of the Iranian funds within U.S. jurisdiction, the Flatow family's efforts to enforce their judgment were quickly derailed.

For the next six years following *Flatow*, a majority of the judges in my district agreed that § 1605(a)(7) and the Flatow Amendment created a federal cause of action against state sponsors of terror. During that time we entered a number of judgments against state sponsors of terror. I myself entered judgments in multiple cases involving hostage takings[22] and in one case involving a suicide bus bombing in Jerusalem.[23]

The most significant case I heard in the post-*Flatow* days was *Peterson v. Iran*, a case involving the 1983 Marine Barracks bombing in Beirut.[24] Prior to 9/11, this was the most deadly terrorist attack against Americans—241 servicemen lost their lives, and countless others suffered severe injuries from the blast.[25] Almost 1000 victims and their family members participated in the consolidated *Peterson*

---

14 Flatow v. Islamic Republic of Iran, 999 F. Supp. 1 (D.D.C. 1998).

15 *See id.* at 12–14.

16 *See id.* at 14–15.

17 *See id.* at 32–34.

18 *Id.*

19 Flatow v. Islamic Republic of Iran, 76 F. Supp. 2d 16 (D.D.C. 1999); Flatow v. Islamic Republic of Iran, 74 F. Supp. 2d 18 (D.D.C. 1999).

20 *See Flatow*, 76 F. Supp. 2d at 23.

21 *See Flatow*, 74 F. Supp. 2d at 25–26.

22 *See, e.g.*, Cronin v. Islamic Republic of Iran, 238 F. Supp. 2d 222 (D.D.C. 2002); Jenco v. Islamic Republic of Iran, 154 F. Supp. 2d 27 (D.D.C. 2001); Sutherland v. Islamic Republic of Iran, 151 F. Supp. 2d 27 (D.D.C. 2001); Price v. Socialist People's Libyan Arab Jamahiriya, 110 F. Supp. 2d 10 (D.D.C. 2000).

23 Weinstein v. Islamic Republic of Iran, 184 F. Supp. 2d 13 (D.D.C. 2002).

24 Peterson v. Islamic Republic of Iran, 264 F. Supp. 2d 46 (D.D.C. 2003).

25 *Id.* at 48.

action. In 2003, I issued a judgment holding Iran liable for the bombing, finding that Iran furnished money, weapons, training, and guidance to Hezbollah in carrying out the attack.[26]

In 2005, however, the D.C. Circuit threw a wrench into the practice our Court had developed under the state-sponsored terrorism exception. The D.C. Circuit's decision in *Cicippio-Puleo v. Islamic Republic of Iran* rejected the idea that either the state-sponsored terrorism exception in § 1605(a)(7) or the Flatow Amendment created a substantive federal cause of action against foreign states.[27] Our Circuit held that § 1605(a)(7) was merely jurisdictional,[28] and that the Flatow Amendment provided a cause of action only against individual officials, employees, and agents of a foreign state, but not against the foreign state itself.[29] Thereafter, plaintiffs were forced to use the terrorism exception as a "pass-through" to causes of action found in state tort law.[30]

The *Peterson* case was still pending at the time of *Cicippio-Puleo*. As a result, I was forced to examine the claims in *Peterson* under a number of sources of state law, and eventually awarded over $2.6 billion dollars to the victims of the Beirut bombings and their families.[31] This award remains one of the largest judgments ever awarded in a FSIA action pursuant to the state sponsor of terrorism exception.

But while a larger majority of plaintiffs in actions post-*Cicippio-Puleo* were able to use the pass-through approach to find relief, hundreds of other equally deserving plaintiffs had their claims denied because they were domiciled in jurisdictions that did not afford them a substantive claim. In the *Peterson* case, for example, some family members of the Marines and other servicemen were barred from asserting intentional infliction of emotional distress claims (IIED) because they lacked standing under the applicable state tort law.[32] Consequently, I had to dismiss the IIED claims of family members who were domiciled in either Pennsylvania or Louisiana at the time of the terrorist attack because those jurisdictions would not permit IIED claims by family members who were not physically present at the site of the incident that gave rise to the emotional distress.[33] Thus, the Pennsylvania and Louisiana plaintiffs in *Peterson* were effectively denied their day in court, and yet they watched as many other similarly-situated plaintiffs (including some of their own family members) from different state jurisdictions

---

26 *Id.* at 59–62.

27 Cicippio-Puleo v. Islamic Republic of Iran, 353 F.3d 1024 (D.C. Cir. 2004).

28 *Id.* at 1032.

29 *Id.* at 1033.

30 *In re Islamic Republic of Iran Terrorism Litigation*, 659 F. Supp. 2d 31, 779 (D.D.C. 2009).

31 Peterson v. Islamic Republic of Iran, 515 F. Supp. 2d 25, 60 (D.D.C. 2007).

32 *Id.* at 45.

33 *Id.* at 44–45.

advanced and ultimately prevailed with their IIED claims. For those plaintiffs who were denied relief as so many others succeeded based on precisely the same kinds of claims, based on the same horrific and unquestionably traumatic incident, I lamented that the result was both arbitrary and unfair.

In addition to the unfairness caused by a lack of uniformity in the underlying state sources of law, the pass-through approach proved cumbersome and tedious in practical application. In any given case based on a single terrorist incident, I was forced to resolve choice of law problems and then proceed through a lengthy analysis of tort claims under the laws of numerous different state jurisdictions. For example, in the *Heiser* case, a large consolidated action involving the Khobar towers bombing, I issued a 209-page opinion in which I ultimately applied the laws of eleven different state jurisdictions.[34] In *Peterson*, I had to apply the laws of nearly forty different jurisdictions in order to resolve the victims' claims.[35] To efficiently manage these terrorism cases under the pass-through regime imposed by *Cicippio-Puleo*, I was forced to have one of my law clerks almost exclusively work on Iranian FSIA cases.

Another consequence of the *Cicippio-Puleo* decision[36] was that the Flatow Amendment could not serve as an independent basis for punitive damages awards against Iran. As the Court of Appeals found that the amendment was not intended to provide for claims against foreign states, the bar on punitive damages in § 1606 of the FSIA remained intact, even with respect to state sponsors of terrorism.[37] Accordingly, large awards of punitive damages, like the award I granted in *Flatow* to deter Iran from sponsorship of terrorist groups, were no longer available in actions under the terrorism exception. If you cannot tell by now, I was not a fan of the *Cicippio-Puelo* decision.

Even for those plaintiffs who managed to receive awards under state causes of action, attachment of assets to satisfy the judgments proved near impossible. The same problems continued to exist as before *Cicippio*. The United States would not waive sovereign immunity for any Iranian assets held in U.S. Treasury Accounts, the Algiers Accords had swept up most Iranian assets and rendered them untouchable, and the President granted waivers nullifying statutes that otherwise would have expanded the pool of Iranian assets available for attachment. I began to refer to the FSIA judgments as "Pyrrhic Victories" and expressed my dismay that the rule of law was being frustrated by the executive's actions.[38]

---

34 *See* Estate of Heiser v. Islamic Republic of Iran, 466 F. Supp. 2d 229, 271–356 (D.D.C. 2006).

35 *See Peterson*, 515 F. Supp. 2d 25.

36 Cicippio-Puleo v. Islamic Republic of Iran, 353 F.3d 1024 (D.C. Cir. 2004).

37 *Id.*

38 *See, e.g.*, Eisenfeld v. Islamic Republic of Iran, 172 F. Supp. 2d 1, 9 (D.D.C. 2000); Flatow v. Islamic Republic of Iran, 76 F. Supp. 2d 16, 27 (D.D.C. 1999).

In 2008, Congress finally implemented a series of major reforms when it repealed the old § 1605(a)(7) and created the new § 1605A state-sponsored terrorism exception.[39] My first chance to deal with the new state sponsorship exception came in 2009 and was the first major decision interpreting the statute. In my 109-page omnibus opinion entitled *In re Islamic Republic of Iran Terrorism Litigation*,[40] I discussed four significant changes contained in the new state-sponsored terrorism exception: first, it created a federal cause of action against foreign states;[41] second, it made punitive damages available in those actions;[42] third, it authorized compensation for special masters;[43] and fourth, it implemented new measures designed to facilitate the enforcement of judgments.[44]

However, in that opinion I also needed to consider whether Congress had prescribed duties to the courts in § 1605A that violated separation of powers principles.[45] I noted that in the realm of foreign affairs, our Courts must attach a strong presumption of validity to actions in which both the Congress and President are in agreement.[46] As our Circuit has emphasized time and again, the FSIA terrorism exception represents a "delicate legislative compromise."[47] I therefore held that this new compromise involved foreign affairs policies best left to the political branches of our Federal Government.[48] Indeed, President Bush vetoed the first attempt by Congress to enact § 1605A.[49] At that time, the President expressed concerns about how these reforms to the FSIA terrorism exception would negatively impact Iraq's economy and reconstruction efforts as the United States worked to help that nation rebuild.[50] Shortly thereafter, Congress redrafted its proposed legislation to accommodate the President's concerns by adding a provision that authorized the President to waive any part of the Act with respect to Iraq.[51] As a result, the President signed the 2008 amendments into law on January 28, 2008, thereby enacting the sweeping reforms to the FSIA contained

---

39 National Defense Appropriations Act for Fiscal Year 2008 ("2008 NDAA"), Pub. L. No. 110–181, § 1083, 122 Stat. 3, 338–44, codified at 28 U.S.C. § 1605A.

40 *In re* Islamic Republic of Iran Terrorism Litig., 659 F. Supp. 2d 31 (D.D.C. 2009).

41 *Id.* at 59–61.

42 *Id.* at 61.

43 *Id.*

44 *Id.* at 61–62.

45 *Id.* at 68–91.

46 *Id.* at 81.

47 *See, e.g., Cicippio-Puleo*, 353 F.3d at 1035; Price v. Socialist People's Libyan Arab Jamahiriya, 294 F.3d 82, 89 (D.C. Cir. 2002).

48 *In re* Islamic Republic of Iran Terrorism Litig., 659 F. Supp. 2d 31, 81 (D.D.C. 2009).

49 *See* President George W. Bush, Memorandum to the House of Representatives Returning Without Approval the "National Defense Authorization Act for Fiscal Year 2008," 43 Wkly. Comp. Pres. Doc. 1641 (Dec. 28, 2007).

50 *Id.*

51 *See* 2008 NDAA, Pub. L. No. 110–181, § 1083, 122 Stat. 3, 338–44, codified at 28 U.S.C. § 1605A.

in § 1605A.[52] When both the President and Congress—the two branches vested with responsibility for our conduct of foreign affairs—are working together toward a common foreign policy objective, the Judicial Branch should be extremely hesitant about intervening in a way that would unravel those efforts.

Since my 2009 omnibus opinion, a number of cases under the federal cause of action have been brought to judgment. Among the many cases I have heard, I have issued five judgments totaling more than $7.4 billion against Iran for cases arising out of the 1983 Marine Barracks bombing.[53] However, Iran is not the only country to face such lawsuits. Let me now spend a few minutes addressing non-Iranian FSIA-related cases that have passed through our district.

III. Specific Examples of Non-Iranian Cases in the D.C. District Court

A. *Iraq*

After the invasion of Iraq in April 2003, Congress enacted the Emergency Wartime Supplemental Appropriations Act, which in part authorized the President to "make inapplicable with respect to Iraq [any] provision of law that applies to countries that have supported terrorism."[54] President Bush exercised that authority to its fullest extent in May 2003. In 2004, the D.C. Circuit in *Acree v. Iraq* held that President Bush's waiver authority did not include the authority to waive liability under the original state-sponsored terrorism exception.[55] However, in light of its recent ruling in *Cicippio-Puleo*, the Circuit Court vacated the judgment against Iraq because no claim could be stated for a federal cause of action under the then-existing state sponsor of terrorism exception.[56]

The jurisdictional question was revisited by our district in the 2006 case, *Vine v. Iraq*.[57] In that case, American citizens who were held hostage in Kuwait and Iraq during the First Gulf War had sued Iraq to recover damages for their time in captivity.[58] Judge Kennedy ruled that Iraq could be held liable under various state laws for actions committed when it was designated a state sponsor of terror

---

52 *See id.*

53 *See* Anderson v. Islamic Republic of Iran, 839 F. Supp. 2d 263 (D.D.C. 2012); Taylor v. Islamic Republic of Iran, 10-cv-844, 2012 WL 3126774 (D.D.C. Aug. 2, 2012); Fain v. Islamic Republic of Iran, 10-cv-628, 2012 WL 3095308 (D.D.C. July 31, 2012); Murphy v. Islamic Republic of Iran, 740 F. Supp. 2d 51 (D.D.C. 2010); Valore v. Islamic Republic of Iran, 700 F. Supp. 2d 52 (D.D.C. 2010).

54 Emergency Wartime Supplemental Appropriations Act § 1503, Pub. L. No. 108–11, 117 Stat. 559, 579 (2003).

55 Acree v. Republic of Iraq, 370 F.3d 41 (D.C. Cir. 2004).

56 *Id.*

57 Vine v. Republic of Iraq, 459 F. Supp. 2d 10 (D.D.C. 2006).

58 *Id.*

in 1990.[59] On appeal, the D.C. Circuit addressed the intervening enactment of the 2008 National Defense Authorization Act (NDAA) and its impact on the case.[60] The NDAA contained a provision allowing the President to waive the applicability to Iraq of the new federal cause of action against state sponsors of terror.[61] The Circuit Court held that neither the NDAA nor the President's waiver of its provisions with regard to Iraq deprived courts of jurisdiction over cases which were pending under § 1605(a)(7) when the NDAA went into effect.[62]

However, in 2009, the Supreme Court's 9–0 decision in *Republic of Iraq v. Beaty* put the brakes on further FSIA state sponsorship cases against Iraq.[63] Justice Scalia authored an opinion holding that the 2003 Emergency Wartime Supplemental Appropriations Act[64] authorized the President to waive the original FSIA state sponsorship exception's application to Iraq.[65] This opinion not only reversed the D.C. Circuit in *Vine*, but also expressly abrogated the D.C. Circuit's 2004 *Acree* opinion.[66] Thus, the Supreme Court quickly struck down any interference from federal courts hearing FSIA cases and minimized the possible implications these suits could have had on our new relationship with Iraq.

B. *Libya*

A number of Libyan cases involving the new terrorism exception were also heard by the recently retired Judge Henry Kennedy. On January 15, 2008, Judge Kennedy issued an opinion and order awarding $6 billion in damages to the families and the owners of Flight 772, which was bombed on September 19, 1989.[67] On August 14, 2008, however, the United States government entered an agreement with Mommar Gaddafi including a provision for the settlement of U.S. nationals' claims against Libya arising out of certain terrorist incidents occurring prior to June 30, 2006—including the Lockerbie bombing and the bombing of Flight 772.[68] In exchange, Gaddafi agreed to make a $1.5 billion lump sum payment to a compensation program administered through the Foreign Claims Settlement Commission. By statute, the decisions of the Commission are final and conclusive on all questions of fact and law and are not subject to review by

59 *Id.* at 18–19.
60 Simon v. Republic of Iraq, 529 F.3d 1187 (D.C. Cir. 2008).
61 2008 NDAA § 1083(d)(1).
62 *Simon*, 529 F.3d at 1194.
63 Republic of Iraq v. Beaty, 556 U.S. 848 (2009).
64 Pub. L. No. 108–11, 117 Stat. 559 (2003).
65 *Id.* at 854–63.
66 *Id.*
67 Pugh v. Socialist People's Libyan Arab Jamahiriya, 530 F. Supp. 2d 216 (D.D.C. 2008).
68 *See* Claims Settlement Agreement Between the United States of America and the Great Socialist People's Libyan Arab Jamahiriya, art. I (Aug. 14, 2008).

any other official, department, or agency of the United States, or by any court by mandamus or otherwise.[69]

My December 2011 opinion in *La Reunion Aerienne v. Libya* discusses these issues.[70] Plaintiff was a French partnership representing the interests of a group of insurance companies.[71] The partnership sued six high-ranking Libyan government officials in their personal capacities, as well as Libya and its external security service.[72] The partnership sought to recover payments it made to compensate victims' estates and families for losses arising from the explosion of Flight 722.[73]

Earlier, Judge Kennedy had dismissed the claims against Libya, various agencies of the Libyan government, and the individual defendants in their official capacities, but agreed with the partnership that the Act did not require dismissal of the claims against the individual defendants in their personal capacities.[74] After Judge Kennedy's retirement, the case was reassigned to me. The United States then asked me to reconsider Judge Kennedy's earlier ruling that the partnership's claims could proceed against the individual defendants in their personal capacities.[75]

I stood by Judge Kennedy's original ruling that the terms of the 2008 Libyan Claims Resolution Act, by themselves, did not deprive the partnership of a cause of action against the defendants in their personal capacities.[76] However, the United States raised a new argument that the subsequent Executive Order signed by President Bush[77] and the Claims Settlement Agreement with Libya[78] mandated dismissal of the partnership's claims.[79] The partnership contended that the President did not have the power to settle these claims without explicit congressional authorization.[80]

I found a line of cases holding it indisputable that the President's control of foreign relations includes the settlement of claims.[81] Although most of the cases

69 Libyan Claims Resolution Act ("LCRA"), Pub. L. No. 110–301, 122 Stat. 2999 (2008).

70 La Reunion Aerienne v. Socialist People's Libyan Arab Jarmahiriya, 05-cv-1932, 2011 WL 6197504 (D.D.C. Dec. 14, 2011).

71 *Id.*

72 *Id.*

73 *Id.*

74 La Reunion Aerienne v. Socialist People's Libyan Arab Jamahiriya, 477 F. Supp. 2d 131 (D.D.C. 2007).

75 *La Reunion Aerienne*, 2011 WL 6197504, at *2.

76 *Id.*

77 Exec. Order No. 13,477 § 1 (2008).

78 Claims Settlement Agreement Between the United States of America and the Great Socialist People's Libyan Arab Jamahiriya, art. I (Aug. 14, 2008).

79 *La Reunion Aerienne*, 2011 WL 6197504 at *2.

80 *Id.*

81 *Id.* (citing Medellin v. Texas, 552 U.S. 491, 531 (2008); Am. Ins. Ass'n v. Garamendi, 539 U.S. 396, 415 (2003); Dames & Moore v. Regan, 453 U.S. 654, 679–83 (1981); United States v. Pink, 315 U.S. 203, 240 (1942) (Frankfurter, J., concurring); United States v.

establishing this power involved claims against foreign governments, the Supreme Court in *Medellin v. Texas* said that its claims-settlement cases endorse "the making of executive agreements to settle civil claims between American citizens and ... foreign nationals."[82] This is a sensible interpretation of well-established doctrine, because, as the Supreme Court also said in *American Insurance Association v. Garamendi*, "[w]hile a sharp line between public and private acts works for many purposes in the domestic law, insisting on the same line in defining the legitimate scope of the Executive's international negotiations would hamstring the President in settling international controversies."[83] I thus rejected plaintiff's argument that the President lacked the authority to settle claims against Libyan officials in their personal capacities.[84]

In addition, I held that the purpose of the Claims Settlement Agreement was to "further the process of normalization of relations" between the United States and Libya.[85] The agreement therefore fell squarely within the President's foreign relations powers, and President Bush had the authority to settle the claims of American nationals against Libya and its officials without any authorization from Congress. He did so. I was therefore required by precedent and separation of powers concerns to dismiss the case.[86]

C. *Sudan*

Only a few weeks ago I entered judgment in the case of *Harrison v. Republic of Sudan*.[87] The case arose out of the October 12, 2000, bombing of the USS Cole. My case was a follow-on case. The original case was heard by Judge Doumar of the Eastern District of Virginia and was styled *Rux v. Republic of Sudan*.[88] In that case, Judge Doumar had awarded almost $8 million dollars to a number of victims.[89] Since the *Rux* case was brought under the Flatow Amendment, Judge Doumar relied on the Death on the High Seas Act[90] to create the substantive cause of action.[91]

Belmont, 301 U.S. 324, 330–31 (1937); Roeder v. Islamic Republic of Iran, 333 F.3d 228, 235 (D.C. Cir. 2003)).

82 *Medellin*, 552 U.S. at 531.

83 *Garamendi*, 539 U.S. at 416.

84 *La Reunion Aerienne*, 2011 WL 6197504, at *3.

85 *Id.*

86 *Id.*

87 Harrison v. Republic of Sudan, 10-cv-1689, 2012 WL 1066683 (D.D.C. Mar. 30, 2012).

88 Rux v. Republic of Sudan, 495 F. Supp. 2d 541 (E.D. Va. 2007).

89 *Id.*

90 46 U.S.C. § 30302.

91 495 F. Supp. 2d at 559–60.

My decision in *Harrison* was based on the new federal cause of action in § 1605A.[92] In that judgment, I awarded $314 million in damages.[93] You might notice that this award is exponentially higher than Judge Doumar's $8 million award in *Rux*. Judge Doumar was confined by the damages framework under the Death on the High Seas Act, which only allows recovery for pecuniary loss and does not allow punitive damages or solatium.[94] This disparity is yet another example of the inconsistent awards that were caused by the post-*Cicippio* pass-through regime.

The *Rux* plaintiffs refiled their case after the 2008 NDAA in an attempt to gain access to the damages and cause of action available under FSIA § 1605A.[95] However, in *Kumar v. Republic of Sudan*, decided last September, Judge Doumar disagreed with my 2009 omnibus opinion and reasoned that both res judicata and the prohibition on legislative reopening of final judgments barred their claims.[96] Judge Doumar's decision is on appeal before the Fourth Circuit, and Sudan has yet to enter an appearance. Sudan recently missed the Fourth Circuit's March 30, 2012 deadline to file a response brief, so it appears that a decision will be rendered without Sudan's participation.

D. *Syria*

Currently pending before me is a case entitled *Wultz v. Islamic Republic of Iran*.[97] Iran, Syria, and the Bank of China have all been defendants in this case. The case arose out of the April 17, 2006, suicide bombing attack at a restaurant in Tel Aviv, Israel. The explosion killed eleven people and wounded dozens of others. Among the wounded were two of the plaintiffs, Daniel Wultz and his father Tuly Wultz. The Wultz family brought suit against the foreign states under § 1605A and against the Bank of China under the Antiterrorism Act. Iran, as usual, defaulted. Syria, represented by Ramsey Clark, participated in the litigation through the motion to dismiss stage and then defaulted. The Bank of China participated fully in the litigation.

First, I rejected Syria's arguments and held that § 1605A did not violate the UN Charter's principle of sovereign equality, does not raise political questions, and does not violate the separation of powers.[98] Second, I held that the Bank of China

---

92 *Harrison*, 2012 WL 1066683.

93 *Id.* at *25.

94 *Rux*, 495 F. Supp. 2d 541.

95 Kumar v. Republic of Sudan, 2011 WL 4369122 (E.D. Va. Sept. 19, 2011).

96 *Id.* at *10–11.

97 One month after this speech was delivered, I entered default judgment against defendants. Wultz v. Islamic Republic of Iran, 08–CV-1460 RCL, 2012 WL 1664027 (D.D.C. May 14, 2012).

98 Wultz v. Islamic Republic of Iran, 08–cv-1460, 2010 WL 4190277 at *1–3 (D.D.C. Oct. 20, 2010).

did not qualify as an instrumentality of the Chinese government and therefore was not entitled to immunity.[99] I also held that the Wultz family had adequately pled claims against the Bank of China under the Antiterrorism Act—specifically claims that the bank provided material support for terrorism and funds with knowledge that the funds would be used in a terrorist attack.[100]

On reconsideration, I revisited my decision that the Bank of China was subject to personal jurisdiction in the District of Columbia. I reversed myself and held that I did not have personal jurisdiction over the Bank of China.[101] I had originally evaluated the Bank of China's contacts with the U.S. as a whole, rather than the standard practice of looking at the Bank's contacts with the District of Columbia. However, upon further review, I held that access to the Antiterrorism Act's nationwide service provision could only be accessed through proper invocation of its venue provision.[102] Since the venue provision could not be satisfied, I was forced to analyze the Bank's contact with D.C., which were lacking.[103] Therefore, I transferred the Wultz's claims against the Bank of China to the Southern District of New York,[104] which is wading through choice of law questions at the moment.[105]

I have recently conducted a trial of the Wultz's claims against Syria and Iran, and I expect to rule on that case in the near future.[106]

E. *Russia*

I also currently have pending before me a case entitled *Agudas Chasidei Chabad of the United States v. Russian Federation*.[107] Because it is still before me and I cannot extensively comment on it, I will confine my remarks to a brief background of the case and the motions currently pending. Plaintiff Chabad is a New York non-profit religious corporation that on November 9, 2004 sued defendants the Russian Federation, the Russian Ministry of Culture and Mass Communication, the Russian State Library, and the Russian State Military Archive.[108] Chabad alleged that defendants possessed and obtained, in violation of international law, a collection of invaluable religious books and manuscripts of which plaintiff is

---

99 Wultz v. Islamic Republic of Iran, 755 F. Supp. 2d 1, 29–30 (D.D.C. 2010).
100 *Id.* at 45–48.
101 Wultz v. Islamic Republic of Iran, 762 F. Supp. 2d 18, 25–29 (D.D.C. 2011).
102 *Id.*
103 *Id.* at 30.
104 *Id.* at 31–33.
105 Wultz v. Bank of China Ltd., 11-cv-1266, 2012 WL 70341 (S.D.N.Y. Jan. 9, 2012).
106 Default judgment was entered in favor of plaintiffs on May 14, 2012. *Wultz*, 2012 WL 1664027.
107 *See* Agudas Chasidei Chabad of U.S. v. Russian Fed'n, 798 F. Supp. 2d 260 (D.D.C. 2011); Agudas Chasidei Chabad of U.S. v. Russian Fed'n, 729 F. Supp. 2d 141 (D.D.C. 2010); Agudas Chasidei Chabad of U.S. v. Russian Fed'n, 466 F. Supp. 2d 6 (D.D.C. 2006).
108 Factual history of the case is at *Chabad*, 466 F. Supp. 2d at 10–14.

and always has been the rightful owner. Chabad sought return of the Collection under the "expropriation" exception of the Foreign Sovereign Immunities Act. This Collection held by defendants consists of two separate groups of religious writings: 12,000 books and manuscripts seized during the Bolshevik Revolution and Russian Civil War between 1917 and 1925 ("the Library"), and 25,000 pages of handwritten teachings and other writings of the Rebbes (the Chabad religious leaders), which were seized by Nazi Germany during the 1941 invasion of Poland, subsequently transferred by the Soviet Red Army to Russia as "trophy documents" and "war booty," and are still held in Russia ("the Archive").[109]

Russia moved to dismiss for lack of jurisdiction. On December 4, 2006, I granted dismissal as to the Library but denied the motion as to the Archive.[110] Both sides appealed to the D.C. Circuit. On June 13, 2008, Circuit Court found that I properly possessed jurisdiction over plaintiff's claims concerning both the Library and Archive and found that these claims were not barred by sovereign immunity under the FSIA, by defendants' forum non conveniens, or act of state defenses.[111] Russia's petition for rehearing en banc was denied on October 6, 2008, and no petition for writ of certiorari was filed with the United States Supreme Court.[112]

On remand, Russia filed an Answer, but rather than respond to plaintiff's discovery requests, on June 26, 2009, Russia informed me that it declined to participate further in the litigation and believed that I had no authority to enter orders with respect to the property.[113] On October 27, 2009, I ordered entry of default.[114] I also ordered that plaintiff should "move for judgment on the default with proof satisfactory to the Court" pursuant to the FSIA.[115] On July 30, 2010, I granted default judgment and ordered the Russian Federation to "surrender ... the complete collection of religious books, manuscripts, documents and things that comprise the 'Library' and the 'Archive.'"[116] Chabad later moved for civil contempt sanctions, and I issued an order to show cause.[117] Russia, to date, has not appeared to contest the show cause order. At plaintiff's request, I granted two voluntary stays to facilitate negotiations between plaintiffs and the Russian Federation. However, on March 5 plaintiff informed me that the negotiations have not reached a resolution, and renewed its motion for sanctions. The motion is now pending.[118]

---

109 *Id.*

110 *Chabad*, 466 F. Supp. 2d 6.

111 Agudas Chasidei Chabad of U.S. v. Russian Fed'n, 528 F.3d 934 (D.C. Cir. 2008).

112 *Id.*

113 *Chabad*, 729 F. Supp. 2d at 144.

114 *See id.*

115 *See id.*

116 *Id.* at 144–48.

117 *Chabad*, 798 F. Supp. 2d at 272–74.

118 On January 16, 2013, I issued civil contempt sanctions against defendants in the amount of $50,000 per day until they complied with the Court's order. *Chabad v. Russian Fed'n*, 05-cv-1548 RCL, 2013 WL 164071 (D.D.C. Jan. 16, 2013).

F. Doe v. Exxon Mobile

The final case I will highlight is an Alien Tort Statute case that was before me captioned *Doe v. Exxon Mobile*. This suit was filed in June 2001 by eleven Indonesian citizens against defendants Exxon Mobil Corporation and PT Arun LNG Company ("PT Arun").[119] Plaintiffs allege that defendants violated the Alien Tort Statute, the Torture Victim Protection Act, and committed various common-law torts in the course of protecting and securing defendants' liquid natural gas extraction pipeline and liquification facility in Arun, Indonesia.[120] The Plaintiffs allege that during an on-going conflict with the Indonesian government and Achenese rebels, defendants contracted with a unit of the Indonesian national army to provide security for the pipeline. Defendants allegedly conditioned payment on providing security, made decisions about where to build bases, hired mercenaries to train the security troops, and provided logistical support. Plaintiffs claim that Exxon and PT Arun are liable for the alleged actions of the Indonesian soldiers because of the training and equipment they provided.

In 2005, Judge Oberdorfer dismissed the statutory claims brought under the ATS and the TVPA.[121] Judge Oberdorfer relied on ATS precedent calling for a "more searching merits-based inquiry" into the alleged facts.[122] He held that liability for aiding and abetting violations of international law was not actionable and that Congress should be deferred to with respect to innovative interpretations of the ATS.[123] In 2009, I dismissed a separate suit containing common law tort claims. I ruled that the doctrine of prudential standing prevented me from hearing the case.[124] I relied on *Berlin Democratic Club*[125] and what I believed precedent held concerning the general rule that non-resident aliens have no standing to sue in the United States courts absent certain exceptions, which did not exist in this case.[126]

On appeal, the D.C. Circuit reversed my opinion and held that the doctrine of prudential standing did not apply.[127] It also took up, in the first instance, the question of whether a corporation can be held liable for a violation of the ATS.[128] The Circuit Court rejected the idea from the earlier *Sosa* case[129] that ATS

---

119 Doe v. Exxon Mobil Corp., 393 F. Supp. 2d 20, 22 (D.D.C. 2005).

120 *Id.*

121 *Id.*

122 *Id.* at 24 (citing Walsh v. Ford Motor Co., 588 F. Supp. 1513, 1519 (D.D.C. 1984)).

123 *Id.* at 24–27.

124 John Doe VIII v. Exxon Mobil Corp., 658 F. Supp. 2d 131 (D.D.C. 2009).

125 410 F. Supp. 144 (D.D.C. 1976).

126 *John Doe VIII*, 658 F. Supp. 2d at 134 (citing Boumediene v. Bush, 553 U.S. 723 (2008)).

127 Doe v. Exxon Mobil Corp., 654 F.3d 11, 65–71 (D.C. Cir. 2011).

128 *Id.* at 39–57.

129 Sosa v. Alvarez-Machain, 542 U.S. 692 (2004).

tribunals should not recognize private claims under federal common law for violations of any international law norm which did not exist when the ATS was enacted.[130] The Court concluded that "neither the text, history, nor purpose of the ATS supports corporate immunity for torts based on heinous conduct allegedly committed by its agents in violation of the law of nations."[131] Citing the *Kiobel* decision[132] that is presently before the Supreme Court, the D.C. Circuit also indicated that the notion that corporations could be held liable for their torts would not have been surprising to the First Congress that enacted the ATS because corporate liability in tort was by 1789 an accepted principle of tort law in the United States. The Circuit examined the text of the ATS which it found made it clear that the corporate nature of a person cannot shield it from being brought to Court with a defendant status.[133]

Reargument is scheduled in the *Kiobel* case this fall at the Supreme Court on the question of the extraterritorial reach of the ATS.[134] The D.C. Circuit has stayed consideration of Exxon's petition for a rehearing en banc until the Supreme Court finishes its consideration of *Kiobel.*

G. Mohamad v. Palestinian Authority

As you might have heard, the companion case to *Kiobel,* which was styled *Mohamad v. Palestinian Authority,* was decided yesterday.[135] Justice Sotomayor's 11-page unanimous opinion held that nothing in the text or history of the Torture Victims Protection Act (TVPA) suggested that Congress intended for organizations to be held liable under that statute.[136] Justice Scalia refused to join her discussion of the legislative history of the statute,[137] and Justice Breyer concurred while making the point that in other statutes the word "individual" could sometimes apply to corporations.[138] Thus, the scope of possible claims under the TVPA has been narrowed significantly by the Court.

---

130 *Doe,* 654 F.3d at 65–71.

131 *Id.* at 15.

132 Kiobel v. Royal Dutch Petroleum Co., 621 F.3d 111 (2d Cir. 2010).

133 *Doe,* 654 F.3d at 65–71.

134 Oral Argument was held on October 1, 2012. *See* Transcript of Oral Argument, Kiobel v. Royal Dutch Petroleum Co., 10–1491 (Oct. 1, 2012) *available at* http://www.supremecourt.gov/oral_arguments/argument_transcripts/10-1491rearg.pdf.

135 Mohamad v. Palestinian Auth., 132 S. Ct. 1702 (2012).

136 *Id.* at 1706–08.

137 *Id.*

138 *Id.* at 1711 (Breyer, J., concurring).

IV. Concluding Remarks on the Role of Courts in Foreign Affairs

In light of these cases, I would like to conclude my remarks today with a few general reflections on the role of the Courts in foreign affairs. Most of my views are contained in my 2009 Iranian omnibus opinion,[139] but recent developments have caused me to reconsider some of my former doubts of the merits of civil suits against state sponsors of terror.

The Executive Branch, in its dealings with Congress and in litigation before me, often takes the position that civil actions against state sponsors of terror threaten to undermine United States foreign policy and national security interests, both with respect to Iran specifically, as well as with respect to our relations with other nations more broadly. The victims in these cases counter with what are often extremely emotional retorts to the Executive Branch's opposition. In frustration and anger, the victims, their lawyers, and even some members of Congress, have accused the Executive of defending Iran and siding with terrorists. While such extreme rhetoric undoubtedly reveals the depth of the frustration experienced by the victims in these civil actions against Iran, it inaccurately characterizes the position of the Executive Branch and the true nature of the interests at stake in these important actions. What the victims, their attorneys, and backers in Congress apparently fail to see, or perhaps conveniently overlook, is that these actions frequently run into direct conflict with other sources of law, including bilateral Executive agreements, multilateral treaty obligations, and numerous other statutory and regulatory authorities relating to foreign policy and the President's powers to manage national security crises.

Nonetheless, the victims in these lawsuits are right to feel abandoned and frustrated to a certain extent. After all, these Americans are merely pursuing justice under the terms of a federal statute that, twice now, the Congress has passed and two Presidents have signed. Yet, in taking action in accordance with that federal law, these victims are all too frequently stopped in their tracks by their own Government, which quickly and poignantly reveals in open Court that the promise of justice that they thought they had achieved in the FSIA terrorism exception is nothing more than an illusion.

As Congress usually backs the victims in their desire to press forward with lawsuits against Iran in the courts, the FSIA terrorism exception has had another unfortunate consequence of turning these already extraordinary lawsuits against a foreign power into high stakes contests between the two political branches. As this inter-branch feud over terrorism suits has heated up over the years, the Executive Branch and Congress have in essence waged a war by proxy against one another through these FSIA terrorism lawsuits. As difficult separation-of-powers problems and other challenging legal questions loom large in these supercharged

[139] *See In Re* Islamic Republic of Iran Terrorism Litig., 659 F. Supp. 2d 31 (D.D.C. 2009).

actions, the victims are often relegated to the role of bystanders, stuck in the middle, caught up, and emotionally torn up in the cross-fire of an inter-branch political feud turned-litigation event.

But it is not only the victims who are caught up in the middle of this volatile political mix; the Court itself is also stuck in the middle and forced to referee these highly charged and highly political disputes. Like the victims, the Court finds itself relegated to the role of a powerless and frustrated bystander at times because under Article III courts have neither foreign affairs powers nor any of the plenary authorities that are rightly vested in the political branches under our Constitution. It is these powers of governance, and not the powers of the courts, that must be used to help these victims overcome the significant challenges they face. Thus, courts are caught in something of a political quagmire in which they are called upon to consume judicial resources chewing on novel legal issues and jurisprudential problems while carefully dodging delicate political questions. All the while the victims in these actions are no closer to justice. More fundamentally, respect for the Courts and for the rule of law is undermined as judges in these actions are cast as the perennial bearers of bad news and as the designated apologists for the meaningless charade that our the political branches have created.

All these problems might be easy enough to ignore if it were not for the real people involved. As I and others continue to wrestle with and mete out judicial solutions to the variety of legal issues that stem from this delicate political compromise that is the terrorism exception to foreign sovereign immunity, it can be all too easy to lose sight of the human beings whose lives have been torn apart. These victims have poured much of their emotional energy and time, to say nothing of their financial resources, into these civil cases in the hope of finding justice for themselves and for the loved ones they have lost due to terrorist violence. Over the last decade, I have listened to live testimony of these victims in dozens of tragic cases, and I will not forget—and no one familiar with the harsh and intimate details of these cases could ever forget—the stories these victims have to tell of lives destroyed by unjustifiable violence committed against them or their family members and against the laws of all civilized nations.

The truth is that both the victims of terrorism and the federal government each have valid concerns—and both sides are ultimately seeking to achieve the same broad objectives of holding terrorists accountable and eliminating terrorism against United States nationals. In 2009 I noted that "the private litigation model for resolving these terrorism claims has had the very unfortunate consequence of casting the United States Government and American victims of terrorism as constant and bitter adversaries. This cold reality will undoubtedly continue under § 1605A."[140]

[140] *Id.* at 126–27.

In 2009, I also suggested that the President consider renewing efforts to move forward with the establishment of a terrorism claims settlement commission with respect to Iran.[141] This, I said, would be consistent with the historical role of the political branches taking the lead in ensuring compensation for Americans injured by the acts of foreign states. However, $1.8 billion in Iranian funds were recently blocked by OFAC as they transited through New York banks. It is true that this is only a portion of the more than $7 billion in judgments now outstanding in Iranian cases. But if the plaintiffs manage to collect the $1.8 billion, this would represent an exponential leap forward in the effectiveness of FSIA suits in procuring compensation for victims of terrorism. Should such a success occur, I might be willing to reconsider my past doubts on the effectiveness of the current model.

Professor Moore has proposed that a protocol be added to the various United Nations Conventions on Terrorism to require that signatory states create civil damages actions under their national law against state sponsors of terror.[142] I commend Professor Moore for his creativity. However, the skeptic in me—having seen judgment after judgment unable to be enforced—has reservations that such an international convention could change the status quo. These judgments implicate political, economic, and military considerations of the highest magnitude for an enforcing state, and the judiciaries of foreign states may be ill equipped to entertain such considerations. Only time will tell if more meaningful and substantial justice can be accomplished for these victims. The important point is that the political branches cannot continue shirking their responsibilities to these victims and placing the onus on the Courts. This only serves to damage the rule of law and undermine the proper separation of powers in our government.

---

141 *Id.* at 133–37.

142 John Norton Moore, "Civil Litigation Against Terrorism: Neglected Promise" *in* LEGAL ISSUES IN THE STRUGGLE AGAINST TERROR 231–234, (John Norton Moore & Robert F. Turner eds., 2010).

POLICY OPTIONS FOR THE OBAMA ADMINISTRATION: ENFORCEMENT PROVISIONS OF THE FOREIGN SOVEREIGN IMMUNITIES ACT AS A TOOL AGAINST STATE SPONSORS OF TERRORISM

Steven R. Perles and Edward B. MacAllister[1]

The Foreign Sovereign Immunities Act,[2] as amended in 2008, provides an exploitable policy lever for the Obama administration as it seeks to deal with threats posed by state sponsors of terror such as Iran and Syria. Supporting private causes of action by victims of terror is both just and good policy.

The dramatic and successful evolution in civil litigation against foreign sovereign sponsors of terrorism since the late 1990s[3] supports the argument that the U.S. government should cooperate with victims in their efforts to sue the parties that injured them and to collect any damages awarded. Recent successes have confirmed this thesis, but there is further room for cooperation. Today, U.S. victims of international terrorism have robust legal rights in U.S. federal courts against state sponsors of terrorism, after a protracted battle in the courts and Congress as to the scope of those rights. Now that the benefits of such litigation have become clearer, the Executive Branch should cooperate with victims of terrorism to ensure that they are able to collect on their damage awards, which would facilitate U.S. foreign policy goals.

The existence of the rights of victims of terrorism has not meant that they have been exercised as effectively as Congress intended. Congress created a legislative regime in 1996 to allow civil litigators to pursue state sponsors of terrorism by

---

1 Perles Law Firm, PC, Washington, DC. This paper was the foundation of the oral presentation and comments by Mr. Perles at the 2012 Sokol Colloquium on the topic of "Enforcement Provisions of the FSIA". Additionally, this is an update and expansion of a paper written in 2008 by the coauthors and Major Gabriel Lajeunesse of the United States Air Force (whose input did not necessarily reflect the views of the Department of Defense or its components).

2 28 U.S.C. § 1602, *et seq.*

3 In the late 1990s, the first successful cases brought by U.S. citizens against state sponsors of terrorism, such as *Flatow v. Islamic Republic of Iran*, 999 F. Supp. 1 (D.D.C. 1999), *Eisenfeld v. Islamic Republic of Iran*, 172 F. Supp 2d 1 (D.D.C. 2000), and *Jenco v. Islamic Republic of Iran*, 154 F. Supp 2d 27 (D.D.C. 2001).

John Norton Moore (ed.) Foreign Affairs Litigation in United States Courts, pp. 21–48
 ISBN 978-90-04-25727-6

obtaining damages for U.S. victims of terrorism in order to both deter further acts of terrorism and compensate the victims of past acts. Two factors thereafter imperiled the efforts by private civil litigators: structural problems in the statutory regime and insufficient support from the Executive Branch and law enforcement and investigatory officials.

Prior to 1996, the only precedent in U.S. federal courts from cases brought by victims of terrorism seemed to suggest to victims of international terrorism that they should not bother to bring a lawsuit against either foreign states[4] or the terrorist groups[5] that had injured them. After the passage of a new "state-sponsored terrorism exception" to foreign sovereign immunity in 1996, there were now statutes creating subject matter jurisdiction against foreign states that sponsored acts of terrorism against U.S. citizens,[6] as well as non-state actors,[7] but a few harmful court decisions arising out of structural deficiencies in the key statutes created difficulties for the civil litigators seeking to represent U.S. citizens who had suffered death and personal injury as a result of international terrorism. A line of cases brought against the Islamic Republic of Iran, beginning with *Flatow v. Islamic Republic of Iran*,[8] brought the concept of using civil litigation to win redress against sponsors of international terrorism to a wider audience of attorneys and victims. The hesitation to litigate diminished as several attorneys and firms successfully acquired sufficient information to withstand the rigors of trial in a U.S. federal court and win a judgment against a foreign state sponsor of terrorism. The subsequent difficulties the Flatows experienced in satisfying their judgment identified the obstacles that needed to be removed before anti-terrorism civil litigation could near its goals of deterrence and compensation.

Despite this, the field of anti-terrorism litigation has stabilized. An increasingly sophisticated knowledge of international terrorism adds fuel to the cycle of innovation by civil litigators and their successes have encouraged further support from Congress. The hesitation from the Executive Branch does lead one to ask whether these lawsuits complement U.S. foreign policy goals. But the fact that the

4 "Although Libya's alleged participation, if true, in this tragedy is outrageous and reprehensible and the human suffering involved is heartbreaking, this Court may not rightly obtain jurisdiction over Libya for the purposes of these private rights of action. Libya's alleged terrorist actions do not fall within the enumerated exceptions to the Foreign Sovereign Immunity Act and therefore Libya must be accorded sovereign immunity from suit." *Smith v. Socialist People's Libyan Arab Jamahiriya*, 886 F. Supp. 306, 315 (E.D.N.Y. 1995) (rejecting the first lawsuit against Libya for the bombing of Pan Am 103).

5 "I believe, as did the district court, that, in the circumstances presented here, appellants have failed to state a cause of action sufficient to support jurisdiction under either of the statutes on which they rely." *Tel-Oren v. Libyan Arab Republic*, 726 F.2d 774, 799 (D.C. Cir. 1984).

6 28 U.S.C. § 1605(a)(7).

7 18 U.S.C. § 2333.

8 999 F. Supp 1 (D.D.C. 1998).

litigation has continued to achieve notable successes, despite the hesitation of the Executive Branch, its utility to actors in the U.S. government's foreign policy apparatus should be recognized.

Success in both obtaining a judgment and collecting against the foreign sovereign debtor is critical to the effort against state sponsors of terrorism. State sponsors of terrorism ignore these lawsuits unless their assets are vulnerable to the US judgment holders. While legislative reform has greatly aided the ability of civil litigators to secure large judgments in court and to attach the assets of liable state sponsors of terrorism, the cooperation of the Executive Branch is necessary before victims of terrorism may yet secure justice and anti-terrorism civil litigation may maximize its impact.

I. Early Promises—The Beginning of Anti-Terrorism Civil Litigation

There was a time when U.S. victims of terrorism had no explicit civil recourse for acts of international terrorism. In 1984, the United States Circuit Court for the District of Columbia Circuit decided *Tel-Oren v. Libyan Arab Republic*, and victims of horrendous attacks learned that they had no suitable remedy despite identifiable defendants.[9] On March 11, 1978, thirteen heavily armed members of the Palestine Liberation Organization landed by boat in Israel and captured two buses, and a few carloads of hostages.[10] They tortured them, shot them, wounded them and murdered them. Before the Israeli police could stop the massacre, 22 adults and 12 children were killed, and 73 adults and 14 children were seriously wounded.[11]

In a per curiam opinion with three concurring written decisions, the appellate court found that the trial court correctly dismissed the case for lack of subject matter jurisdiction.[12] The appellate court agreed that there was no jurisdictional basis for the trial court to adjudicate these acts of international terrorism[13] and the case was dismissed. The claimants who brought the lawsuit originally included the sovereign state supporter of the attack, but the trial court ruled that it had no subject matter jurisdiction over the case and those claims were abandoned in the appeal.[14] The result in this case laid bare the complete inability of U.S. citizens to file civil suits against the terrorists or their supporters injured them in acts of international terrorism. Congress would resolve this problem by enacting

9 *Tel-Oren v. Libyan Arab Republic*, 726 F.2d 774 (D.C. Cir. 1984).
10 *Id.* at 776.
11 *Id.*
12 *Id.*
13 *Id.* at 795, 796, 798.
14 *Id.* at 799 n. 3.

two statutes into law: one that allowed U.S. citizens injured in his or her person, property, or business by reason of an act of international terrorism"[15] to sue to recover damages and the second one to allow U.S. citizens to peel back the sovereign immunity that protected foreign state sponsors of terrorism from lawsuits by private individuals in the United States.[16]

In 1992, Congress passed 18 U.S.C. § 2333, allowing a person "injured in his or her person, property, or business by reason of an act of international terrorism" to sue to recover damages. 18 U.S.C. § 2333 relies upon another statute for the controlling definition of "international terrorism"—18 U.S.C. § 2331 defines it as "activities that involve violent acts or acts dangerous to human life that are a violation of the criminal laws of the United States." Civil litigation against state sponsors of terrorism also required action by Congress. Courts in the United States possess subject matter jurisdiction over foreign sovereigns only to the extent granted by the Foreign Sovereign Immunities Act ("FSIA").[17] The FSIA therefore "provides the sole basis for obtaining jurisdiction over a foreign state in the courts of this country."[18] From early on, federal common law generally provided foreign states with absolute immunity from suit.[19] With the rise of state trading companies in the twentieth century, exceptions began to be made under a theory of "restrictive immunity," which was formally adopted as United States policy by the Department of State in the so-called Tate Letter of May 1952.[20] Under this theory, immunity was confined to suits involving the foreign sovereign's public acts, and did not extend to cases arising out of a foreign state's strictly commercial acts.[21] Administration of the restrictive-immunity theory proved problematic. Courts deferred to State Department recommendations on immunity questions, which forced this executive agency to assume a judicial function that often conflicted with its primary mission of conducting American foreign policy: foreign nations frequently pressured the State Department to recommend immunity, and political considerations sometimes led to recommendations of immunity in cases where immunity would not have been available under the restrictive theory.[22]

---

15 18 U.S.C. § 2333.

16 28 U.S.C. § 1605(a)(7).

17 28 U.S.C. § 1330 ("The district courts shall have original jurisdiction without regard to amount in controversy of any nonjury civil action against a foreign state as defined in section 1603").

18 *Argentine Republ. v. Amerada Hess Shipping Corp.*, 488 U.S. 428, 443 (1989).

19 *See, e.g., The Schooner Exchange* v. *M'Faddon*, 11 U.S. (7 Cranch) 116 (1812).

20 Letter from Jack B. Tate, Acting Legal Advisor, Department of State to Acting Attorney General Philip B. Perlman (May 19, 1952), *reprinted in* 26 Department of State Bulletin 984–85 (1952) *and in Alfred Dunhill of London, Inc.* v. *Cuba*, 425 U.S. 682, 711 (1976) (Appendix 2 to opinion of White, J.). *See Verlinden B.V.* v. *Central Bank of Nigeria*, 461 U.S. 480, 486–87 (1983).

21 *Id.* at 487.

22 *Id.*

The State Department, moreover, did not participate in every case, which left the courts to make their own decisions in that class of cases. As a result, "the governing standards were neither clear nor uniformly applied."[23] In 1976, Congress responded to these problems by enacting the Foreign Sovereign Immunities Act, 28 U.S.C. §§ 1330, 1602–1611, which specified seven exceptions to the general rule of immunity for foreign states (including the "commercial activities exception"), and assigned the interpretation of those exceptions to the courts.[24] Subsequent amendments added two additional exceptions to the general rule (including the 1996 addition of the "state sponsored terrorism exception").[25]

The FSIA provides for immunity, subject to its enumerated exceptions: "a foreign state shall be immune from the jurisdiction of the courts of the United States and of the States except as provided in sections 1605–1607 of this chapter".[26] A U.S. citizen cannot file a lawsuit against a foreign state in the United States unless the allegations contained in his or her complaint meet the requirements found within the several enumerated exceptions, listed at 28 U.S.C. § 1605–1607. Hence the result in *Tel-Oren.*

Results such as *Tel-Oren* and *Smith v. Socialist People's Libyan Arab Jamahiriya* in the Eastern District of New York in 1995, led to the formation of political coalitions that successfully advocated on the behalf of the rights of victims of terrorism. In 1996, as part of the Antiterrorism and Effective Death Penalty Act ("AEDPA"), Congress reacted by amending the Foreign Sovereign Immunities Act ("FSIA") to create a judicial forum for adjudicating the claims of victims of terrorist acts committed by foreign states that the U.S. State Department has designated as state sponsors of terrorism.[27] AEDPA created the "state-sponsored terrorism exception" to the sovereign immunity that is ordinarily enjoyed by foreign states under the FSIA. 28 U.S.C. § 1605(a)(7). Under AEDPA, countries officially designated by the Department of State as terrorist states can be held liable for personal injuries or deaths if the foreign state commits a terrorist act, or provides material support and resources to an individual or entity that commits

---

23 *Id.* at 488 (citations omitted).

24 The originally enacted exceptions to immunity of foreign states from the courts of the United States were waiver, commercial activity, expropriation, gifts in immovable property in the United States, torts occurring within the United States, 28 U.S.C. § 1605(a)(1)–(5), suits in admiralty to enforce maritime liens, 28 U.S.C. § 1605(b), and counterclaims against foreign state plaintiffs, 28 U.S.C. § 1607.

25 In 1988, Congress added an exception to immunity for actions to enforce arbitration agreements and awards. 28 U.S.C. § 1605(a)(6). In 1996, Congress added the "state-sponsored terrorism exception" to immunity for actions arising from a foreign state's acts of torture, extrajudicial killing, hostage-taking, aircraft sabotage or material support for such an act which results in the injury or death of United States nationals. 28 U.S.C. § 1605(a)(7).

26 28 U.S.C. § 1604.

27 Pub. L. No. 104–132, § 221, 110 Stat. 1241 (1997).

such an act.[28] Congress next addressed the issue of remedies for plaintiffs in these cases. A provision called "Civil Liability for Acts of State-Sponsored Terrorism" was enacted on September 30, 1996 as part of the 1997 Omnibus Consolidated Appropriations Act.[29] This provision is commonly referred to as the "Flatow Amendment."[30] The Flatow Amendment established the measure of damages available in suits under the "state-sponsored terrorism" provision of the FSIA.[31] After passage of the Flatow Amendment, victims of terrorism moved quickly to take advantage of the new tools provided by Congress to fight back against the sovereign states that injured them. Stephen Flatow filed a wrongful death complaint against the Islamic Republic of Iran ("Iran") and its officials on February 26, 1997, in the United States District Court for the District of Columbia and on March 11, 1998, the district court entered a historic default judgment against Iran in favor of the Flatows in the amount of $247,513,220.[32]

There have been numerous cases since *Flatow* that have documented the ties between Iran, Iraq, Syria, the Sudan, and Libya and individual acts of terrorism.

II. Flatow's Promise Broken?

Almost immediately, court decisions that were at odds with the congressional intent behind the Flatow Amendment threatened to radically undermine anti-terrorism civil litigation. The Flatow Amendment was critical to the early development of anti-terrorism civil litigation for two principle reasons: increasing the measure of damages available to victims in order to create deterrence through massive penalties for the proscribed behavior[33] and providing a uniform measure

---

28 *Id.*

29 Pub. L. No. 104–208, § 589, 110 Stat. 3009 (1997).

30 The Flatow Amendment was named after the murdered daughter of lead Plaintiff Stephen Flatow whose case resulted in the decision *Flatow v. Islamic Republic of Iran.* 999 F. Supp. 1 (D.D.C. 1998). 20-year Alisa was riding in a bus that was attacked by a Palestine Islamic Jihad suicide bomber, who drove a van loaded with explosives and shrapnel. *Id.* at 7. Alisa died shortly after the bombing, from a fatal head wound. *Id.* at 8.

31 *Id.* at 12–13. This holding was overruled by the United States Circuit Court of Appeals for the District of Columbia Circuit in *Cicippio-Puleo v. Islamic Republic of Iran*, which found that the Flatow Amendment only provided a cause of action against officials of a foreign state under certain circumstances. 353 F.3d 1024, 1033 (D.C. Cir. 2004). This holding was overturned by Congress in 2008 by the codification of a new exception to foreign sovereign immunity at 28 U.S.C. § 1605A and an explicit federal right of action against the foreign state itself, with punitive damages, at 28 U.S.C. 1605A(c). P.L. 110–181, § 1083.

32 999 F. Supp. at 32.

33 *Id.* at 12–13 ("The brief explanation of the Flatow Amendment's purpose in the House Conference Report explicitly states that it was intended to increase the measure of damages available in suits under 28 U.S.C. § 1605(a)(7)."). (citing to H.R. CONF. REP. 863, 104TH CONG, 2ND SESS. 1996, reprinted at 1996 U.S.C.C.A.N. 924).

of damages by creating a federal cause of action. A foreign sovereign that is supporting acts of terrorism against U.S. citizens is unlikely to pay attention to damage awards against it unless the damages are significant:

> The state-sponsored terrorism exception, however, was enacted explicitly with the intent to alter the conduct of foreign states, particularly towards United States nationals traveling abroad. Congressman Saxton, the Chairman of the House Task Force on Counterterrorism and Unconventional Warfare, was convinced that the only way to accomplish this goal was to impose massive civil liability on foreign state sponsors of terrorism whose conduct results in the death or personal injury of United States citizens. As compensatory damages for wrongful death cannot approach a measure of damages reasonably required for a foreign state to take notice, Congressman Saxton sponsored the Flatow Amendment in order to make the availability of punitive damages indisputable.[34]

Are punitive damages appropriate for these types of cases? Punitive damages are traditionally used to both punish particularly heinous conduct and to deter future wrongdoing.[35] The provision of material support to terrorists who detonate high explosives wrapped with nails and ball bearings on packed buses or in crowded civilian shopping malls would seem to be an act uniquely deserving of an award of punitive damages.[36]

> The evidence shows that Syria supported, protected, harbored, and subsidized a terrorist group whose modus operandi was the targeting, brutalization, and murder of American and Iraqi civilians. Premeditated violence against civilian targets is not a legitimate action by any government. Civilized society cannot tolerate states whose partnership with terrorist surrogates, like Zarqawi's terrorist network, is formed for the purpose of achieving political victory through heinous acts of barbarism.[37]

The second purpose behind the codification of a federal cause of action for use in actions against state sponsors of terrorism was equally important. This was to provide a uniform measure of damages for all victims of terrorism irrespective of where the act of terrorism took place or of the place of residence of the victim of terrorism. The alternative in place of a federal cause of action would

---

34 999 F. Supp. at 25–26.

35 "Punitive damages are awarded to punish a defendant for particularly egregious conduct, and to serve as a deterrent to future conduct of the same type." *Eisenfeld v. Islamic Republic of Iran*, 172 F. Supp. 2d 1, 9 (D.D.C. 2000); *see also Pacific Mut. Life. Ins. Co. v. Haslip*, 499 U.S. 1, 15 (1991).

36 *See, e.g., Cronin v. Islamic Republic of Iran*, 238 F. Supp. 2d 222, 235 (D.D.C. 2002) ("Here, the Court has no difficulty finding that the depraved and uncivilized conduct of the Iranian Ministry of Information and Security constitutes 'outrageous' conduct. The defendant organized, trained, and funded Amal, Islamic Amal, and Hizbollah so that the organizations could torture and take individuals like the plaintiff hostage. Under even the most restrictive interpretation of the term, the defendant's actions in this matter are clearly "outrageous" and warrant the imposition of punitive damages.").

37 *Gates v. Syrian Arab Republic*, 580 F. Supp. 2d 53, 75 (D.D.C. 2008).

be dependant upon the choice-of-law analysis conducted by each court, which might lead to widely varying recoveries or, worse, to an unfortunate circumstance where some families might recover but others might not in a single mass tort case due to the vagaries of the law applicable to each family.

The importance of the Flatow Amendment was underscored after the United States Circuit Court for the District of Columbia Circuit issued a ruling that effectively nullified it.[38] *Cicippio-Puleo* held that the "Flatow Amendment does not authorize a cause of action against foreign states"[39] despite the holding of *Flatow*, the overwhelming weight and uniformity of subsequent authority[40] and the logic behind these decisions.

The Flatow Amendment is a hollow right unless the state sponsor of terrorism itself can be held liable. Allowing the parents of a murdered US citizen to sue the driver of the truck that detonated a bomb that killed their child does not have any effect or impact upon the calculations of the foreign state that paid for the driver's training, the bomb that incinerated the U.S. citizen, and the funds that sustain the organization that planned and executed the horrific act itself. The policy goals of anti-state sponsored terrorism litigation, as codified by Congress, are to compensate the victims of terrorism and to staunch the flow of money from foreign states to the terrorist organizations that fight proxy wars on behalf of the foreign states. This policy cannot be effectively achieved without a federal cause of action against the state itself, and the subsequent ability to collect money judgments against the terrorists, their organizations, their funders, and the U.S. State Department designated state sponsors of terrorism.

The ruling created a brake on litigation against state sponsors of terrorism as litigators were not only stripped of the right to seek punitive damages against foreign sovereigns, but the question of what, if any, law would supply any cause of action against a foreign sovereign became paramount. A prime example of the

---

38 *Cicippio-Puleo v. Islamic Republic of Iran*, 353 F.3d 1024 (D.C. Cir. 2004).

39 *Id.* at 1032.

40 Nine district court decisions considered the question of whether Congress intended to create a federal cause of action against foreign states, and each have concluded that Congress intended to do so when it enacted the 1996 FSIA amendments. *Kilburn v. Socialist People's Libyan Arab Jamahiriya*, 2003 U.S. Dist. LEXIS 14347, at *35–51 (D.D.C. Aug. 8, 2003); *Price v. Socialist People's Libyan Arab Jamahiriya*, 2003 U.S. Dist. LEXIS 12428, at *15–36 (D.D.C. July 21, 2003); *Pugh v. Socialist People's Libyan Arab Jamahiriya*, 2003 U.S. LEXIS 19327 at *6–7 (D.D.C Oct. 27, 2003); *Regier v. Islamic Republic of Iran*, 2003 U.S. Dist. LEXIS 15523, at *28–34 (D.D.C. Sept. 8, 2003); *Dammarell v. Islamic Republic of Iran*, 2003 U.S. Dist. LEXIS 1564, at *253–59 (D.D.C. Sept. 8, 2003); *Acree v. Republic of Iraq*, 2003 U.S. Dist. LEXIS 11421 at *99 (D.D.C. July 7, 2003); *Weir v. Islamic Republic of Iran*, Civil Action No. 01–1303, slip op. at 6 (D.D.C. Apr. 29, 2003); *Kerr v, Islamic Republic of Iran*, 245 F.Supp.2d 59, 63 n. 9 (D.D.C. 2003); *Cronin v. Islamic Republic of Iran*, 238 F.Supp.2d 222, 230–33 (D.D.C. 2002); *Smith v. Islamic Emirate of Afghanistan*, 262 F.Supp.2d 217, 227 (S.D.N.Y. 2003).

potential for mischief is illustrated by the decision issued in the case brought by the families of the deceased U.S. service personnel murdered in the 1983 bombing of the Marine barracks in Beirut, Lebanon. In 1982, a multi-national peacekeeping force including U.S. and French troops, with the concurrence of the United Nations, deployed to Beirut.[41] The U.S. troops were from the 24th Marine Amphibious Unit,[42] which included men and women from all over the country, including non-U.S. nationals. In *Peterson v. Islamic Republic of Iran*, the court found that Iran organized and planned the attack that destroyed the Marine barracks.[43] The enormously complex question remained of what law to apply to determine damages for nearly one thousand plaintiffs from numerous different states. "In order to ensure that the Court determines the appropriate amount of damages available to each plaintiff under the law, it must first ensure that each plaintiff has a valid claim under state law."[44]

Without the ability to utilize the Flatow Amendment, the plaintiffs were forced to resort to whatever other sources of law were available. It is important to remember that 28 U.S.C. § 1605(a)(7) merely prescribed the requirements that a plaintiff's lawsuit must meet before a U.S. court may assert subject matter jurisdiction over the case. 28 U.S.C. § 1606 further provides that "the foreign state shall be liable in the same manner and to the same extent as a private individual under like circumstances...." Thus, once a plaintiff pierces the immunity of a foreign state under 28 U.S.C. § 1605(a)(7), and a court asserts its subject matter jurisdiction, 28 U.S.C. § 1606 defines the sources of law that apply to a foreign sovereign. This allows a plaintiff to assert any applicable cause of action against a non-immune foreign state. Under the FSIA, a foreign sovereign "shall be liable in the same manner and to the same extent as a private individual under like circumstances".[45]

> Once a foreign state's immunity has been lifted under Section 1605 and jurisdiction is found to be proper, Section 1606 provides that "the foreign state shall be liable in the same manner and to the same extent as a private individual under like circumstances." 28 U.S.C. § 1606. Section 1606 acts as a "pass-through" to substantive causes

---

41 *Peterson v. Islamic Republic of Iran*, 264 F. Supp. 2d 46, 49 (D.D.C. 2003) ("The rules of engagement issued to the servicemen of the 24th MAU made clear that the servicemen possessed neither combatant nor police powers. In fact, under the rules, the servicemen were ordered not to carry weapons with live rounds in their chambers, and were not authorized to chamber the rounds in their weapons unless (1) they were directly ordered to do so by a commissioned officer or (2) they found themselves in a situation requiring the immediate use of deadly force in self-defense.").

42 *Id.*

43 *Id.* at 61.

44 *Peterson v. Islamic Republic of Iran*, 515 F. Supp. 2d 25, 38 (D.D.C. 2007).

45 28 U.S.C. § 1606.

of action against private individuals that may exist in federal, state or international law.[46]

The *Peterson* court therefore performed a choice-of-law analysis through an application of the choice-of-law rules of the forum.[47] The court employed the District of Columbia's "modified government interest analysis" to decide that the law of the plaintiffs' domicile at the time of the attack has "the greatest interest in providing redress to its citizens."[48] This meant that the law of the domicile of the service person at the time of the attack would provide the applicable law for the wrongful death claims and for the battery claims of the surviving service persons.[49] For the family members with intentional infliction of emotional distress claims, 753 plaintiffs, the court would look to the domicile of the plaintiff at the time of the attack.[50] This led the court to analyze the various laws of:

> Alabama, California, Connecticut, District of Columbia, Florida, Georgia, Illinois, Indiana, Kansas, Kentucky, Louisiana, Maryland, Massachusetts, Michigan, Minnesota, Mississippi, Missouri, Nebraska, New Jersey, New Mexico, New York, North Carolina, Ohio, Oklahoma, Pennsylvania, Rhode Island, South Carolina, South Dakota, Tennessee, Texas, Vermont, Virginia, Washington, West Virginia, and Wisconsin.[51]

Aside from the enormous expenditure of judicial resources, this also resulted in a tragic outcome for those plaintiffs whom happened to have been situated in states that did not allow for recovery for intentional infliction of emotional distress under the factual circumstances of the case. Plaintiffs from Louisiana and Pennsylvania therefore were unable to recover for their damages.[52] Had there been a uniform measure of damages in a federal cause of action, those plaintiffs would have not been left out.

III. Failed Attempts to Capitalize on 28 U.S.C. § 1605(a)(7)

The tale of the Flatows' attempts to enforce their judgment against Iran further illustrated the obstacles that remained to hinder litigators and provided a primer for the legislators who would set out to remove those obstacles. Among other Iranian assets inside the country,[53] the Flatows targeted the former Iranian

46 *Heiser v. Islamic Republic of Iran*, 466 F. Supp. 2d 229, 265–66 (D.D.C. 2006) (*quoting Dammarell v. Islamic Republic of Iran*, 2005 U.S. Dist. LEXIS 5343, at *27–32 (D.D.C. Mar. 29, 2005)).

47 515 F. Supp. 2d at 38.

48 *Id.*

49 *Id.* at 39–40.

50 *Id.* at 41.

51 *Id.*

52 *Id.* at 45.

53 The Flatows waived their right to pursue Iranian assets outside of the United States as a part of an agreement signed with the U.S. Treasury Department to accept partial

embassy and former Iranian embassy officials' residences. The Department of Justice appeared in court to defend the Iranian assets from attachment by arguing that the attachments would impermissibly conflict with the obligations of the United States under the Vienna Convention on Diplomatic Relations, a treaty to which the United States is a signatory.[54] The Department of Justice also defended against the attachment of any funds in the U.S. Treasury owed to Iran or under dispute in litigation between the U.S. government and Iran in other tribunals by arguing that any Iranian funds sitting in U.S. accounts are protected by U.S. sovereign immunity, and the courts agreed.[55]

The asset hunt therefore expanded to include Iranian assets remaining in the United States yet outside U.S. government control. An insuperable obstacle quickly arose: courts began to apply the common law presumption of respect for the corporate form of juridically separate government instrumentalities, enunciated in *First National City Bank* v. *Banco Para El Comercio Exterior de Cuba*,[56] and known as *Bancec* doctrine. This created an impossible obstacle to the statutory scheme through which Congress had sought to deter state-sponsored terrorism against American citizens.

First National City Bank had enunciated an equitable, common law principle under which duly created instrumentalities of a foreign state are ordinarily entitled to a presumption of independent status. *First National City Bank* also made it clear, however, that this presumption must not be used to undermine countervailing congressional policies. "In particular, the Court has consistently refused to where it is interposed to defeat legislative policies."[57] Congress enacted both the "state-sponsored terrorism exception" to the FSIA and the Flatow Amendment in order to deter state-sponsored terrorism.[58] The "state-sponsored terrorism" exception, however, "was enacted explicitly with the intent to alter the conduct of foreign states, particularly towards United States nationals traveling abroad."[59] The Flatow Amendment, in turn, sought to achieve deterrence by increasing the damages available for plaintiffs suing foreign state sponsors of terrorism.[60]

---

payment of their judgment from the U.S. Treasury subrogated against Iranian assets frozen in the United States. *Ministry of Defense and Support for the Armed Forces of the Islamic Republic of Iran v. Cubic Defense Systems, Inc.*, 385 F.3d 1206, 1213 (9th Cir. 2004) *reversed on other grounds, Ministry of Defense and Support for the Armed Forces of the Islamic Republic of Iran v. Elahi*, 546 U.S. 450 (2006).

54 The Vienna Convention on Diplomatic Relations, T.I.A.S. 7502, 23 U.S.T. 3227 (1964).

55 *Flatow v. Islamic Republic of Iran*, 74 F.Supp.2d 18 (D.D.C. 1999).

56 *First National City Bank v. Banco Para El Comercio Exterior de Cuba*, 462 U.S. 611 (1983).

57 *Id.* at 630 (citing *Anderson v. Abbot*, 321 U.S. 349, 362–63(1944)).

58 *Flatow*, 999 F. Supp. at 12, 25.

59 *Id.*

60 *Id.* at 12–13.

Congress intended to create massive civil liability for proven state sponsors of terrorism under 28 U.S.C. § 1605(a)(7) as a way of altering their behavior.[61]

Furthermore, in 1996, when Congress amended 28 U.S.C. § 1605 to include the "state-sponsored terrorism exception" to foreign sovereign immunity, it also amended 28 U.S.C. § 1610 to permit attachment of assets irrespective of the assets' involvement in the underlying incident that provided the right for attachment.[62] These amendments were intended to ease the process of attachment and execution for 28 U.S.C. § 1605(a)(7) judgment creditors. Prior to the amendments, victims of state-sponsored terrorism who obtained judgments under the then-existing provisions of the FSIA could not attach or execute upon the assets owned by the foreign state, unless they could prove the asset sought for execution or attachment was involved in the underlying incident.[63]

The harsh limitations this requirement placed upon successful plaintiffs' ability to satisfy their outstanding judgments were illustrated in *Letelier v. Republic of Chile*.[64] In *Letelier*, the victims of a bombing and assassination, sponsored by Chile and carried out in the United States, sought to execute upon the Chilean national airline, Linea Aerea Nacional-Chile ("LAN"), to satisfy their default judgment against Chile.[65] The court found that the property was not used for the commercial activity upon which the claim was based and denied execution against LAN.[66] In doing do, the court made clear the reason for its ruling: "Congress did not provide for execution against a foreign state's property under the circumstances of this case. Congress provided for execution against property used in commercial activity upon which the claim is based."[67] The 1996 amendment to 28 U.S.C. § 1610 was to ensure that victims of terrorism with outstanding 28 U.S.C. § 1605(a)(7) judgments did not fall into the *Letelier* trap.

The *Letelier* trap may have been avoided, but was quickly replaced by emergence of the *Bancec* trap in the Ninth Circuit decision *Flatow v. Islamic Republic of Iran*.[68] The Flatows had "obtained a writ of execution for $247,513,220.00 on property in Carlsbad, California, owned by California Land Holding Company" a wholly-owned subsidiary of Bank Saderat Iran,[69] which an Iranian national bank wholly owned by the state of Iran, as are all banks in Iran, due to the nationalization of banks in 1979 after the revolution. The Ninth Circuit affirmed the decision by the federal court in the Southern District of California by finding that the

---

[61] H.R. Rep. 106–733, at 25 (2000).

[62] Antiterrorism and Effective Death Penalty Act, Pub. L. No. 104–132, § 221, 110 Stat. 1241 (*codified at* 28 U.S.C. § 1610 (1997)).

[63] 28 U.S.C. § 1610(a)(2).

[64] 748 F.2d 790, 791 (2d Cir. 1984).

[65] *Id.* at 792.

[66] *Id.* at 795–98.

[67] *Id.* at 799.

[68] 308 F.3d 1065 (9th Cir. 2002).

[69] *Id.* at 1067.

Bancec doctrine prevented execution against an entity established separate from the state by the state, unless the plaintiff can show that Iran exercises extensive or "day-to-day control" over Bank Saderat Iran.[70] "The court found that Flatow had not shown that BSI operates as an arm of the Iranian government or that BSI's mission is to further the policies of the Iranian government."[71] The U.S. government entered a statement of interest and "took the position that the amendments to the FSIA did not alter the Bancec presumption because Bancec and the FSIA govern two separate questions of law: liability and jurisdiction."[72]

The mistake of the Ninth Circuit was to formulate a federal common law rule regarding the attribution of liability under the FSIA that defeated the congressional intent behind the anti-terrorism legislation. Congress decided that financial penalties should be exacted upon those foreign states that sponsor acts of terrorism against United States citizens, and Congress deliberately constructed a legislative scheme to fulfill its goal of deterrence. The Ninth Circuit mechanically construed *Bancec* to block the attachment of assets otherwise available to satisfy outstanding judgments resulting from litigation that Congress has specifically sought to encourage, and thus upset Congress's carefully crafted scheme.

In applying the *Bancec* doctrine, the Ninth Circuit adopted a "day-to-day control" test developed by other courts under the rubric of a *different* statutory provision: the FSIA's "commercial activities exception" to sovereign immunity, 28 U.S.C. § 1605(a)(2). This was a serious mistake because the history and purposes of the two exceptions are quite different. The "day-to-day control" test is completely incongruous when applied to cases arising under the "state-sponsored terrorism exception," found in 28 U.S.C. § 1605(a)(7). The *Bancec* test, which is broadly consistent with analogous rules in American corporate law,[73] has an obvious appeal in light of the purpose and history of the "commercial activities exception." In establishing a separate corporation to pursue specific commercial activities, a foreign government is making trade-offs similar to those that an American corporation makes when it establishes an independent subsidiary. There being no obvious reason for applying different rules of attribution in these two highly analogous situations, courts have been inclined to treat them alike.

The legislative intent behind 28 U.S.C. § 1605(a)(7), the "state-sponsored terrorism exception, " however, is quite different from that underlying 28 U.S.C. § 1605(a)(2), the "commercial activities exception." The difference is illustrated, for example, by the explicit and profound difference between the corresponding provisions for attachment in aid of execution. When the claim is brought under the "state-sponsored terrorism exception," judgment creditors do not have

[70] *Id.* at 1072–74.

[71] *Id.* at 1072.

[72] *Id.* at 1071 n. 10.

[73] *See, e.g., Hester Int'l Corp.* v. *Federal Republic of Nigeria*, 879 F.2d 170, 177–78 (5th Cir. 1989).

to prove that property sought for attachment in aid of execution was involved in the underlying claim. 28 U.S.C. § 1610(a)(7). This stands in contrast to judgment creditors holding a judgment from a claim under the "commercial activities exception," who are required by statute to prove that the asset sought for attachment in aid of execution was involved in the commercial activity that their underlying claim was based on. 28 U.S.C. § 1610(a)(2).

Whatever justification there is for the "day-to-day control" test under the FSIA's "commercial activities exception," it has no justification whatsoever under the "state-sponsored terrorism exception" that is at issue in this case.[74] Unlike the "commercial activities exception," the statutory provision at issue in this case cannot be regarded as a device for facilitating legitimate commercial intercourse among the community of nations. While the "commercial activities" exception represents the codification of the restrictive doctrine of immunity, the "state-sponsored terrorism exception" is not based on the restrictive theory, and instead denies immunity for the indisputably 'sovereign' act of waging war or conducting a violent foreign policy. The purpose of the "state-sponsored terrorism exception," quite unlike that of the "commercial activities exception," is to penalize foreign states for grossly unacceptable conduct against American citizens.

The U.S. government has now come to view Bank Saderat Iran as a key cog for Iranian support for terrorism. "Stuart Levey, the Treasury's under-secretary for terrorism and financial intelligence, announced... [Bank Saderat Iran] had been blacklisted because 'this bank, which has approximately 3,400 branch offices, is used by the government of Iran to transfer money to terrorist organisations.'"[75] In any event, time would be required before the advocates for the victims of international terrorism could successfully press for the legislative reforms necessary to address the *Bancec* doctrine.

The Flatows' attachment efforts can now be seen as correct in retrospect in another case: *Flatow v. Alavi Foundation.*[76] In that decision, the Fourth Circuit affirmed a trial court's quashing of writs of execution against property of the Alavi Foundation in Maryland that Flatow alleged were controlled by Iran. On November 13, 2009, the U.S. government moved to seize an entire sky scraper in New York City as well as properties around the country belonging to two non-profit foundations under civil forfeiture statutes.

> The forfeiture action is part of an investigation into the Alavi Foundation, which the government says has sent millions of dollars to Iran's Bank Melli. In March, the

[74] We do not necessarily endorse the "day-to-day control" test for all cases arising under the "commercial activities exception." Our point here is only that the "day-to-day control" test is clearly *not* appropriate under the "state-sponsored terrorism exception," whatever its merits may be elsewhere.

[75] BBC News website, News, Business, http://news.bbc.co.uk/2/hi/business/5329326.stm (September 8, 2006).

[76] *Flatow v. Alavi Found.*, 2000 U.S. App. LEXIS 17753 (4th Cir. July 24, 2000).

> US Treasury Department called the bank a key fundraising arm for Iran's nuclear program.[77]

Utilization of the public-private partnership in 1998 would have prevented years of Iranian money laundering in Maryland subsequent to the quashing of the writs in 1998.

In 2001, Congress passed the Terrorism Risk Insurance Act ("TRIA") in an attempt to clarify the ability of the victims of terrorism to seize frozen assets in the United States.[78] The law however did not sufficiently address the *Bancec* doctrine. The imposition of the *Bancec* doctrine has no place where foreign governments seek to use the corporate form to protect their assets from victims of acts of terrorism. A legislative solution to the *Bancec* problem and the problem created by the decision in *Cicippio-Puleo* were desperately needed if anti-terrorism litigation was not going to die a premature death.

IV. Flatow's Promise Upheld—Needed Legislative Reform

For advocates representing American victims of international terrorism, 2008 was a year of significant developments. In January 2008, Congress passed the 2008 National Defense Authorization Act ("NDAA"), P.L. 110–181, § 1083,[79] amending the FSIA to provide an explicit, private right of action against state sponsors of terrorism.[80] The legislation was designed to address a 2004 opinion issued by the United States Circuit Court of Appeals for the District of Columbia Circuit that held the FSIA provided a cause of action against individual agents in their personal capacity only, rather than against the foreign state itself—forcing claimants to seek remedies under domestic state law, if available.[81] The 2008 amendment to the FSIA created a federal cause of action that allowed for the recovery of monetary damages to include economic damages, solatium, pain and suffering, and

---

77 *Alavi Foundation: Complaint comes at delicate time for US, Iran*, Michael B. Farrell http://www.csmonitor.com/2009/1113/p02s17-usfp.html.

78 Pub. L. No. 107–297, 116 Stat. 2322, Nov. 26, 2002.

79 Congress passed the law after providing for Presidential waiver authority to the application of the law to the Government of Iraq following a veto over concerns of how the legislation would affect the fledgling democracy in Iraq.

80 P.L. 110–181, § 1083(a)(1), modifying Chapter 97 of Title 28, U.S.C. § 1605A. In 1996, Congress amended the FSIA, 28 U.S.C. §§ 1602 *et seq.*, to allow civil suits by U.S. victims of acts state-sponsored terrorism such as torture, extrajudicial killing, aircraft sabotage, and hostage taking under 28 U.S.C. § 1605(a)(7), which has now been replaced by 28 U.S.C. § 1605A. Congress subsequently created a cause of action via a further amendment against "an official, employee, or agent of a foreign state designated as a state sponsor of terrorism", which was known as the Flatow Amendment. "Civil Liability for Acts of State-Sponsored Terrorism," P.L. 104–208, Title I, § 101(c) [Title V, § 589] (September 30, 1996), 110 Stat. 3009–172; codified at 28 U.S.C. § 1605 note.

81 *Cicippio-Puleo v. Islamic Republic of Iran*, 353 F.3d 1024 (D.C. Cir. 2004).

punitive damages; "in any such action, a foreign state shall be vicariously liable for the acts of its officials, employees, or agents."[82]

An early application of the amended law was seen on September 26, 2008, when Judge Rosemary M. Collyer, of the U.S. District Court for the District of Columbia, handed down a judgment for over $400 million to the survivors of Jack Armstrong and Jack Hensley, two American contractors who were brutally murdered by Al Qaeda in Iraq ("AQI") in *Gates v. Syrian Arab Republic.*[83] The judgment was rendered against the Arab Republic of Syria—held liable for the murders via the federal cause of action under the amended FSIA for Syria's material support to Zarqawi and AQI.[84] The use of the federal cause of action avoided any problem that may have been presented by using different state laws to prescribe the rules for the causes of action or damages in the case. Additionally, the new federal cause of action allowed the court to award punitive damages for the unusually heinous nature of the murders at issue.[85]

The amended FSIA also contains a critical new provision that a judgment may be enforced against any property "titled in the name of any defendant, or titled in the name of any entity controlled by any defendant" expanding the scope of liability to state-owned enterprises.[86] This remedy of the *Bancec* trap, in cases involving judgments against state sponsors of terrorism, will make FSIA judgments significantly more threatening to state sponsors than in prior experience, particularly if the judgments can be registered and enforced in foreign jurisdictions.

State sponsors of terrorism had been able to use the *Bancec* doctrine to shield their investments in the United States from U.S. citizens who hold judgments against them. Congress enacted both the "state-sponsored terrorism exception" to

---

82 28 U.S.C. § 1605A(c).

83 *Gates v. Syrian Arab Republic,* 580 F. Supp. 2d 53 (D.D.C. 2008).

84 *Id.* at 75.

85 *Id.* at 73 ("The medical evidence corroborates the video: each man was alive when his captors began to saw upon his neck with a sharp-bladed, but relatively short tool. Williams T-2-58; Welch T-2-25. Both were physically restrained during the ordeal, with handcuffs holding their hands behind their backs, and ropes binding their ankles. Williams T-2-49-50 & 58; Welch T-2-24 & 32. As the expert testimony made clear, the ability to sense pain depends upon the brain receiving input from the spinal cord. It was not easy to sever fully the spinal cords of Mr. Armstrong or Mr. Hensley because of the methods and tools used by their murderers, as evidenced by the markings on their spinal vertebrae. Williams T-2-60 ("it required considerable effort and movement and length of time to cut through both the soft tissue and bone"); Welch T-2-29 ("the blade hit the spinal column in...11 different places"). The cutting began on the right side of each man's neck and continued, around the back of the neck without severing the spinal cord, until it reached the left carotid artery; only then did Mr. Armstrong and Mr. Hensley bleed to death and lose sensation of pain. *See* Williams T-2-54 ("So consciousness with just one carotid artery [] compromised would remain for a while."). It was, quite obviously and scientifically, "a very cruel and inhumane method of causing death." *Id.* at 63.").

86 28 U.S.C. § 1605(g)(1).

the FSIA and the Flatow Amendment in order to deter state-sponsored terrorism by financially penalizing the state sponsors of terrorism. Although dozens of U.S. citizens hold judgments resulting from litigation brought under these enactments against the government of Iran for hundreds of millions of dollars, it can avoid collection claims from victims of terror if it actively invests money in the United States through shell corporations, foreign subsidiaries and other properly layered entities. The *Bancec* doctrine allowed these foreign states to invest and litigate in the United States, before the eyes of their victims, even those victims with valid final outstanding judgments against those foreign states. US citizens who have lost loved ones to senseless acts of violence cannot comprehend why the United States would allow Iranian business investment in the United States to be shielded from attachment when Iran has killed and injured hundreds of United States citizens since 1980.

While premised upon international trade concerns, the *Bancec* doctrine frustrated Congress's effort to deter state sponsors of terrorism. Instead, the victims of terrorism are deterred from bringing suits of the type that Congress deliberately sought to encourage. While the *Bancec* doctrine is perfectly sensible in the realm of commercial activity and should be invoked to protect legitimate commercial undertakings by foreign governments, trade between the United States and state sponsors of terrorism should not take priority over compensating the victims of terrorism and penalizing the sponsors of terrorism.

V. Executive Branch Cooperation Furthers U.S. Foreign Policy Goals

In addition to the expanded relief afforded by the amended FSIA, 2008 saw unprecedented support from the political branches of government in holding Libya accountable for its past support of terrorism. In January 2008, the U.S. District Court for the District of Columbia ruled on behalf of a group of American families under the FSIA, awarding a $6 billion judgment against Libya in connection with the 1989 bombing of UTA Flight 772.[87] Libya, anxious to reestablish relations with the United States, was unable to make much progress as State Department officials and members of Congress blocked rapprochement until the claims were satisfied.[88] In August, the governments of Libya and the U.S. reached an agreement where Libya agreed to pay the U.S. $1.5 billion in settlement of all outstanding claims.[89] Though many victims were dissatisfied with this result and felt that the U.S. government made a politically expedient settlement at the expense of fair compensation of all victims and survivors of Libyan terrorism,

---

87 See *Pugh v. Socialist People's Libyan Arab Jamahiriya*, 530 F.Supp.2d 216 (D.D.C. 2008).

88 For background see Families Who Sued Libya See Their Victory Voided U.S. Pact Nullifies $6 Billion Award in '89 Bombing Over Africa By Kimberly Kindy Washington Post Staff, Tuesday, December 23, 2008.

89 Libyan Claims Resolution Act, Pub. L. No. 110–301, 122 Stat. 2999 (2008).

the level of U.S. government participation in the vindication of private causes of action was unique. While it may have been preferable to see more done on behalf of victims, U.S. government support for the Libyan cases was vital to their eventual settlement.

In the past, the Executive Branch has typically taken a dim view of private actions against state sponsors of terrorism under the FSIA; viewing them as interfering with the President's foreign affairs powers: "undermin[ing] the President's ability to combat international terrorism and other threats to national security by permitting the wholesale attachment of blocked property, thereby depleting the pool of blocked assets and depriving the U.S. of a source of leverage…"[90] President Clinton's infamous reversal of policy—on the one hand supporting the creation of the Flatow Amendment,[91] which was initially construed as a cause of action against state supporters of terrorism until the 2004 opinion issued by the United States Circuit Court of Appeals for the District of Columbia Circuit, while later sending the Department of Justice to file briefs on behalf of Iran to protect Iranian assets located in the United States against the efforts of the Flatow family to satisfy their judgment against Iran in U.S. court—provides another example of the kind of political football that can often occur.[92]

Last year's resolution of the Libya cases for its past acts of state sponsorship of terrorism provides an illustration of how advocates for victims of state sponsorship of terrorism can provide ammunition to the State Department in its advancement of U.S. policy and how the two can work together to achieve their goals. The primary cases that drove the agreement with Libya forward were the Lockerbie Pan Am 103 bombing, the LaBelle discotheque bombing case and the UTA Flight 177 bombing. It had been U.S. government policy to bring Libya into the community of law abiding nations on the condition that its government take the requisite steps towards responsible governance—by giving up their WMD program, ending support to groups of terrorists and accepting liability for past terrorist actions, and increasing diplomatic and commercial ties between our countries. As isolated as Libya was, however, the U.S. Executive Branch had few

---

90 Jennifer K. Elsea, *Report on Suits Against Terrorist States*, Congressional Research Service, 31 Jul 2008, 13 (quoting *Terrorism: Victims' Access to Terrorist Assets—Hearing Before the Senate Committee on the Judiciary*, 106th Cong., 1st Sess. (October 27, 1999) (S. 106–941) (statement of Sen. Mack); *Justice for Victims of Terrorism Act: Hearing Before the Subcommittee on Immigration and Claims of the House Committee on the Judiciary*, 106th Cong., 2d Sess. (April 13, 2000) (statement submitted by Treasury Deputy Secretary Eizenstat, Defense Under Secretary for Policy Slocombe, and State Under Secretary Pickering).

91 Civil Liability for Acts of State-Sponsored Terrorism," P.L. 104–208, Title I, § 101(c) [Title V, § 589] (September 30, 1996), 110 Stat. 3009–172; codified at 28 U.S.C. § 1605 note.

92 For background see *Clinton Shields Iran from U.S. Justice Blocks Restitution to Families of Victims Murdered By State-Sponsored Terrorists*, Western Journalism Center, 28 Sep 2000 available online at http://www.wnd.com/news/article.asp?ARTICLE_ID=20214.

levers with which to influence their behavior and to finalize the resolution of the cases against Libya.

Despite this lack of leverage, a unique United States private-public partnership succeeded in negotiating the transfer of $1.5 billion in Libyan funds to compensate past victims of Libyan acts of state-sponsored terrorism. The partnership was comprised of Jim Kreindler and Perles Law Firm, PC as the legal counsel for two of the largest groups of victims, and Jonathan Schwartz of the State Department, Deputy Legal Advisor for Near Eastern Affairs. This partnership should serve as a model for future reconciliation with other countries currently outside the community of law abiding nations. Such a partnership does not happen often because of the absence of an institutional voice for victims of terrorism at the State Department. One way to fix this is to statutorily create an office for terror victims' assistance, ("LTVA"), based upon LCID—which would deal with providing assistance for U.S. victims of terrorism as LCID provides assistance to U.S. companies with foreign investment disputes.

What is referred to as the "Libya model" worked well because Mr. Schwartz, Mr. Kreindler and Perles Law worked toward the ultimate goal of victim compensation, even in difficult times when the partnership was strained by inherently divergent interests. The creation of the LTVA office would lay the groundwork for the future replication of the successful results of the Libya model. The Libya model worked in this case because Mr. Schwartz took the unusual step of effectively serving as a quasi-institutional voice for victims of Libyan terrorism at the State Department. Irrespective of the establishment of an office such as LTVA, the public-private partnership should be repeated for the benefits of the victims of terrorism and to further U.S. foreign policy interests.

One of the byproducts of the Libya-United States settlement over all past acts of terrorism is the Executive Branch espousing the claims of all plaintiffs in U.S. courts who had filed suit against Libya, thereby putting an end to their litigation efforts in return for varying levels of compensation, which included a possible result of zero compensation for some plaintiffs. It cannot be doubted that the President has the authority to settle claims or take the lead in foreign affairs. Precedents for the President's power to enter into agreements with foreign nations to settle monetary claims by U.S. citizens are seen in cases such as *Dames & Moore v. Regan*[93] or *United States v. Pink*.[94] Nonetheless the Executive

---

[93] *Dames & Moore v. Regan*, 453 U.S. 654, 687 (1980) (stating in upholding the Iran-U.S. Settlement that the "fact that the President has provided such [an alternative] forum here means that the claimants are receiving something in return for the suspension of their claims, namely, access to an international tribunal before which they may well recover something on their claims.").

[94] *United States v. Pink*, 315 U.S. 203 (1942) (where the United States was acting pursuant to an Executive Agreement with the former Soviet Union that required it to collect the remaining assets from the New York branch of a Russian insurance company that were allegedly owed to foreign creditors).

Branch's constitutional prerogative over these private causes of action does not automatically mean that it is good policy to exercise the power and trump the private claim. In addition to the moral rationale—doing our very best to make victims of horrific acts of terrorism whole—there is a significant public policy reason for supporting these actions. If state sponsors of terrorism come to realize that there is a cost for their malicious activities, they may reevaluate their policies. Even if private causes of action do not cause an immediate shift in state policy, these lawsuits provide another avenue for attacking the malign influence of state sponsors of terrorism such as Syria and Iran. As recently described by journalist Robin Wright, the U.S. Treasury Department has found that private industry itself provides a significant financial tool against terror.[95] If industry is convinced that doing business with a state sponsor poses greater risk than benefit, they will simply stop doing business.

The amended FSIA provides leverage in this arena by providing an expansion of means to recover from foreign state-owned assets and enterprises. The threat of a judgment creditor attaching such properties would make industry wary of doing business with state sponsors of terror, particularly in countries which provide for full faith and credit to foreign civil judgments. While the Libyan desire for rapprochement provided a unique point of leverage, U.S. officials can still do much to aid in cases with unrepentant state sponsors of terror by simply taking a non-obstructive posture towards civil actions, and allowing private judgment creditors to pressure the state sponsors of terrorism. Further, the U.S. government could help by identifying state-owned assets in the United States and, in conjunction with U.S. allies abroad. These properties are often hidden in a web of front companies that victims would have difficulty identifying.[96]

Should the Executive Branch follow the Libya model, thereby reversing its trend of resisting the successful resolution of private actions against state sponsors of terrorism, and choose to use these private suits as levers against state sponsors, the FSIA could have an impact in not only compensating victims, but causing state sponsors of terror to recalculate the costs of their behaviors. The Obama administration should seriously consider the value of this potential tool in the continued struggle against violent extremists and the states that support them.

The Obama Administration should consider another example of the benefits that flow from cooperation with advocates for victims of state-sponsored terrorism. As a result of efforts by private claimants, the state sponsor of the Khobar

---

95 Robin Wright, *Stuart Levey's War*, N.Y. Times, 31 October 2008.

96 For example, a high rise in New York City was recently seized by US authorities—owned on paper by the Assa Corporation but which acted on behalf of the Treasury designated terror facilitator, Iran's Bank Melli. *See* Lee Ross, *Feds Seize New York Office Building Tied to Iranian Government*, Fox News, 17 Dec 08, available online at http://www.foxnews.com/story/0,2933,468804,00.html.

Towers bombing was publicly exposed by trial lawyers after the FBI was prevented from investigating the attack by the Saudi government. As Louis Freeh detailed in a *Wall Street Journal* op-ed in July 2006, the United States government decided not to pursue the investigation into the Iranian angle due to prevailing geopolitical considerations. President Clinton was supporting the rise of then Iranian President Khatami, the Iranian reformist in hopes (in retrospect, unfounded) that Khatami could usher in a new era of US-Iranian relations. The Executive Branch is constitutionally privileged to sacrifice private interests in the pursuit of foreign policy and national security objectives of the U.S. Luckily for the Khobar Towers victims and the U.S. government, the FSIA allows for lawsuits against those designated as state sponsors of terrorism. Here, a law firm took the case and pursued it—resulting in a judgment against Iran. This allowed for the public exposure of that regime's guilt, something the Clinton administration could not investigate or pursue at the time. Nonetheless, because of the FSIA incentives, victims of that horrendous attack and their counsel were able to investigate the attack and expose its perpetrators before the world. The exposure by private litigants allowed the U.S. government to disclaim responsibility in its dialogue with the Iranian government as President Clinton pursued rapprochement.

Many cases have publicized the state sponsors of infamous attacks where the U.S. government was unwilling or unable to devote resources to the investigation, or where geopolitical considerations constrained their overt involvement. One example is seen in a case successfully brought in the District Court for the District of Columbia against Iran for its complicity in the 1983 Marine barracks bombing in Beirut, Lebanon that caused the death of over 240 servicemen, captioned *Peterson v. Islamic Republic of Iran*. Judge Royce Lamberth authored a May 30, 2003 opinion that adjudged Iran liable based upon the clear and convincing evidence linking Iran to the 1983 attack.[97] Subsequently, Judge Lamberth entered a judgment against Iran in excess of $2.6 billion.[98]

This important case exposed Iran's involvement in the 1983 Beirut attack. While those in intelligence circles were aware of Iran's complicity, that fact did not reach wider public circulation until the court awarded this judgment. The news was carried on CNN.com and went around the world. The attack happened so long ago that it was almost forgotten, but this is an important terrorist attack to remember for another reason. Bin Laden was inspired to bomb the two U.S. embassies in Africa in 1998 by the Marine barracks bombing. American soldiers are "paper tigers," Osama bin Laden told ABC News in 1998.[99] "[T]he Marines fled

97 *Peterson v. Islamic Republic of Iran*, 264 F. Supp. 2d 46 (D.D.C. 2003).

98 *Peterson v. Islamic Republic of Iran*, 515 F. Supp. 2d 25 (D.D.C. 2007).

99 http://www.nytimes.com/1998/08/23/weekinreview/the-world-osama-bin-laden-in-his-own-words.html.

after two explosions."[100] Our withdrawal from Lebanon led Bin Laden to believe that he could blast the United States out of Africa to protect his then home base in the Sudan. And while Bin Laden himself withdrew from the Sudan in the late 1990s, Al Qaeda activity in the horn of Africa remains a top U.S. foreign policy concern.

VI. Missed Opportunities?

In view of these promising developments in anti-terrorism civil litigation, the Executive Branch should increase its cooperation with victims' enforcement efforts. On September 7, 2007 the plaintiffs in *Peterson v. Iran*,[101] recovered a $2.7 billion judgment against Iran arising out of the Marine Barracks bombing of October 23, 1983. Post-judgment remedies permit the *Peterson* plaintiffs, the judgment creditor, to seize assets of Iran, the judgment debtor, that are in the hands of any third parties. This process is traditionally called a garnishment, in which a third party is obligated to turn over to a US Marshal money or "property" due to the judgment debtor. Various subsets of the legal process compel the surrender of the debtor's property in the third party's hands, including the service of a writ of execution, a full blown creditor's suit to enforce the judgment, subpoena of records belonging to third parties to trace the assets of the judgment debtor, and an order compelling a physical appearance before a judge to testify and produce documents. While the *Peterson* plaintiffs' judgment originated in the United States District Court for the District of Columbia, this judgment can be registered in any judicial district in the United States.

The *Peterson* plaintiffs promptly registered their judgments in various other judicial districts in an effort to seize Iranian assets throughout the country. These districts included the Northern District of California[102] and the Northern District of Illinois.[103] In both proceedings, the issue of the extent to which the foreign

---

[100] *Id.* ("We have seen in the last decade the decline of the American Government and the weakness of the American soldier who is ready to wage cold wars and unprepared to fight long wars. This was proven in Beirut when the Marines fled after two explosions.").

[101] *Peterson v. Islamic Republic of Iran*, 515 F. Supp. 2d 25, 38 (D.D.C. 2007).

[102] The *Peterson* plaintiffs sought to enforce their judgment against Iran against various third parties holding Iranian assets in the Northern District of California by registering their judgment in that District on March 11, 2008. *Peterson v. Islamic Republic of Iran*, 08-mc-80030 (JSW), *Registration of Foreign Judgment in the amount of $2,656,944,877.00 in favor of plaintiff and against defendant* (N.D. Cal. Filed March 11, 2008).

[103] The *Peterson* plaintiffs sought to enforce their judgment against Iran in the Northern District of Illinois by a motion for intervention. *Rubin v. Islamic Republic.* 03-cv-09370 (BMM), *Motion to Intervene by Deborah Peterson, et al.* (N.D. Il. filed July 7, 2008). The motion to intervene was granted on October 16, 2008.

sovereign itself must be made to submit to discovery by the *Peterson* plaintiffs for the purpose of enforcing the underlying judgment has been raised. Discovery into the holdings of various third parties holding or transferring Iranian assets would necessarily provide information on one of the most important topics in U.S. national security circles today. Appeals have been entered in both proceedings and in both circuit courts, the U.S. government has filed a statement of interest siding with Iran as a party to the proceeding in the Northern District of Illinois and a statement of interest siding with the third party in possession of Iranian assets in the Northern District of California.[104] Despite the gravity of permitting a private party to proceed with broad-based non-jurisdictional discovery, neither FSIA on its face or TRIA prohibits such an endeavor nor has any court banned such practices.

What is well known is that Iran has been using national banks to fund its WMD program through an overseas network of shell companies. In 2006 and 2007 the U.S. Treasury began blacklisting various Iranian state-owned banks and international companies in an attempt to announce these entities' ties to international terrorism and more importantly to nuclear proliferation and WMD acquisition:

> The Department of the Treasury today designated Bank Sepah, a state-owned Iranian financial institution for providing support and services to designated Iranian proliferation firms… "Bank Sepah is the financial linchpin of Iran's missile procurement network and has actively assisted Iran's pursuit of missiles capable of carrying weapons of mass destruction," said Stuart Levey, Treasury's Under Secretary for Terrorism and Financial Intelligence (TFI).[105]

The discovery of information, at issue now in the *Peterson* plaintiffs' litigation in Northern District of California and the Northern District of Illinois, could facilitate U.S. government efforts to break up proliferation networks and support for international terrorism. The potential for the serious interruption of financial support for the Iranian weapons and terrorism pipeline is illustrated by the groundbreaking restraint of over $2 billion in Iranian funds at a financial institution in New York City, which is now the subject of an ongoing garnishment action.[106]

Under the Obama administration, the U.S. Treasury has expanded sanctions against Iran to further cripple Iran's financial and industrial sectors. The first major step taken by the Obama administration against the Iranian regime went into effect on June 24, 2010 with the creation of the Comprehensive Iran Sanctions, Accountability, and Divestment Act of 2010 ("CISADA"). CISADA limited

---

104 Existent case law supports broad based discovery against an agency or instrumentality of a foreign state. *Richmark Corp. v. Timber Falling Consultants*, 959 F.2d 1468 (9th Cir. 1992).

105 http://www.ustreas.gov/press/releases/hp219.htm (January 9, 2007).

106 The matter remains under seal and subject to a protective order. *Peterson v. Islamic Republic of Iran*, CA 01-2094 docket Entry #439 (RCL) (September 30, 2009).

Iran's ability to import refined petroleum and other industrial goods that enable the Islamic Republic's civil and military industrial capacities.[107] Further sanctions banning U.S. entities from dealing with the National Iranian Tanker Company took effect in July, 2012 along with other restrictions on Iranian crude oil distribution, all contributing to a substantial one-third drop in the exchange value of Iran's currency against the U.S. dollar in October 2012. The U.S. government estimates that crude oil sales account for roughly half of Iran's national annual revenue.[108]

In a concerted effort to destabilize Iran's central banking structure and promote non-proliferation, the National Defense Authorization Act for 2012 gave the first provisions sanctioning the Central Bank of Iran, Bank Markazi, by restricting U.S. entities from doing business with it.[109] In an unprecedented move against the Iranian financial structure, President Obama issued Executive Order 13599 on February 5, 2012, blocking and freezing all assets of the Central Bank of Iran held in the U.S. or by any U.S. citizen.[110] Freezing assets tied to Iran's Central Bank opens doors for victims of terrorism who have secured judgments against Iran in U.S. courts currently searching for assets to compensate their civil judgments.

Those plaintiffs seeking compensation in judgments against Iran were given momentum on August 10, 2012 when President Obama signed into law Section 502 of the Iran Threat Reduction and Syria Human Rights Act of 2012, part of the newest Iran sanctions, the "Iran Threat Reduction and Syria Human Rights Act of 2012." Section 502, entitled "Interests in Certain Financial Assets of Iran," stripped the immunity previously provided under the FSIA from assets of the Central Bank of Iran discovered in U.S. banks. The new provision established that Iranian Central Bank assets discovered in the *Peterson* case in New York banks "shall be subject to execution or attachment... to satisfy any judgment to the extent of any compensatory damages awarded against Iran."[111] Securing the funds is still an ongoing legal battle, but Section 502 gives the *Peterson* plaintiffs a clearer route to securing compensation. The supportive political provisions are certainly useful, but without more comprehensive support from the Obama administration in cases against state sponsors of terrorism, plaintiffs will continue to struggle to compensate their judicial victories.

---

107 http://www.whitehouse.gov/the-press-office/remarks-president-signing-iran-sanctions-act (July 1, 2010).

108 http://www.reuters.com/article/2012/10/23/us-iran-oil-idUSBRE89M0EP20121023 (October 23, 2012).

109 http://www.washingtonpost.com/politics/obama-signs-defense-bill-pledges-to-maintain-legal-rights-of-terror-suspects/2011/12/31/gIQATzbkSP_story.html (December 31, 2011).

110 Exec. Order No. 13,599, 77 Fed. Reg. 6659 (February 8, 2012).

111 http://www.reuters.com/article/2012/08/24/us-usa-iran-idUSBRE87N0TM20120824 (August 24, 2012).

In perhaps the greatest nod to the success of these lawsuits in advancing the cause of victims of terrorism, a senate and house bill has been advanced by Canadian legislators to largely replicate the U.S. system for lawsuits against state sponsors of terrorism.[112] If the Canadian government agrees with the efficacy of the program advanced by U.S. private advocates for victims of terrorism, then the U.S. government should support these efforts and cooperate with its victims of terrorism in their search for assets to satisfy any outstanding judgments. Only by overcoming the obstacles that have prevented victims from collecting upon their judgments can the anti-terrorism litigation scheme prove its utility. And only the utilization of the public-private partnership has succeeded thus far in procuring that level of success. The Chief Judge of the District Court for the District of Columbia recently issued an opinion that noted the endemic obstacles that have continuously hobbled victims of terrorism:

> Despite the best intentions of Congress and moral statements of support from the Executive Branch, the stark reality is that the plaintiffs in these actions face continuous road blocks and setbacks in what has been an increasingly futile exercise to hold Iran accountable for unspeakable acts of terrorist violence. [113]

VII. The Use of TRIA as an Enforcement Tool

The Terrorism Risk Insurance Act of 2002 TRIA was adopted as Pub. L. No. 107–297, 116 Stat. 2322 (2002) and is codified at 28 U.S.C. § 1610, Note. Congress enacted TRIA in 2002 as a footnote to 28 U.S.C. § 1610 in order to facilitate the ability of the victims of terrorist attacks to collect upon their judgments. In relevant part, TRIA Section 201(a) provides:

> *Notwithstanding any other provision of law*... in every case in which a person has obtained a judgment against a terrorist party on a claim based upon an act of terrorism, or for which a terrorist party is not immune under section 1605(a)(7) of title 28 United States Code, the blocked assets of that terrorist party (*including the blocked assets of any agency or instrumentality of that terrorist party*) shall be subject to execution or attachment in aid of execution in order to satisfy such judgment to the extent of any compensatory damages for which such terrorist party has been adjudged liable.

TRIA § 201(a) (emphasis added). Thus, to execute upon the blocked assets of a "terrorist party", a plaintiff must establish the following facts: (1) they have obtained judgments for compensatory damages; (2) against a "terrorist party"; (3) on a claim based upon an "act of terrorism, or for which a terrorist party is not immune under"; and (4) the blocked assets are "the blocked assets of" a "terrorist party" or "the blocked assets of any agency or instrumentality of" a "terrorist

112 Victor Comras, *A Bulwark Against Terror*, National Post, editorial (September 11, 2009).
113 *In re Islamic Republic of Iran Terrorism Litig.*, 659 F. Supp. 2d 31, 35–36 (D.D.C. 2009).

party".[114] Conflicting approaches in the statutory interpretation of the provisions of TRIA in the Second Circuit has illustrated how courts evaluate the different policy considerations implicated by the utilization of TRIA.

In the beginning of 2013, the Second Circuit is set to hear the appeals in *Hausler v. JPMorgan Chase Bank*, 845 F. Supp. 2d 553 (S.D.N.Y. 2012) and *Calderon-Cardona v. JPMorgan Chase Bank*, 2011 WL 6155987 (S.D.N.Y. Dec. 7, 2011) jointly. The analysis of the TRIA in each line of cases differs in three key areas: (1) the statutory construction of the phrase "blocked assets of the terrorist party," (2) the underlying policy rationales that inform the interpretation, (3) whether TRIA preempts state law regarding ownership of property/assets.

The key distinctions between the opinions focus on the statutory interpretation of the phrase "blocked assets of that terrorist party." The *Hausler* line reads TRIA in conjunction with the appropriate regulatory scheme to comprehensively define which blocked assets can be attached and therefore preempt state property law. This approach is more victim-focused and emphasizes that the purpose of the statute is to provide comprehensive compensation for victims of terrorism. Furthermore, it asserts that using state law could lead to inconsistent judgments where some states allow the attachment of certain types of property while other states do not. The *Calderon-Cardona* approach breaks the phrase into two components and finds that TRIA does not define ownership sufficiently. Consequently, state law must supplement the federal scheme, and the petitioner cannot establish the second component because EFTs are not properly owned by the state or its instrumentalities under state law. This approach also defers to the executive and does not want to read TRIA broadly because it may negatively impact the executive's ability to negotiate on the international stage.

In *Hausler I*, the court found that TRIA in conjunction with the CACRs preempted state property law in establishing ownership.[115] The court relied on reading the two together because the CACRs provide an explicit and broad definition of what constitutes a property interest or asset.[116] The plain language of the statute indicates that blocked assets are determined in reference to the CACRs. The court additionally looks to the legislative history of TRIA which indicates Congress had a broad purpose intended to "deal comprehensively with the problem of judgments rendered on behalf of victims of terrorism in any court of competent jurisdiction.[117] The court construed the definition of blocked assets very

114 *See* TRIA § 201(a); *see also Weinstein v. Islamic Republic of Iran*, 624 F.Supp.2d 272, 274 (E.D.N.Y. 2009), *aff'd*, 609 F.3d 43 (2d Cir. 2010); *Weininger v. Castro*, 462 F. Supp. 2d 457, 479 (S.D.N.Y. 2006) (listing elements of a TRIA claim).

115 *Id.* at 530–31.

116 *Id.* at 532–33 (noting that according to the C.F.R. "the term 'interest' when used with respect to property shall mean an interest of any nature whatsoever, direct or indirect.").

117 *Id.* at 531 (citing H.R. Conf. Rep. No. 107–779 at 27).

broadly to refer to any asset seized or frozen under the CACRs.[118] The focus here is on the broad remedial purpose of providing a remedy for victims of terrorism.

Hausler II was decided in February 2012, after *Calderon-Cardona* and *Levin*. The court reaffirmed its original finding that state law was preempted by the definition of blocked assets in TRIA.[119] The court distinguished *Calderon-Cardona* saying that the court incorrectly splits the analysis of the phrase "blocked assets of that terrorist party" into two pieces: "blocked assets" and "of that terrorist party." *Id.* The *Hausler II* court asserts that in reading the phrase as a whole it demonstrates that assets blocked pursuant to the particular regulation or administrative action directed at the particular terrorist party are available for attachment.[120] This limits a party seeking a judgment against Iran from executing against funds blocked pursuant to the CACRs because those are targeted at Cuba, not Iran.

The *Levin* court, following *Hausler*, asserts that TRIA must be read in context with the overarching statutory scheme of the FSIA.[121] Furthermore, the court noted that in *Asia Pulp*, the Second Circuit held that *Jaldhi* instructs that whether or not midstream EFTs may be attached or seized depends upon the nature and the wording of the statute to which attachment or seizure is sought, and in this case, TRIA defines which assets are subject to attachment by reference to regulations pursuant to which the assets are blocked.[122] Essentially, *Levin* and *Hausler I* and *II* look at TRIA in the greater context of regulations against the country. In each case, the states in question were Cuba and Iran, both state sponsors of terrorism with aggressive statutory regulations in place restricting trade and imposing sanctions.

Calderon-Cardona, took a different approach, splits the phrase "blocked assets of that terrorist party" into two components and asserts that the petitioners cannot establish that North Korea or one of its agencies or instrumentalities actually owns the EFTs in question.[123] The court asserts that TRIA does not specifically define property or property ownership leaving a gap in the law that should be filled by reference to state law.[124] The court does acknowledge that the CACRs are functionally equivalent to the NKSRs.[125] The NKSRs, in the court's view, do not properly define ownership leaving "ample room for state law to supplement this federal regime."[126] The analysis here hangs on the meaning of the word "of"

---

118 *Id.* at 533.
119 *Id.* at 566.
120 *Id.* at 568.
121 *Id.* at 10.
122 *Id.* at 16–17.
123 *Id.* at 8.
124 *Id.* at 9.
125 *Id.* at 10.
126 *Id.* at 12.

regarding ownership. The court finds that EFTs do not qualify as an asset "of" or belonging to North Korea so they are not attachable.

Calderon-Cardona actually decided the case based on the fact that North Korea is no longer declared a state sponsor of terrorism. The court shows deference to the Executive Branch in being able to use TRIA judgments as part of bargaining with a state sponsor of terrorism.[127] Essentially, executive foreign policy trumps the victims' interest in judgment recovery.

We will follow the resolution of these cases very closely considering that the final decision from the Second Circuit might have an impact on terrorism victims' enforcement efforts in the United States, depending of course on how the opinion is written. Undoubtedly, the loser will seek review at the Supreme Court.

VIII. Conclusion

These types of cases significantly increase the cost of state sponsorship of terror through punitive and compensatory damages and expose what would otherwise be secret networks for the facilitation of terror. These cases also make doing business more difficult, as financial institutions increasingly scrutinize transactions. These cases may act as a type of private sanction—forcing corporations doing business with state sponsors of terror to think twice if their actions could make them liable in U.S. courts. Based upon past experience, the Obama administration should expand its cooperation, even if in an unofficial capacity, because these lawsuits further U.S. government foreign policy goals, by creating serious disincentives for the continuity of state sponsorship of terror.

---

127 *Id.* at 6.

ADJUDICATING ACTS OF STATE

Chimène I. Keitner*

I. Introduction

An apparent paradox lies at the heart of modern transnational human rights litigation. On the one hand, relevant actors in the international community have agreed that certain actions performed by individuals on behalf of states are so offensive to basic notions of human freedom and dignity that no state's officials should be able to engage in them with impunity. On the other hand, the principles of sovereign equality and non-interference in the affairs of other states (absent U.N. Security Council authorization) continue to animate basic understandings of the structure of international society and the limits of international law.

One of the central puzzles for international law remains the problem of enforcement. Increasingly, where individual actors violate international legal norms, interested parties seek to use the judicial machinery of foreign states to impose legal consequences for such violations. I have referred to this phenomenon as "horizontal" enforcement because, legally speaking, states are situated on an equal or horizontal plane vis-à-vis each other.[1] Some view horizontal enforcement as presumptively illegitimate, based on the idea that one sovereign cannot sit in judgment on the acts of another sovereign. Others maintain that recognition of the idea of "universal jurisdiction" to prescribe, adjudicate, and enforce prohibitions on certain types of specifically defined and universally condemned conduct (such as torture, genocide, war crimes, crimes against humanity, and

* Professor of Law, University of California Hastings College of the Law. This paper expands on the author's remarks on *Suing Foreign Officials in U.S. Courts* at the 2012 Sokol Colloquium, held at the University of Virginia School of Law. The author wishes to thank all those who attended the colloquium for their contributions to the discussion, which helped to shape this written intervention.

1 *See* Chimène I. Keitner, Germany v. Italy *and the Limits of Horizontal Enforcement: Some Reflections from a U.S. Perspective*, 11 J. Int'l Crim. Just. 167 (2013).

John Norton Moore (ed.) Foreign Affairs Litigation in United States Courts, pp. 49–66
 ISBN 978-90-04-25727-6

piracy) necessarily entails an acceptance of horizontal enforcement by foreign states, in addition to "vertical" enforcement by international bodies. Courts and commentators continue to grapple with defining the circumstances under which horizontal enforcement may be warranted.

This contribution focuses on horizontal enforcement in the form of civil proceedings against current or, more often, former foreign officials. It focuses on the practice of the United States, although civil proceedings (and criminal proceedings joined by *parties civiles*) have also been brought against foreign officials in other countries. Part II sets forth the distinction between status-based (*ratione personae*) and conduct-based (*ratione materiae*) immunity for individual officials. Part III traces the late nineteenth-century origins of the act of state doctrine in U.S. courts to earlier, eighteenth-century understandings of conduct-based immunity. Although the act of state doctrine subsequently took on a different, narrower meaning in litigation involving foreign expropriations, Part IV concludes by suggesting that understanding the connection between early formulations of the act of state doctrine and claims to conduct-based immunity can help define the circumstances under which U.S. courts can and should impose legal consequences on foreign defendants for internationally unlawful conduct.

II. Conduct-based vs. Status-based Immunity

International law distinguishes between status-based immunities (*ratione personae*) and conduct-based immunities (*ratione materiae*). Status-based immunities shield incumbent officials (such as diplomats and heads of state) from foreign legal proceedings that would interfere with their ability to conduct international relations.[2] Conduct-based immunities shield certain acts performed by incumbent officials who do not have status-based immunity (such as consular officials) from foreign legal proceedings relating to those acts.[3] They also shield former foreign officials from legal proceedings based on certain acts performed in their official capacity during their tenure in office. The scope of conduct-based immunity from foreign legal proceedings for acts that amount to international crimes remains a subject of debate.[4]

This contribution approaches the question of the scope of conduct-based immunity from a different angle by examining legal proceedings brought against

---

[2] *See, e.g.*, Arrest Warrant of 11 April 2000 (Dem. Rep. Congo v. Belg.), 2002 I.C.J. 3 (Feb. 14) (finding status-based immunity for an incumbent foreign official).

[3] *See, e.g.*, Vienna Convention on Consular Relations, Apr. 24, 1963, 21 U.S.T. 77, 596 U.N.T.S. 261, art. 43(1), 53(4), 71(1) (providing current and former consular officials with conduct-based immunity for acts performed in the exercise of their consular functions).

[4] For an overview, see Chimène I. Keitner, *Transnational Litigation: Jurisdiction and Immunities*, *in* Oxford Handbook of Human Rights (forthcoming 2013).

foreign officials in U.S. courts in the eighteenth and nineteenth centuries. It builds on my earlier work unearthing U.S. practice from the late eighteenth century.[5] As I suggested in that work, the common wisdom tracing the origins of sovereign immunity jurisprudence to Chief Justice John Marshall's opinion in *The Schooner Exchange* actually misses two decades of earlier practice involving proceedings against individuals who acted on behalf of foreign states.[6] Differentiating between early cases that involved claims to status-based immunity for ambassadors and public ships, and cases that involved claims to conduct-based immunity for officials who were not ambassadors, enables us to better understand the development of common law immunity doctrines. The Supreme Court has recently held that these common law doctrines continue to apply to proceedings brought against foreign officials in U.S. courts.[7]

The Schooner Exchange followed an earlier decision involving the *Cassius*, a French ship of war.[8] In that case, the Supreme Court enjoined the Pennsylvania district court from adjudicating claims against the *Cassius*. It did so based in part on a "suggestion" filed by U.S. Attorney William Rawle arguing that *in rem* proceedings against a French ship of war impermissibly impleaded France itself,[9] because the "[p]rocess of information and seizure indirectly brings the sovereign to submit to the tribunal, or to abandon the property."[10] Following Rawle's lead, U.S. Attorney Alexander Dallas and Attorney General William Pinkney argued to the Supreme Court in 1812 that a French public ship of war was entitled to immunity akin to the absolute, status-based immunity of a diplomat or foreign head of state: "We claim for this vessel, an immunity from the ordinary jurisdiction, as extensive as that of an ambassador, or of the Sovereign himself; . . . ."[11] The Supreme Court found that the ship was entitled to immunity because the United States had "impliedly consented to wa[i]ve its jurisdiction" over friendly foreign public ships entering U.S. ports.[12] Chief Justice Marshall reasoned that this consensual waiver of territorial jurisdiction could be presumed unless the United States gave "notice" to the contrary.[13]

---

5 Chimène I. Keitner, *The Forgotten History of Foreign Official Immunity*, 87 N.Y.U. L. Rev. 704 (2012).

6 *Id.* at 750–51.

7 *See* Samantar v. Yousuf, 130 S. Ct. 2278 (2010).

8 *See* United States v. Peters, 3 U.S. (3 Dall.) 121, 129 (1795).

9 *See* Keitner, *supra* note 5, at 751 & n. 263.

10 Statement of W. Rawle [to Timothy Pickering] (Dec. 21, 1796), *in* 1 American State Papers: Foreign Relations 637 (Walter Lowrie & Matthew St. Clair Clarke eds., 1833), *available at* http://memory.loc.gov/cgi-bin/ampage?collId=llsp&fileName=001/llsp001.db&recNum=4.

11 The Schooner Exchange v. M[c]Faddon, 11 U.S. (7 Cranch) 116, 132 (1812).

12 *Id.* at 146.

13 *Id.* at 137, 141.

Litigation involving the *Cassius* and the *Schooner Exchange* provided the jurisprudential foundation for the practice of seeking "suggestions" of status-based immunity from the Executive Branch to confirm the "fact" of a particular ship's status as "a public armed ship, in the service of a foreign sovereign, with whom the government of the United States is at peace."[14] Beginning in the 1790s, another line of cases emerged that can be viewed as providing the jurisprudential foundation for claims to conduct-based immunity in U.S. courts. The foundational case, *Waters v. Collot,* involved a suit against the former Governor of Guadeloupe for allegedly abusing his authority as Governor to confiscate an American ship.[15] *Waters* has been cited by several scholars as an early example of the act of state doctrine,[16] which provides a substantive defense on the merits, rather than immunity from jurisdiction.[17] In *Waters,* the Pennsylvania Supreme Court found that the defendant was not immune from U.S. jurisdiction notwithstanding the "official" nature of his acts, whether or not he could be found "ultimately liable" on the merits.[18]

Two centuries after *Waters,* in *W.S. Kirkpatrick v. Environmental Tectonics Corporation,* the U.S. Supreme Court characterized the act of state doctrine as "merely requir[ing] that, in the process of deciding, the acts of foreign sovereigns taken within their own jurisdictions shall be deemed valid."[19] However, in a pre-*Kirkpatrick* world, when a foreign official claimed conduct-based immunity from proceedings in a U.S. court, she was essentially saying that her conduct amounted to an act of state for which she could not be held personally liable. Conceptualizing conduct-based immunity as a variation of the act of state doctrine underscores

---

14 *Id.* at 147.

15 Waters v. Collot, 2 U.S. (2 Dall.) 247 (Pa. 1796); Waters v. Collot, 2 Yeates 26 (Pa. 1795); *see also* Keitner, *supra* note 5, at 713–24 (discussing this case).

16 *E.g.,* Penelope Dalton, *The Right of the State Department and the Duty of the Court,* 6 Wm. & Mary L. Rev. 70, 81 (1965) (indicating that *Waters v. Collot* "introduced" the act of state doctrine); L.F.E. Goldie, *The Sabbatino Case: International Law Versus the Act of State,* 12 UCLA L. Rev. 107, 108 n. 4 (1964–1965) (citing *Waters v. Collot* as an example of an "act of state type of situation"); Louis Henkin, *The Foreign Affairs Power of the Federal Courts:* Sabbatino, 64 Colum. L. Rev. 805, 805 n. 2 (1964) (citing *Waters v. Collot* as an early example of the act of state doctrine); Michael Zander, *Act of State Doctrine,* 53 Am. J. Int'l L. 826, 829–30 (1959) (describing *Waters v. Collot* as a classical application of the act of state doctrine); Charles B. Hagan, *The Act of State,* 23 Minn. L. Rev. 446, 476 n. 24 (1938–1939) (citing *Waters v. Collot* as an early example of the idea that "the agents of another state shall not be held liable in the courts of the United States for acts done in the course of their duties in other States").

17 *See* Republic of Austria v. Altmann, 531 U.S. 677, 700 (2004) ("Unlike a claim of sovereign immunity, which merely raises a jurisdictional defense, the act of state doctrine provides foreign states with a substantive defense on the merits.").

18 *Waters,* 2 U.S. (2 Dall.) at 248 (determining that the defendant could be held to bail, without prejudging the question of whether he could be found "ultimately liable").

19 W.S. Kirkpatrick v. Environmental Tectonics Corp., 493 U.S. 400, 409 (1990).

its origin as an affirmative defense on the merits.[20] It also suggests that judicial recognition of conduct-based immunity might appropriately be calibrated to the degree of acceptance by the international community of the conduct-regulating norm at issue. As the Supreme Court observed in *Banco Nacional de Cuba v. Sabbatino,* a classic decision involving the act of state doctrine, "[i]t should be apparent that the greater the degree of codification or consensus concerning a particular area of international law, the more appropriate it is for the judiciary to render decisions regarding it. . . ."[21] The case for horizontal enforcement is at its strongest when the alleged conduct rises to the level of a universally recognized violation for which individuals bear personal responsibility.

III. Acts of State from McLeod to *Underhill*

In the late eighteenth century, claims to conduct-based immunity did not succeed as a defense to jurisdiction over a current or former official who was present on U.S. territory, even if the alleged conduct occurred overseas.[22] In the early nineteenth century, judicial elaboration of common law notions of sovereign immunity continued to expand, primarily in the context of *in rem* proceedings against foreign ships and their cargo, rather than suits against foreign officials. In his 1822 opinion in *The Santissima Trinidad,* Justice Story interpreted the precedent in the *Cassius* and a subsequent case[23] as "furnish[ing] a rule for the exemption of a public ship from proceedings *in rem,* in our Courts for illegal captures on the high seas, in violation of our neutrality," but as "in no degree exempt[ing] her *prizes* in our ports from the ample exercise of our jurisdiction."[24] He concluded:

> It may therefore be justly laid down as a general proposition, that all persons and property within the territorial jurisdiction of a sovereign, are amenable to the jurisdiction of himself or his Courts: and that the exceptions to this rule are such only

---

20 *See* Keitner, *supra* note 5, at 755–57.

21 Banco Nacional de Cuba v. Sabbatino, 376 U.S. 398, 428 (1964). Accordingly, the Restatement (Third) of Foreign Relations suggests that "[a] claim arising out of an alleged violation of fundamental human rights—for instance, a claim on behalf of a victim of torture or genocide—would (if otherwise sustainable) probably not be defeated by the act of state doctrine, since the accepted international law of human rights is well established and contemplates external scrutiny of such acts." Restatement (Third) of the Foreign Relations Law of the United States § 443 cmt. c (1987). *See also* Kenneth C. Randall & Chimène I. Keitner, *Sabbatino, Sosa, and "Super Norms", in* Looking to the Future: Essays on International Law in Honor of W. Michael Reisman (Martinus Nijhoff, 2010).

22 *See* Keitner, *supra* note 5, at 757–58. For more on early cases against foreign defendants for foreign conduct, see Chimène I. Keitner, *State Courts and Transitory Torts in Transnational Human Rights Cases,* 3 U.C. Irvine L. Rev. 81 (2013).

23 L'Invincible, 14 U.S. (1 Wheat.) 238 (1816).

24 The Santissima Trinidad, 20 U.S. (7 Wheat.) 283, 351 (1822) (emphasis in original).

> as by common usage, and public policy, have been allowed, in order to preserve the peace and harmony of nations, and to regulate their intercourse in a manner best suited to their dignity and rights.[25]

The Supreme Court in the *Santissima Trinidad* found no applicable exception to territorial jurisdiction and affirmed the decree restoring the disputed cargo to its original Spanish owners.[26]

Although Justice Story acknowledged in *The Santissima Trinidad* that some "inconvenience... from reasons of state policy or executive discretion" could grow out of the long-standing practice of allowing recovery in tort by private parties in cases of captures based on violations of U.S. neutrality, he noted that "it is competent for Congress to apply at its pleasure the proper remedy."[27] The Executive Branch likewise disavowed the ability to halt private litigation, even if the pursuit of private claims might adversely affect the conduct of foreign relations.[28]

A. *The Case against Alexander McLeod*

The case of Alexander McLeod tested the Executive Branch's policy of non-intervention in civil suits that did not involve ambassadors or public ships. McLeod faced criminal and civil charges in New York state court for his alleged involvement in the 1837 attack on the steamboat *Caroline*, in which Buffalo citizen Amos Durfee was killed.[29] In seeking discharge from his arrest and detention in a Niagra county jail, McLeod filed an affidavit claiming that the attack on the *Caroline* had "since been approved and adopted by the national government of Great Britain, as a necessary act of self defence on the part of the authorities of

---

25 *Id.* at 353–54.

26 *Id.* at 284.

27 *The Santissima Trinidad*, 20 U.S. (7 Wheat.) at 349–50.

28 *See, e.g.*, Letter from Timothy Pickering to Philippe de Létombe (Nov. 30, 1797) (manuscript copy on file with author), *reprinted in* 8 The Documentary History of the Supreme Court of the United States, 1789–1800, at 84–85 (Maeva Marcus ed., 1998); *see also* Keitner, *supra* note 5, at 727 (emphasizing the Executive Branch's belief that it did not have authority to stop private litigation in either federal or state court, in line with separation of powers principles); David J. Bederman, *The Cautionary Tale of Alexander Mcleod: Superior Orders and the American Writ of Habeas Corpus*, 41 Emory L.J. 515, 526 (1992) (citing *Waters v. Collot* as one of the early cases when a "state had prosecuted a foreigner under circumstances that were likely to result in a diplomatic incident... [, and] Attorney General William Bradford concluded that the federal government could not intervene in the case and that Collot had to present his defense before the state court, where, it was assumed, it would be favorably received").

29 People v. McLeod, 25 Wend. 483 (N.Y. Sup. Ct. 1841). For additional discussion, see John E. Noyes, The Caroline*: International Law Limits on Resort to Force, in* International Law Stories 263 (John E. Noyes, Laura A. Dickinson & Mark W. Janis, eds., 2007); Bederman, *supra* note 28.

the province of Upper Canada."[30] He asked the court to take judicial notice of the ongoing public correspondence about the attack on the *Caroline* and McLeod's arrest between the British Minister, Henry Fox, and two successive Secretaries of State (John Forsyth and Daniel Webster), which he appended to his affidavit.

In that correspondence, British Minister Fox claimed the attack on the *Caroline* "cannot justly be made the ground of legal proceedings in the United States against the individuals concerned, who were bound to obey the authorities appointed by their own government."[31] He therefore asked Forsyth to "caus[e] the present immediate release of Mr. McLeod."[32] Forsyth replied that the President could not intervene on two grounds. First, he claimed that "[t]he jurisdiction of the several states, which constitute the Union, is, within its appropriate sphere, perfectly independent of the federal government."[33] Because McLeod had allegedly acted within New York territory, Forsyth said the federal government was powerless to intervene. Second, he indicated that, even if such a power existed over the states, nothing in Fox's protest would justify the federal government exercising it. He explained:

> The president is not aware of any principle of international law, or, indeed, of reason or justice, which entitles such offenders to impunity before the legal tribunals, when coming voluntarily within their independent and undoubted jurisdiction, because they acted in obedience to their superior authorities, or because their acts have become the subject of diplomatic discussion between the two governments.[34]

He further indicated:

> If the destruction of the *Caroline* was a public act of persons in his Majesty's service, obeying the order of their superior authorities, … it will be for the court which has taken cognizance of the offence with which Mr. McLeod is charged, to decide upon its validity when legally established before it.[35]

In other words, Forsyth took the position that McLeod was not entitled to claim jurisdictional immunity, although he could attempt to present an affirmative defense.

Frustrated in his attempts to secure McLeod's release, Fox escalated his rhetoric in a subsequent letter to Forsyth's successor, Daniel Webster, making it perfectly clear that he was demanding "formally, in the name of the British government, the immediate release of Mr. Alexander McLeod" on the grounds that

---

30 Alexander McLeod, Affidavit of May 6, 1841, *as reprinted in McLeod*, 25 Wend. 483.

31 Letter from Mr. Fox to Mr. Forsyth (Dec. 13, 1840), *as reprinted in McLeod*, 25 Wend. 483.

32 *Id.*

33 Letter from Mr. Forsyth to Mr. Fox (Dec. 26, 1840), *as reprinted in McLeod*, 25 Wend. 483.

34 *Id.*

35 *Id.*

"those subjects of her Majesty, who engaged in that transaction [of attacking the *Caroline*], were performing an act of public duty, for which they cannot be made personally and individually answerable to the laws and tribunals of any foreign country."[36] He again attempted to differentiate questions subject to diplomatic resolution from those subject to adjudication, and he argued that claims arising from the *Caroline* incident belonged exclusively in the former category. Fox also appealed to the idea of combatant immunity, whereby individuals "engaged in military or naval enterprises in their country's cause" should not bear individual responsibility for their actions, and he warned that holding McLeod individually responsible would "bring back into the practice of modern war, atrocities which civilization and Christianity have long since banished."[37]

Webster responded by reminding Fox that "in the United States, as in England, persons confined under judicial process can be released from that confinement only by judicial process," and that, with respect to the civil proceedings against McLeod, "it is quite clear that the executive government cannot interfere to arrest a civil suit, between private parties, in any stage of its progress; but that such suit must go on to its regular judicial termination."[38] That said, Webster noted that, given Fox's formal declaration that any act committed by McLeod was "an act of public force, by the British authorities,"[39] the President would furnish to McLeod's counsel "authentic evidence of the avowal by the British government, of the attack on and destruction of the *Caroline*, as acts done under its authority," and he expressed confidence that the New York court would discharge McLeod on the grounds of his "immunity from personal responsibility by virtue of the law of nations."[40] In other words, Webster believed that McLeod's affirmative defense would succeed because the international law of the time did not attribute personal responsibility to McLeod for combatant activities ordered and ratified by the United Kingdom.

The argument for an affirmative defense based on a lack of personal responsibility is different from the argument for status-based immunity from jurisdiction. Indeed, New York State Attorney General Willis Hall argued passionately against discharging McLeod from custody on status-based immunity grounds:

> It has been attempted to place the case of the prisoner on the footing of an ambassador. There is however little or no analogy between this man, acting under the order of the British government and an ambassador from that nation. They stand on distinct grounds.... The ambassador's privileges arise from the necessity of nations, and to

[36] Letter from Mr. Fox to Mr. Webster (Mar. 12, 1841), *as reprinted in McLeod*, 25 Wend. 483.

[37] *Id.*

[38] Letter from Mr. Webster to Mr. Fox (Apr. 24, 1841), *as reprinted in McLeod*, 25 Wend. 483.

[39] *Id.*

[40] *Id.*

> avoid interminable war. But these reasons do not apply to the prisoner. They apply to none but an ambassador, and much less to one who is *hostis humani generis*, or in other words, a murderer.[41]

Unlike Webster, Hall maintained that McLeod could not disavow personal responsibility for his actions on the grounds that he had been acting within the scope of official authority:

> There is also evidence which goes to show that the prisoner, was the very man who pursued and wantonly and inhumanly shot Durfee upon our territory, as he was flying unarmed from the boat. If these facts should be established on investigation, the British nation would be first to repudiate the act and to declare that it was not done by their authority.[42]

The United Kingdom did not, in fact, "repudiate the act." Nevertheless, a unanimous three-judge panel of the New York Supreme Court of Judicature (the highest court of general jurisdiction in New York at the time), which included future U.S. Supreme Court Justice Samuel Nelson,[43] denied that McLeod was entitled to immunity, either on the grounds of status-based immunity or on the grounds of a lack of personal responsibility for the alleged acts.[44] Although his claim to immunity failed, McLeod presented an alibi defense at trial and was ultimately acquitted by the jury.[45]

McLeod raised the question of whether an act performed on U.S. soil under the orders of a foreign government, and subsequently ratified by that government, could give rise to personal responsibility on the part of the defendant. The New York Supreme Court found that it could. In later cases involving conduct performed within a foreign country's own territory, however, U.S. judges proved less willing to exercise their adjudicatory authority to impose legal consequences on individuals for conduct performed under color of foreign law. Two cases, *Hatch*

---

41 *McLeod*, 25 Wend. 483, 537–38.

42 *Id.*

43 *See* Bederman, *supra* note 28 at 523 (citing 5 CARL SWISHER, HISTORY OF THE SUPREME COURT OF THE UNITED STATES: THE TANEY PERIOD 1836–64, at 186 (1974)).

44 Subsequent criticism of the N.Y. Supreme Court's opinion insisted that the N.Y. Supreme Court's discussion of whether or not it had jurisdiction over McLeod was "a waste of labour and learning" because the court so obviously had jurisdiction. DANIEL BRYANT TALLMADGE, REVIEW OF THE OPINION OF JUDGE COWEN, OF THE SUPREME COURT OF THE STATE OF NEW YORK, IN THE CASE OF ALEXANDER MCLEOD 9 (1841). That said, Daniel Bryant Tallmadge, a judge on the superior court for the city of New York, argued that the Supreme Court should have discharged McLeod because McLeod's actions did not constitute "a crime according to the law of nations," *id.* at 10, and that McLeod was therefore "entitled to the impunity of a soldier in time of war," *id.* at 11, and bore no "individual responsibility" for the alleged acts, *id.* at 18, which were committed "under lawful authority." *Id.* at 19.

45 *See* Bederman, *supra* note 28, at 526.

v. Baez[46] and *Underhill v. Hernandez*,[47] illustrate this development, as discussed below.

B. *The Case against Buenaventura Baez*

Davis Hatch, the agent for a New York company, travelled to the Dominican Republic and obtained the concession to a salt mountain from the Spanish government; the concession was confirmed by General José Maria Cabral Luna, who took power in September 1866.[48] In May 1868, supporters of Buenaventura Baez forced Cabral out of power and reinstated Baez. Baez believed that Hatch had been supporting Cabral loyalists, and ordered Hatch arrested on August 28, 1869.[49] On October 1, Hatch was tried by court-martial and sentenced to death, but Baez commuted the sentence to banishment three days later.[50] Despite the commutation, Hatch remained under confinement. U.S. consul and commercial agent Raymond Henry Jones Perry, who arrived in November 1869, reported to Secretary of State Hamilton Fish that "I have requested the release of Mr. Hatch several times since my arrival, and the government promised to comply with my request, but they have kept their word no better in this matter than in many others."[51] The Senate committee subsequently charged with investigating Hatch's trial and detention seemed persuaded that he was not, in fact, entitled to immediate release:

> Mr. Hatch, we say again, had voluntarily fixed his abode in the republic, and subjected himself to its laws. He could not, therefore, complain of wrong done him if he found himself detained according to those laws for intermeddling to prevent the consummation of a great national measure [the annexation of the Dominican Republic to the United States], which not only that republic, but the United States, his own government, was seeking to bring about. We cannot, of course, approve the principle of restraining him of his liberty on account of his publications or intended publications; but we are compelled to admit, that if such a power of detention is warrantable in any case it was justly applied to Mr. Hatch.[52]

---

46 Hatch v. Baez, 14 N.Y. Sup. Ct. 596 (Gen. Term 1876).

47 Underhill v. Hernandez, 65 F. 577, 580 (2d Cir. 1895).

48 Letter from John Sommers Smith to Hamilton Fish (Sept. 4, 1869), *reprinted in* MESSAGE OF THE PRESIDENT OF THE UNITED STATES COMMUNICATING, IN COMPLIANCE WITH A RESOLUTION OF THE SENATE OF FEBRUARY 21, 1870, CORRESPONDENCE RELATING TO THE IMPRISONMENT OF MR. DAVIS HATCH BY THE DOMINICAN GOVERNMENT, 41ST Cong., 2d Sess., Ex. Doc. No. 54 at 2 (1870) [hereinafter MESSAGE OF THE PRESIDENT].

49 REPORT OF THE SELECT COMMITTEE APPOINTED TO INVESTIGATE THE MEMORIAL OF DAVIS HATCH, 41st Cong., 2d Sess., S. Rep. No. 234, at 2 (1870) [hereinafter SELECT COMMITTEE REPORT]; *see also* Letter from Smith to Fish, *supra* note 48, at 2.

50 SELECT COMMITTEE REPORT, *supra* note 49, at 2.

51 Letter from Raymond Henry Jones Perry to Hamilton Fish (Feb. 8, 1870), *reprinted in* MESSAGE OF THE PRESIDENT, *supra* note 48, at 7.

52 SELECT COMMITTEE REPORT, *supra* note 49, at 12.

In the end, Hatch was released on March 17, 1870 and allowed to return to the United States.[53]

Hatch sought the interposition of the U.S. government to seek "damages in the sum of fifty thousand dollars from [the Dominican] government, which sum he believes to be justly due him for what he has suffered in person, character, and influence in being deprived of his liberty six months and twenty days,"[54] in addition to "the further sum of $8,547.12, for spoliation of his property by the army of Baez in that republic."[55] The Senate committee was not persuaded by Hatch's claims. With respect to his first claim, the committee indicated:

> We do not conceive it to be the duty of our government to interpose in [Hatch's] behalf in respect to that transaction. We know of no principle of the law of nations that justifies our government in demanding reparation. Had he been wantonly seized and subjected to a mere mock-trial and condemned without a hearing, and without testimony; in short, had he been treated with manifest wantonness, tyranny, and cruelty, we could not hesitate to recommend a demand for satisfaction; but the facts do not show that such was the character of the proceedings, but they were, on the contrary, in accordance with the laws of the republic. The committee, therefore, see no ground for this branch of his claim.[56]

With respect to Hatch's claim for damages arising from the alleged seizure and confiscation of his property, the committee noted the irregularity in Hatch's appealing to the legislative branch for redress, rather than to the U.S. State Department.[57] The committee suggested that Hatch was motivated by a desire to cast adverse publicity on the annexation treaty that President Ulysses S. Grant had concluded with President Baez, and for which Grant was seeking support in the Senate.[58] The committee concluded that the alleged spoliation "was nothing but the ordinary ravages of war,"[59] and that "to hold the government responsible for all damages that may occur to individuals in the necessary use of military means to repel an invasion or subdue an insurrection would be to demand of it what would be in very many cases utterly unreasonable and impracticable."[60]

---

53 *Id.* at 14.

54 *Id.* at 1.

55 *Id.*

56 *Id.* at 22. Of course, such wanton seizure is precisely what Hatch alleged. *See id.* at 2.

57 *Id.* at 23.

58 *Id.* at 23; *see also id.* at 25 ("We cannot but regard this unusual course as an attempt by Mr. Hatch, in making his alleged grievances public, to prevent a fair consideration of the treaty of annexation; to arouse unfounded prejudices against it, and finally to defeat it.").

59 *Id.* at 24.

60 *Id.*

The committee thus concluded that the Baez government did not bear legal responsibility for the damage to Hatch's property.[61]

Hatch was undeterred in his quest for reparations. Meanwhile, the political situation in the Dominican Republic remained volatile. In January 1874, Baez was again forced to leave office, and he made his way to New York.[62] Hatch filed a civil suit against him, and Baez was arrested and compelled to respond to the suit.[63] The order of arrest was ultimately vacated and set aside, and Hatch appealed.[64]

Attorney Nelson Cross argued on behalf of Hatch in the appeal before the New York Supreme Court. He argued that any offenses committed by Baez had been committed in his private, rather than his representative, capacity:

> No unjust or oppressive act committed by his direction upon any one of his subjects, or upon others entitled to protection, is in any true sense the act of the executive in his public and representative capacity, but of the *man* simply, rated as other men are rated in private stations; for in the perpetration of unauthorized offenses of this nature, he divests himself of his "regal prerogatives," and descends to the level of those untitled offenders, against whose crimes it is the highest purpose of government to afford protection.[65]

Cross thus attempted to assimilate Baez's unlawful acts to private acts for which he could and should be held responsible by the New York court.

The law firm of Evarts, Southmayd & Choate represented Baez. Baez did not contest that he was subject to the personal jurisdiction of the New York court for his alleged acts in the Dominican Republic, but he argued that the nature of his acts removed them from the purview of judicial scrutiny by a U.S. court. He argued:

> It is clear that the sovereign of another nationality is not amenable to any court of this State, for acts so done in his governmental capacity within his own territory. The municipal courts of one country cannot thus sit in review of the acts of state of another nation.... Not only the inherent limits of municipal jurisdiction forbid it, but the universal comity of nations prohibits the courts of one to sit in judgment upon the continental acts of another, and for that purpose to take advantage of the accidental presence on our soil of one who, at the time of the acts complained of, exercised sovereign powers, of which he has been since deprived.[66]

---

[61] *Id.* (noting that "[w]e do not find in recognized treaties of the law of nations and of war such a principle").

[62] Hatch v. Baez, 14 N.Y. Sup. Ct. 596, 596 (Gen. Term 1876) (indicating that Baez was arrested in a civil suit "while residing in New York"); *id.* at 597 ("It is not denied that the defendant took up his temporary residence in this State voluntarily, and that he was residing here at the time of his arrest.").

[63] *Id.*

[64] *Id.*

[65] *Id.* at 596–97 (emphasis in original).

[66] *Id.* at 598–99.

In support, Baez invoked the U.K. House of Lords' decision in *Duke of Brunswick v. King of Hanover*, in which the House of Lords refused to adjudicate a dispute over a guardianship arrangement for the Duke of Brunswick's fortune that involved conflicting claims to legitimate authority in the Duchy.[67]

The three-judge panel of the New York court, comprised of presiding justice Joseph F. Barnard and justices Jackson O. Dykman and Jasper W. Gilbert, agreed with Baez. In an opinion authored by Gilbert, the court expressed "no doubt" that it had subject-matter jurisdiction because the action was "transitory" and personal jurisdiction because the defendant had been "served with process here."[68] However, the court proceeded to articulate the view that "by the universal comity of nations and the established rules of international law, the courts of one country are bound to abstain from sitting in judgment on the acts of another government done within its own territory."[69] Consequently, "[t]he only remedy for such wrongs must be sought through the intervention of the government of the person injured, or by an appeal to the sense of justice of that, which inflicted the injury"[70]—two remedies that the court surely knew Hatch had pursued without success. (Given the notoriety of the Senate proceedings surrounding Hatch's reparations claims, the court might have been concerned about effectively overruling a prior determination by a different branch of government.) The court, citing *The Duke of Brunswick* as well as *The Schooner Exchange* and *The Santissima Trinidad*, ultimately concluded that Baez enjoyed immunity based on "the capacity in which the acts were done,"[71] which protects "the individual who did them, because they emanated from a *foreign and friendly* government."[72] The court ordered Hatch to pay Baez's legal costs, and Baez returned to the Dominican Republic, where he enjoyed one final stint as President before being deposed yet again and sent into exile in Puerto Rico. The court's emphasis on comity left unanswered the question of what immunity, if any, a former official of a foreign and *unfriendly* government might enjoy in a U.S. court.

C. *The Case against Jose Manuel Hernandez*

On November 5, 1893, the *New York Times* reported that General Jose Manuel Hernandez had been arrested at the Victoria Hotel and compelled to post $15,000

---

67 *Id.* at 598 (citing Duke of Brunswick v. King of Hanover, 2 H.L. Cas. 1 9 E.R. 993 (1848) refusing to invalidate a decree of the Germanic Diet depriving the Duke of Brunswick of "the management and administration of his fortune").

68 *Hatch*, 14 N.Y. Sup. Ct. at 599. For a recent exploration of transitory tort jurisprudence and its potential relevance to international human rights cases, see Keitner, *supra* note 22.

69 *Hatch*, 14 N.Y. Sup. Ct. at 599.

70 *Id.* at 599–600.

71 *Id.* at 600.

72 *Id.* (emphasis added).

bail in a suit brought by former U.S. Consul George F. Underhill and his wife.[73] The Underhills alleged that Hernandez, who was second-in-command of the revolutionary army that seized power in 1892 in Venezuela, had imprisoned them there and forced Mr. Underhill to sell his water works "for a pittance."[74] Hernandez responded that "what he did in regard to Underhill was done as a representative of the Government, and he was not responsible personally."[75] Consequently, he argued, "Underhill might prosecute a claim against the Venezuelan Government, but he had no case against him personally."[76]

A jury heard the Underhills' case in support of their claim of false imprisonment and assault and battery, and the trial judge entered a directed verdict for Hernandez.[77] Underhill appealed. A three-judge panel of the Second Circuit comprised of William J. Wallace, E. Henry Lacombe, and Nathaniel Shipman affirmed the directed verdict.[78] In an opinion authored by Judge Wallace, the court of appeals noted that the revolutionary forces commanded by Hernandez had prevailed and had been recognized "as the legitimate government of Venezuela by the government of the United States."[79] Because there was no evidence in the record that Hernandez's action in commandeering Underhill's water works "for the benefit of the community and the revolutionary forces ... was actuated by malice, or any personal or private motive,"[80] the trial judge had properly ruled that Underhill was not entitled to recover damages. In the Second Circuit's view, Hernandez could not be held "civilly responsible" in a U.S. court for the acts of "a military commander, representing the de facto government in the prosecution of a war."[81]

Underhill urged the U.S. Supreme Court to review the Second Circuit's decision on the grounds that "the mere recognition of a new government is not a recognition of the rightfulness of the methods by which it arose."[82] The Supreme Court granted review. Chief Justice Melville Weston Fuller wrote the Court's brief

---

[73] *Bail Came Just in Time*, N.Y. TIMES, Nov. 5, 1893, at 9.

[74] *Id.*

[75] *Id.*

[76] *Id.*

[77] *See* Underhill v. Hernandez, 65 F. 577, 578 (2d Cir. 1895), *aff'd on other grounds*, 168 U.S. 250 (1897). Underhill filed suit in the New York State Supreme Court, but Hernandez had the case removed to the Circuit Court of the United States for the Eastern District of New York. *See* Petition for Writ of Certiorari at 2, Underhill v. Hernandez, 168 U.S. 250 (Feb. 15, 1895). The trial judge was Hoyt H. Wheeler. *Id.*

[78] *Underhill*, 65 F. at 578.

[79] *Id.*

[80] *Id.* at 579.

[81] *Id.; see also id.* at 582 (noting that if acts of military authorities "are done in the legitimate exercise of belligerent powers, they are not ordinarily attended with civil responsibility").

[82] Petition for Writ of Certiorari, *supra* note 77, at 7.

opinion disposing of the case.[83] The opinion began with the proposition that "[e]very sovereign state is bound to respect the independence of every other sovereign state, and the courts of one country will not sit in judgment on the acts of the government of another, done within its own territory."[84] It continued:

> The immunity of individuals from suits brought in foreign tribunals for acts done within their own states, in the exercise of governmental authority, whether as civil officers or as military commanders, must necessarily extend to the agents of governments ruling by paramount force as a matter of fact.[85]

The Court concluded that "[w]here a civil war prevails…, generally speaking, foreign nations do not assume to judge of the merits of the quarrel,"[86] and that "if actual war has been waged, acts of legitimate warfare cannot be made the basis of individual liability."[87] The idea of combatant immunity thus loomed large in the Supreme Court's reasoning. In its view, "acts of legitimate warfare" included Hernandez's treatment of Underhill, which the Supreme Court agreed was intended "'to coerce the plaintiff to operate his waterworks and his repair works for the benefit of the community and the revolutionary forces.'"[88]

The basic ideas that complaints about governmental acts should be resolved through diplomatic channels, and that individuals do not bear personal responsibility for "acts of legitimate warfare," both supported a principle of judicial abstention in this case. U.S. courts continue to trace the first idea to Chief Justice Fuller's opinion in *Underhill*.

IV. Reconnecting the Act of State Doctrine and Conduct-based Immunity

The cases explored above underscore the close connection between conduct-based immunity and what came to be known as the act of state doctrine. Judges who abstained from pronouncing on the acts of friendly foreign sovereigns taken within their own territory thought that diplomatic, rather than judicial, channels should provide redress for injuries allegedly caused by governmental acts. They also emphasized that international law at the time did not make

---

83 Underhill v. Hernandez, 168 U.S. 250 (1897). Fuller had reportedly turned down an earlier offer from President-Elect Grover Cleveland to serve as Secretary of State. Around the time of the *Underhill* case, Fuller was nominated by Venezuelan President Joaquin Crespo to serve on the Panel of Arbitration appointed to resolve a boundary dispute between Venezuela and the United Kingdom.

84 *Id.* at 252.

85 *Id.*

86 *Id.* at 252–53.

87 *Id.* at 253.

88 *Id.* at 254.

individuals personally responsible for certain governmental acts, even if the individual subsequently came within U.S. jurisdiction.

Modern international law attributes personal responsibility to government actors for war crimes, genocide, crimes against humanity, torture, and other universally recognized offenses.[89] This may affect the calculus for U.S. judges contemplating whether or not to exercise their personal and subject-matter jurisdiction to impose legal consequences on individual defendants for violations of universally recognized norms. Unlike their late-nineteenth-century predecessors, late-twentieth-century judges have largely declined to dismiss claims involving governmental abuses on act of state doctrine grounds, particularly where the alleged violations reach a threshold level of specificity and acceptance by the international community.[90]

The Supreme Court's reasoning in *Banco Nacional de Cuba v. Sabbatino* suggests an inverse correlation between the degree of international acceptance of a particular prohibition and the appropriateness of shielding an alleged violation from adjudication in U.S. courts, whether on act of state doctrine or conduct-based immunity grounds. The Court indicated that "the greater the degree of codification or consensus concerning a particular area of international law, the more appropriate it is for the judiciary to render decisions regarding it...."[91] The same could be said of the degree of "codification or consensus" regarding a particular human rights or humanitarian law rule and the appropriateness of a U.S. court imposing legal consequences on a defendant for violating that rule. The

---

[89] *See, e.g.*, Beth Stephens, *Abusing the Authority of the State: Denying Foreign Official Immunity for Egregious Human Rights Abuses*, 44 VAND. J. TRANSNAT'L L. 1163, 1180–81 (2011) (emphasizing that modern international law holds individual officials responsible for international human rights violations, in addition to imputing responsibility to the state itself). *See also id.* at 1182 (indicating that "the individual's personal responsibility for his or her wrongful acts is unaffected by the fact that the acts involved the use or abuse of state authority or by the fact that the state as well is responsible for the wrongful acts"); Beth Stephens, *The Modern Common Law of Foreign Official Immunity*, 79 FORDHAM L. REV. 2669, 2702 (2011) (noting that some human rights treaties "require that states either prosecute or extradite persons accused of violations, including officials who acted under governmental authority").

[90] *See id.* at 2707–09.

[91] Banco Nacional de Cuba v. Sabbatino, 376 U.S. 398, 428 (1964); *see also* Kenneth C. Randall & Chimène I. Keitner, Sabbatino, Sosa, *and "Supernorms," in* LOOKING TO THE FUTURE: ESSAYS ON INTERNATIONAL LAW IN HONOR OF W. MICHAEL REISMAN 559, 5610–62 (Mahnoush H. Arsanjani et al., eds., 2011) (drawing a line of continuity from the reasoning in *Sabbatino* to that in *Sosa v. Alvarez-Machain*, 542 U.S. 692 (2004), to suggest that U.S. courts may appropriately adjudicate claims involving "a norm at the top of the hierarchy of international legal norms—that is, a norm so undisputed, or so fundamental, that its enforcement transcends the ordinary allocation of competence among the domestic branches of government and overrides the usual presumption that the judiciary will not interfere with the acts of sovereign states taken within their own borders").

United States as *amicus curiae* made a similar observation to the Second Circuit in *Filártiga v. Peña-Irala*, citing *Sabbatino*:

> [B]efore entertaining a suit alleging a violation of human rights [under 28 U.S.C. § 1350], a court must first conclude that there is a consensus in the international community that the right is protected and that there is a widely shared understanding of the scope of this protection. *Sabbatino*, 376 U.S. at 428, 430 n. 34. When these conditions have been satisfied, there is little danger that judicial enforcement will impair our foreign policy efforts. To the contrary, a refusal to recognize a private cause of action in these circumstances might seriously damage the credibility of our nation's commitment to the protection of human rights.[92]

The degree of international agreement about an applicable norm can thus inform a court's willingness to recognize a private cause of action for an alleged violation, as well as its willingness to adjudicate a claim on the merits notwithstanding the trans-border character of the claim.

The U.S. State Department has taken the position that the nature of the alleged conduct is a consideration, but not the only factor, in determining conduct-based immunity.[93] The Fourth Circuit Court of Appeals recently went further, holding that a defendant who previously served as Somali defense minister and prime minister is not entitled to conduct-based immunity from civil suit for acts committed while he was in office because "under international and domestic law, officials from other countries are not entitled to foreign official immunity for *jus cogens* violations, even if the acts were performed in the defendant's official capacity."[94] The Fourth Circuit correctly determined that a suggestion of conduct-based immunity from the State Department should inform but not dictate a court's determination of a defendant's immunity or lack thereof.[95] However, the Fourth Circuit's statement that the State Department's assessment of the foreign relations impact of exercising jurisdiction in a particular case "carries substantial weight in our analysis of the issue [of conduct-based immunity]"[96] is difficult to

---

92 Memorandum for the United States as *Amicus Curiae*, Filártiga v. Peña-Irala, 630 F.2d 876 (2d Cir., June 30, 1980) (No. 79–6090), at 22–23.

93 Brief for the United States as *Amicus Curiae* Supporting Affirmance, Samantar v. Yousuf, 130 S. Ct. 2278 (2010) (No. 08–1555), at 7 (listing "the nature of the acts alleged" as one of several factors the Executive "reasonably could find it appropriate to take into account" in deciding whether or not to suggest immunity for a particular defendant); *see also id.* at 25 (indicating that "in this case, the Executive may also find the nature of the acts alleged—and whether they should properly be regarded as actions in an official capacity—to be relevant to the immunity determination").

94 Yousuf v. Samantar, No. 11–1479 (4th Cir., Nov. 2, 2012), *slip op.* at 21–22.

95 *Id.* at 15 (indicating that, with respect to conduct-based immunity, "the Executive Branch still informs the court about the diplomatic effect of the court's exercising jurisdiction over claims against an official of a foreign state," but that such an assessment does not amount to "a controlling determination of whether an individual is entitled to conduct-based immunity").

96 *Id.*

reconcile with its categorical language about the absence of such immunity for alleged *jus cogens* violations.

In *Samantar*, the potential tension between according "substantial weight" to State Department representations and denying conduct-based immunity for alleged violations of *jus cogens* norms was immaterial, because the State Department submitted a suggestion of non-immunity.[97] In a future case, it would be appropriate for a U.S. court to begin with a strong *presumption* of no conduct-based immunity for universally recognized international law violations, but to take into account State Department representations about the likely foreign relations consequences of adjudicating a particular case before deciding whether to proceed. Further judicial elaboration of the circumstances in which the State Department's representation about the diplomatic consequences of a particular case should rebut the presumption against conduct-based immunity would be useful. Courts also require greater guidance if they are to implement the Supreme Court's suggestion in *Sosa v. Alvarez-Machain* that "a policy of case-specific deference to the political branches" in which courts give "serious weight to the Executive Branch's view of the case's impact on foreign policy" might be appropriate in certain cases alleging international human rights violations.[98] In such a case, the issue would not be whether the defendant bears responsibility for the alleged conduct, but rather whether the judicial branch can impose legal consequences for the alleged violation without unduly interfering with the Executive's conduct of foreign relations.

One would hope that the dismissal of a case on foreign relations grounds would not lead to the impunity of the defendant or the absence of redress for victims, but rather to the pursuit of accountability and redress through diplomatic rather than judicial channels. While such a hope might appear naïve, it is consistent with the stated goals of a government whose foreign policy agenda includes "the end of impunity" for human rights violations and the strengthening of monitoring and enforcement mechanisms worldwide.[99] These mechanisms include horizontal enforcement which, as defined above,[100] contemplates an important, if circumscribed, role for domestic courts in enforcing international law.

---

97 *Id.* at 22.

98 *Sosa v. Alvarez-Machain*, 542 U.S. 692, 733 n. 21 (2004).

99 NATIONAL SECURITY STRATEGY (May 2010) at 48, available at http://www.whitehouse.gov/sites/default/files/rss_viewer/national_security_strategy.pdf (stating that "[f]rom Nuremberg to Yugoslavia to Liberia, the United States has seen that the end of impunity and the promotion of justice are not just moral imperatives; they are stabilizing forces in international affairs"); *see also id.* at 39 (indicating that the United States is working "to strengthen human rights monitoring and enforcement mechanisms, so that individuals and countries are held accountable for their violation of international human rights norms").

100 *See supra* note 1 and accompanying text.

SOVEREIGN IMMUNITY AND THE INTERNATIONAL COURT OF JUSTICE: THE STATE SYSTEM TRIUMPHANT

Paul B. Stephan*

The traditional conception of international law depicts it as the product of states. In particular, states alone make treaties and customary law. While proponents of this view hope to see states bring certain values into the project—religious commitments in an earlier day, the greatest manifestations of reason in the modern secular world—they maintain that only states can be the portals for bringing these values into international law.[1]

The constitution of the post-war international system complicated this picture. First, the victorious allies—the United Nations—began creating international organizations endowed with lawmaking power. While these delegations came from states, they left the power to create international law in the hands of the diplomats, bureaucrats and technical specialists who served these organizations.[2] Second, the enormity of the atrocities perpetrated by the defeated states, Nazi Germany in particular, opened up an argument about introducing into international law constraints that transcended mere national interests. Humanity, some argued, must have a seat at the table when international law is made, aside from the states themselves.

For the first thirty years of the post-war period, the argument about transcendental sources of international law concentrated on limiting what international law could do. One strain in the conversation looked at the network of treaties

* John C. Jeffries, Jr., Distinguished Professor and David H. Ibbeken '71 Research Professor, University of Virginia School of Law. I am grateful to Ashley Deeks, Pierre Verdier, and participants in the Sokol Colloquium for comments and criticism. Responsibility for misjudgments, errors and elisions is mine alone.

1 *See, e.g.*, Jeremy Bentham, *Principles of International Law*, in 2 THE WORKS OF JEREMY BENTHAM 550 (John Bowring ed. 1843); J.L. BRIERLY, THE LAW OF NATIONS 1 (6th ed. 1963).

2 *See* Andrew T. Guzman, *Against Consent*, 52 VA. J. INT'L L. 747 (2012); Laurence R. Helfer, *Nonconsensual International Lawmaking*, 2008 U. ILL. L. REV. 71.

John Norton Moore (ed.) Foreign Affairs Litigation in United States Courts, pp. 67–86
©2013 Koninklijke Brill NV, The Netherlands. ISBN 978-90-04-25727-6

constructed by Nazi Germany during its ascendance and argued that the obligations they created should have no legal force.[3] Somewhat later, the Soviet Union and its allies made a different claim, that the fundamental principle of the international legal system must be the prevention of instability in the superpower competition that they characterized as a struggle between socialism and capitalism. This principle, which they called peaceful coexistence, functioned as a check on international law formation. States should regard treaties, as well as custom, that violated this principle as a nullity.[4]

During the 1960s, members of the United Nations turned to this issue as part of a general effort to codify the law of treaties. It is largely the Soviet arguments that prevailed. Countries from the Soviet bloc strongly supported the text that became Article 53 of the Vienna Convention on the Law of Treaties, which states that treaties that contradict peremptory norms of international law have no force.[5] They understood that this formulation provided a portal through which the principles of peaceful coexistence, as understood by their side, would enter international law. The Western states opposed this text for the same reason, the United States and France so much so that they refused to join the treaty.[6]

Only in the late 1970s did there emerge widespread discussion of international law norms that did not depend on state consent, and which operated as positive obligations of states rather than as limits on state lawmaking power. Peremptory norms, proponents argued, now imposed duties, rather than simply constraining the capacity of states to make international law. Principally these norms comprised fundamental human rights, which international law was said to impose on states without the need for state consent. The Final Act of the 1975 Helsinki Conference, although not intended to have any legal force, galvanized an international movement that operated outside of state structures and invoked international law to protect basic human interests. Much of the impetus of this movement was the declining power of the Soviet Union with respect to its satellites and a growing demand for dignity and representation among the captive nations of Central and Eastern Europe, but the movement also had in its sights the authoritarian regimes of Latin America and Africa.[7]

With the collapse of authoritarian regimes in Southern Europe, the break-up of the Soviet Union and the liberation of Central and Eastern Europe, and the end of

---

[3] A precursor of these arguments is Alfred von Verdross, *Forbidden Treaties in International Law*, 31 AM. J. INT'L L. 571 (1937).

[4] For analysis of the theory, see Leon Lipson, *Peaceful Coexistence*, 29 LAW & CONTEMP. PROBS. 871 (1964); *The Rise and Fall of "Peaceful Coexistence" in International Law*, 1 PAPERS ON SOVIET LAW 6 (1977).

[5] Vienna Convention on the Law of Treaties, art. 53, May 23, 1969, 1155 U.N.T.S. 331.

[6] *See* Paul B. Stephan, *The Political Economy of* Jus Cogens, 44 VAND. J. TRANSNAT'L L. 1073, 1083–88 (2011).

[7] *See generally* SAMUEL MOYN, THE LAST UTOPIA—HUMAN RIGHTS IN HISTORY (2010).

authoritarian regimes in Latin American and Africa (South Africa in particular), international relations seemed to have entered a new stage. New international organizations emerged, and old ones took on more authority. At this point it became common to talk of the hollowing out of the state. International economic law and human rights law alike seemed to bind states like never before. Moreover, the process of generating these bodies of law seem to have slipped away from the foreign offices of states, to be taken over by international organizations, independent courts, nongovernmental organizations and individual scholars.[8]

This is the context that frames and gives significance to the decision of the International Court of Justice (ICJ) in *Jurisdictional Immunities of the State (Germany v. Italy)*.[9] The dispute grew out of civil suits brought in Italian domestic courts by Italian nationals who had suffered at the hands of the German Reich during World War II. The plaintiffs were members of the Italian armed forces whom Germany seized at the time of Italy's surrender in 1943, then transported to Germany and conscripted into forced labor. The suits asserted that Germany had committed grave breaches of international humanitarian law and owed compensation.[10] The Italian Corte Suprema di Cassazione allowed the litigation to proceed against Germany, ruling that the traditional immunity accorded a foreign state did not extend to such serious war crimes.[11] After a successful litigant attached Italian real estate belonging to Germany to enforce his judgment, Germany invoked the jurisdiction of the ICJ. In February 2012 the Court ruled that Italy had violated the customary international law of state immunity by allowing its courts to entertain the suits. Three judges dissented.

The ICJ decision unmistakably represents a victory for the traditional conception of international law. The immunity of foreign sovereigns in national courts

---

8 *See* Paul B. Stephan, *Privatizing International Law*, 97 VA. L. REV. 1573 (2011).

9 Jurisdictional Immunities of the State (Germany v. Italy), Judgment (Feb. 3, 2012), *available at* http://www.icj-cij.org/docket/files/143/16883.pdf [hereinafter ICJ Judgment]. For my analysis of the issues presented by the case in advance of the Court's decision, see Paul B. Stephan, *The Political Economy of* Jus Cogens, note 6 *supra*. For criticism of the decision, see Kimberley N. Trapp & Alex Mills, *Smooth Runs the Water where the Brook is Deep: The Obscured Complexities of* Germany v Italy, 1 CAMB. J. INT'L & COMP. L. 153 (2012).

10 In spite of the various peace treaties, which tended to discharge Germany of its obligation to compensate, between 1953 and 2000 Germany adopted increasingly broad (although hardly generous) reparations schemes for various classes of Nazi victims. In particular, it signed two agreements with Italy in 1961 that finalized Germany's obligations to Italian subjects. The German courts interpreted the various compensatory statutes as not extending to persons who had been held as prisoners of war in Germany, even if the Reich had not itself recognized their status as prisoners of war.

11 Ferrini v. Federal Republic of Germany, Cass., sez. un., 11 marzo 2004, n. 5044, Giust. Civ. 2004 II, 1191 (It.), *reprinted in* 87 RIVISTA DI DIRITTO INTERNAZIONALE 539 (2004), *summarized in* Andrea Bianchi, Ferrini v. Federal Republic of Germany, 99 AM. J. INT'L L. 242 (2005).

has ancient roots, argued the Court. Any exceptions have to derive from express state consent through a treaty or implicit consent through a change in state practice accepted as affecting legal obligations. The growing recognition of fundamental human rights does not suffice by itself to create an exception to immunity. Rather, the Court demanded evidence that states separately had equated human rights violations with surrender of immunity. Such evidence, it concluded, did not exist.

This essay proceeds in three parts. First, it discusses the jurisdiction of the ICJ to decide this question. The Court's approach to its jurisdiction, this part will show, indicated early on its emphasis on states as the significant actors in international law and its reluctance to let other considerations detract from that role. The second part describes the Court's analysis in some detail. In its final part, the essay discusses the implications of the decision for the litigation of human rights claims in domestic courts. It also considers the reasons why the ICJ would take a more traditional, not to say conservative, approach to international law formation than do some national courts.

I have argued elsewhere that breaking the link between state consent and international lawmaking risks dangers that advocates of particular outcomes, impatient with the conventional process of norm formation, ignore at their peril.[12] The ICJ's judgment complements that perspective. At its most fundamental level, the judgment indicates that rules of law must have sovereign choices somewhere in their ancestry. Anything else, the judgment suggests, would undermine, not bolster, the international legal system.

I. Jurisdiction of the ICJ

The ICJ, to put it mildly, is not a court of general jurisdiction. Advisory opinions aside, which face their own jurisdictional limits, the Court may address a dispute only if the parties have consented. This consent often is prior to the dispute, in the form of a declaration to accept the Court's jurisdiction in a particular class of cases. In every case, then, the Court must determine whether a declaration exists as well as its extent.

Illustrative is the Court's decision in *Barcelona Traction*.[13] The dispute involved Spain's expropriation of the property of a Canadian company that had mostly Belgian shareholders. Spain in a treaty had consented to ICJ jurisdiction over such disputes with respect to Belgium, but no such treaty existed for Canada. The

---

12 Paul B. Stephan, *Privatizing International Law*, note 8 *supra; The Political Economy of* Jus Cogens, note 6 *supra*.

13 Case Concerning the Barcelona Traction, Light and Power Company, Limited (Belgium v. Spain), [1970] I.C.J. Rpt. 3.

ICJ controversially ruled that the right of foreign investors to diplomatic protection was limited to the direct owners of property, and therefore did not extend to owners of an entity when the entity suffered an injury. As a result, the Court lacked the power to provide any relief to either the company (no jurisdiction) or its shareholders (no right).

The Court is not always this cautious about its jurisdiction, but the instances where it has acted expansively have tended to redound to its detriment. Perhaps the most notorious instance is *Military and Paramilitary Activities in and against Nicaragua*.[14] There the Court's majority simultaneously rejected the United States' withdrawal of consent to jurisdiction, found the terms of the prior U.S. consent satisfied on very problematic grounds, and side-stepped the U.S. reservation with respect to issues involving multilateral treaties by finding norms of customary international law that mimicked the treaties in question.[15]

So that all this creative manufacturing of jurisdiction would not go to waste, the Court then held the United States responsible for what it regarded as illegal use of force against Nicaragua and ordered reparations. The United States blocked enforcement of the Court's judgment in the Security Council, and Nicaragua, after ridding itself of the Sandinista regime, withdrew the suit. Although some observers saw the ICJ's conduct in this episode as courageous, others saw it as ineffectual and feckless.[16]

In *Jurisdictional Immunities*, the existence of some ICJ jurisdiction was unquestioned, but its scope was controversial. Germany and Italy, as parties to the European Convention for the Peaceful Settlement of Disputes, were obligated to

---

14 Military and Paramilitary Activities in and against Nicaragua (Nicaragua v. United States), [1984] I.C.J. Rpt. 392 (admissibility), [1986] I.C.J. Rpt. 14 (merits).

15 Treating the various treaty norms as also constituting custom was not by itself so problematic, but using this strategy to bootstrap jurisdiction in the face of an express reservation was. A useful contrast to *Military and Paramilitary Activities in Nicaragua* is Armed Activities on the Territory of the Congo (New Application: 2002) (Democratic Republic of Congo v. Rwanda), [2006] I.C.J. Rpt. 6 ¶ 64:

> ... [T]he mere fact that rights and obligations *erga omnes* may be at issue in a dispute would not give the Court jurisdiction to entertain that dispute.
>
> The same applies to the relationship between peremptory norms of general international law (*jus cogens*) and the establishment of the Court's jurisdiction: the fact that a dispute relates to compliance with a norm having such a character, which is assuredly the case with regard to the prohibition of genocide, cannot of itself provide a basis for the jurisdiction of the Court to entertain that dispute.

Accordingly, the Court refused to accept jurisdiction over the case, regardless of the gravity of the allegations at issue.

16 For trenchant criticism of the substantive conclusions of the majority, see John Norton Moore, Jus ad Bellum *Before the International Court of Justice*, 52 Va. J. Int'l L. 903, 919–36 (2012).

submit disputes to the ICJ in the absence of any other available juridical forum.[17] Italy did not contest that this treaty gave the ICJ the power to address the legality of its courts' practice in entertaining suits against Germany. It did, however, assert a counterclaim against Germany for compensation on behalf of its nationals.

Italy's counterclaim faced a jurisdictional difficulty. Article 27(a) of the European Convention limited the ICJ's authority by stipulating that it did not extend to disputes relating to "facts and situations" that occurred before the signing of the Convention. The ICJ thus had to decide whether the counterclaim related to the original harmful conduct of Germany, which ended with the war, or instead to the ongoing refusal to compensate the victims, which had continued up to the present.

Every member of the Court except one agreed that it lacked jurisdiction over the counterclaim. Rather than deciding whether the dispute involved the initial war crime or an ongoing duty to compensate, the majority focused instead on Italy's Peace Treaty with the victorious allies. In the view of the majority, the "facts and situations" on which the counterclaim rested necessarily implicated the 1947 Peace Treaty, under which Italy waived any claim to compensation from Germany. It could not address Italy's rights without determining the legal significance of that waiver.[18] Judge Cançado Trindade dissented on this point, foreshadowing his position on the merits.

The differences between the majority and dissenting jurisdictional opinions are instructive. The majority noted Italy's assertion that the dispute concerned the existence and scope of Germany's obligation to compensate, but ruled that this duty depended fundamentally on the meaning of the 1947 waiver.[19] Later decisions by Germany to accord compensation to many victims, but not to those involved here, did not affect the legal obligations as constituted by the Peace Treaty.[20] There were, of course, legitimate arguments as to whether Germany could invoke a provision in a treaty to which it was not a party, and whether Italy had the capacity to waive its nationals' claims. Each of the arguments, however, required resolving a dispute based on events that took place in 1947, well before the European Convention's grant of jurisdiction. Because the dispute thus depended critically on "facts and situations" that occurred before the European Convention's cutoff, the Court could not address it.

Cançado Trindade wrote a lengthy dissent. The dispute, he argued, turned on the duty of Germany to make reparations. The Peace Treaty had no impact on

---

17 European Convention for the Peaceful Settlement of Disputes, art. 1, Apr. 29, 1957, 320 U.N.T.S. 4646.

18 In the Treaty, Italy waived all its claims and those of its nationals. Treaty of Peace with Italy, art. 77(4), Feb. 10, 1947, 61 Stat. 1245.

19 Jurisdictional Immunities of the State (Germany v. Italy), Order, ¶ 26 (July 6, 2010), *available at* http://www.icj-cij.org/docket/files/143/16027.pdf.

20 *Id.* ¶¶ 28–29.

the facts that underlay this duty. By entering into negotiations in 1961 to provide compensation to some Italian victims of Nazi atrocities, Germany had recognized its general duty, notwithstanding Italy's waiver. The real question, he insisted, was whether a right of reparation for war crimes existed. Moreover, the true holders of the claim to reparation were individuals, whose "rights are not the same as their State's rights."[21] This ongoing situation came well within the European Convention's cutoff.

Underlying the gap between these two positions is a profound difference about the significance of the state. For the majority, Italy's actions in 1947 were critical. It could not press its counterclaim without accounting for the legal consequences of its Peace Treaty waiver, and the European Convention did not give the Court competence to consider those issues. That Italy purported to waive the individual rights of its subjects, as well as its rights as a state, presented no problem: It was Italy, and not the victims, who came to the Court to seek relief.

For Cançado Trindade, the focus remained on the individuals who suffered at German hands. Even though only Italy had the power to invoke the Court's jurisdiction, it acted not in its own capacity but rather as the representative of victims of war crimes. To afford these people a hearing, he was willing to stretch the jurisdictional limits grounded in the "facts and situations" language of the Convention. For him, the 1947 waiver was irrelevant because the questions it posed were so easy to answer: Of course Italy could not waive its subjects' right to compensation for grave war crimes.

Here we see in a nutshell the methodological commitments that would play out on the merits. For the majority, jurisdiction depended on state consent and declarations of consent would be interpreted carefully, if not strictly. Cançado Trindade focused primarily on the underlying claim. When faced with a case involving a serious war crime, the Court should seize any opportunity it had to hear it. Even though the Court has jurisdiction only over states, who alone can appear before it, the real parties in interest were individuals. Actions by a state that impaired their interest, such as Italy's purported waiver of any claims against Germany, were to be disregarded.

The Court resolved one other procedural issue before reaching the merits. Greece sought to intervene in the case, but did not claim to be a party to the dispute. Even before the Italian litigation, a Greek court had carved out an exception to sovereign immunity, allowing relatives of victims of German atrocities to sue Germany for damages. But the Greek government had refused permission for enforcement of the judgment, and a special supreme court later ruled that Greece

---

21 *Id.* ¶ 101 (Cançado Trindade, dissenting), *available at* http://www.icj-cij.org/docket/files/143/16031.pdf.

would not recognize any exception to sovereign immunity in war crime cases.[22] Barred from obtaining recourse in either Greece or Germany, the Greek plaintiffs sought to enforce their judgment in Italy. Germany in turned cited these efforts in its claim before the Court. The ICJ's decision thus could have an impact on the ability of Greek nationals to bring an action against Germany in Italy.

The majority noted that the question over which the Court had jurisdiction included the enforceability of Greek judgments against Germany in Italy. Because the Court already was seized of this issue, allowing Greece to participate as a non-party would present no problems.[23] Cançado Trindade concurred. He referred to the significance of the individual rights at stake in the Greek case and the limits of the ability of states to foreclose consideration of such interests.[24] Again, the majority saw its responsibility as adjudicating state rights and obligations, while Cançado Trindade concentrated on individual rights and the imperative of vindicating them.

II. The Decision

In Italy, the question of a foreign sovereign's immunity from judicial process in civil litigation rests exclusively on customary international law, which operates directly in Italian law. Neither Germany nor Italy was party to any treaty that altered this customary international law.[25] The question that the ICJ faced thus was precisely what customary international law requires.

As the Court indicated, the doctrine of state immunity has a long history, but its content has changed over time. In an earlier day states usually enjoyed complete immunity in civil cases. Over the course of the twentieth century, however, at least two exceptions have received widespread, but not universal, acceptance. First, many states, including the United States, now limit immunity to *acta jure*

---

22 Prefecture of Voiotia v. Germany, Areios Pagos [A.P] [Supreme Court] 11/2000 p. 2 (Greece), *summarized in* Maria Gavouneli & Ilias Bantekas, *Sovereign Immunity—Tort Exception—Jus Cogens Violations—World War II Reparations—International Humanitarian Law*, 95 Am. J. Int'l L. 198 (2001); Germany v. Margellos, Anotato Eidiko Dikastirio [A.E.D] [Special Supreme Court] 6/2002 (Greece), *translated in* 129 I.L.R. 525 (2002), *summarized in* Maria Panezi, *Sovereign Immunity and Violation of* Jus Cogens *Norms*, 56 Revue Hellenique de Droit International 199 (2003).

23 Jurisdictional Immunities of the State (Germany v. Italy), Order, ¶¶ 25, 31 (July 4, 2011), *available at* http://www.icj-cij.org/docket/files/143/16556.pdf.

24 *Id.* (Cançado Trindade, concurring), *available at* http://www.icj-cij.org/docket/files/143/16558.pdf.

25 Germany was a party to the European Convention on State Immunity, May 16, 1972, E.T.S. No. 74, 1495 U.N.T.S. 182. Italy, however, was not. Neither Germany nor Italy had signed, much less joined, the United Nations Convention on the Jurisdictional Immunities of States and their Property, Dec. 2, 2004, which in any event had (and has) not gone into effect.

imperii, that is the public acts of sovereigns. Thus, states that engage in commercial transactions often lose their immunity as to such transactions.[26] Second, many states, also including the United States, recognize an exception for public acts that wrongfully result in an injury on the territory of the state where immunity is invoked, that is a domestic tort.[27] Italy argued that customary international law now incorporates these exceptions. Because Germany's misconduct began on Italian territory, where its armed forces seized the plaintiffs in the Italian litigation, Italy maintained that their claims satisfied this widely accepted exception to sovereign immunity.[28]

The majority opinion, supported by twelve of the fourteen permanent members of the Court, found it unnecessary to determine whether customary international law had embraced either the public act limitation or the domestic tort exception. Germany's wrongful conduct involved its armed forces and not any commercial activity. Thus its acts, however wrongful, were public. The majority's review of national practice regarding the domestic tort exception indicated that no state had applied that exception to misconduct by armed forces. The European Convention on State Immunity contains a general carve-out to its immunity exceptions for claims relating to armed forces. The UN Convention, while not addressing the issue directly, comes with clear background evidence of an intention to exclude acts by national militaries. Nor had any state applied the domestic tort exception to military acts, other than the Italian and Greek courts in the cases that triggered the ICJ proceeding. Accordingly, the majority ruled that the domestic tort exception did not apply to the suits at issue.[29]

Having taken care of the legal underbrush, the Court then confronted the central and most compelling question, whether there exists a separate exception to sovereign immunity for violations of peremptory norms of international law. The logic of this argument is clear enough: If international law imposes certain obligations on states regardless of state consent, then it ought to ensure that mechanisms exist to ensure full compliance with those obligations. If the absence of state consent does not impair the obligation, it also should not impair the

---

26 28 U.S.C. § 1605(a)(2).

27 28 U.S.C. § 1605(a)(5).

28 Similarly, the massacre for which the Greek plaintiffs sought compensation occurred on Greek territory.

29 Judge Gaja, the Italian judge *ad hoc* for the case, dissented on this point. Jurisdictional Immunities of the State (Germany v. Italy), Judgment (Feb. 3, 2012) (Gaja, J., dissenting), *available at* http://www.icj-cij.org/docket/files/143/16895.pdf. For a critique of the majority's use of U.S. practice in reaching this conclusion, see Riccardo Pavoni, *The American Anomaly: On the ICJ's Misuse of United States Practice in Jurisdictional Immunities of the State*, 21 ITAL. YB. INT'L L.143 (2012). At least to this U.S. lawyer, the author of the critique, an Italian legal academic, seems to have misunderstood U.S. practice.

remedy. Once peremptory norms enter the system, the very logic of their creation implies that they should be peremptory all the way down.[30]

Conceptually, this argument requires a kind of clumping. The more the right and the remedy are seen as different aspects of the same thing, the more compelling seems the argument for an exception to state immunity. Conversely, the greater the conceptual distance between the right (untethered from state consent) and the remedy (exceptions to sovereign immunity traditionally rested on consent), the easier it is for the right and immunity to coexist.

The majority responded to this challenge first mechanically, then more abstractly. It began by reviewing state practice. Victims of alleged human rights violations had presented variations of Italy's argument to numerous courts and tribunals during the past decade. Aside from Italy, and the one instance in Greece that its highest court later repudiated, every nation's courts had rejected it.[31] Moreover, the European Court of Human Rights, admittedly closely divided, had ruled that the specific obligations of the European Convention on Human Rights did not compel the creation of a peremptory-norm exception to sovereign immunity.[32] In light of this evidence, the majority could not see any basis in state practice for recognizing the exception.

The majority then confronted the logical argument. It emphasized the functional difference between rules of liability and rules of susceptibility to judicial process:

> Assuming for this purpose that the rules of the law of armed conflict which prohibit the murder of civilians in occupied territory, the deportation of civilian inhabitants to slave labour and the deportation of prisoners of war to slave labour are rules of *jus cogens*, there is no conflict between those rules and the rules on State immunity. The two sets of rules address different matters. The rules of State immunity are procedural in character and are confined to determining whether or not the courts of one State may exercise jurisdiction in respect of another State. They do not bear upon the question whether or not the conduct in respect of which the proceedings are brought was lawful or unlawful.[33]

The majority further argued that the governing law as of the time of the atrocities determined the wrongfulness of the conduct, but states were free to apply the contemporary restrictive law of immunity, not the broader rules that existed in

---

30 *See, e.g.*, Cherif Bassiouni, *International Crimes:* Jus Cogens *and* Obligatio Erga Omnes, 59 Law & Contemp. Probs. 63, 65–66 (1996) ("[T[he characterization of certain crimes as *jus cogens* places upon states the *obligatio erga omnes* not to grant impunity to violators of such crimes.").

31 Jurisdictional Immunities of the State, note 9 *supra*, ¶¶ 84–89.

32 *Id.* ¶ 90 (citing Al-Adasani v. United Kingdom, 2001-XI Eur. Ct. H.R. 79). The issue again is before the European Court. Joined Cases, Jones v. United Kingdom, App. No. 34356/06 & 40527/06 (Eur. Ct. H.R. 2010). The European Convention on Human Rights is *lex specialis*, which makes it unnecessary for the European Court to decide what the customary international law of sovereign immunity permits or requires.

33 *Id.* ¶ 93.

the 1940s. Were immunity rules bound up with the underlying right, retroactive application of narrower immunity would violate the legality principle.[34]

Finally, the majority disposed of Italy's argument that, even if no general peremptory-norm exception existed, a state should lose its sovereign immunity once it blocks off all other means of redressing a violation. Not only did this position lack any support in state practice, but it struck the majority as completely unworkable. Given the common approach to post-conflict claims settlement of providing a lump sum to the victim's sovereign, leaving it to the latter to decide how to pay out the proceeds, determining whether redress had occurred or not would beyond the capacity of courts.[35]

As prefigured by his opinions on the preliminary orders, Cançado Trindade dissented on the peremptory norm exception. He commenced with an uncontroversial assertion: The content of customary international law evolves over time. He then argued that, in the wake of World War II, leading theorists realized that state consent had become an inadequate anchor for international law. States could not adequately represent basic human rights and the general interests of humanity. While international law could not dispense entirely with the state, it had to find new ways to bring in transcendental interests and values.[36] Using this lens, international law could not permit a state's waiver of the rights of victims of grave violations of international law. He would construct a categorical exception to state immunity for all international crimes in breach of peremptory norms of international law.[37] More broadly, Cançado Trindade called for the Court "to give *jus cogens* the attention it requires and deserves."[38] Normal consideration of international law, including the principle of sovereign equality, cannot "stand in the way of the *realization of justice*."[39]

---

[34] *Id.* For academic support of this portion of the argument, see Stefan A.G. Talmon, *Jus Cogens after Germany v. Italy: Substantive and Procedural Rules Distinguished*, 25 Leiden J. Int'l L. 979 (2012).

[35] *Id.* ¶¶ 101–102. Judge Keith elaborated on this last point in his concurring opinion. *Id.* ¶¶ 18–19 (Keith, J., concurring), *available at* http://www.icj-cij.org/docket/files/143/16887.pdf. *Id.* One member of the court dissented with respect to this issue. (Yusuf, J., dissenting), *available at* http://www.icj-cij.org/docket/files/143/16893.pdf. For a similar criticism by an Italian legal academic, see Benedetto Conforti, *The Judgment of the International Court of Justice on the Immunity of Foreign States: A Missed Opportunity*, 21 Ital. Yb. Int'l L. 135 (2012).

[36] *Id.* ¶¶ 7–17, 32–40 (Cançado Trindade, J., dissenting), *available at* http://www.icj-cij.org/docket/files/143/16891.pdf.

[37] *Id.* ¶ 184.

[38] *Id.* ¶ 297.

[39] *Id.* ¶ 299 (emphasis in original). For academic criticism of the majority's decision based on arguments advanced by Cançado Trindade's opinion, see Markus Krejewski & Christopher Singer, *Should Judges be Front-Runners? The ICJ, State Immunity and the Protection of Fundamental Human Rights*, 16 Max Planck Yb. U.N. L. 1 (2012); Carlos Espósito, *Jus Cogens and Jurisdictional Immunities of States at the International Court of Justice: A Conflict Does Exist*, 21 Ital. Yb. Int'l L. 161 (2012).

Two general points stand out from Cançado Trindade's extensive and passionately argued opinion. First, no other member of the Court agreed with him. Even though two other judges would have vindicated Italy's right to refuse immunity, none embraced his argument for a categorical peremptory-norm exception. Second, state practice nowhere figured in his argument. Rather, academic claims coupled with moral imperatives did all of the doctrinal work. In particular, prior decisions of the Court that gave priority to procedural rules over peremptory-norms claims were not distinguished, but rather condemned.[40]

In broader perspective, the Court's decision strikes a strong blow for the continuing vitality of state consent in the production of international law. The rise of international organizations and human-rights discourse after World War II, and especially since the end of the Cold War, encouraged imagination of a body of law that legal actors could access and create without any need to obtain the approval of states. Indeed, some argued that efforts by states to erect barriers to the vindication of this body of law, such as by limiting the jurisdiction of international tribunals or recognizing state immunity from national jurisdiction, themselves violate international law. This position was presented fully to the Court, nowhere more forcefully than in Cançado Trindade's dissent. A strong majority resoundingly and unambiguously rejected it.

III. Implications

The ICJ's decision has significant implications both for the law of sovereign immunity and the underlying structure of international law. In particular, it suggests that U.S. practice constitutes a violation of the rights of the very small set of states that come under its terrorism exception to foreign sovereign immunity.[41] More generally, it indicates structural limits on the recognition of nonstate actors in the formation of international law.

A. *U.S. Practice*

Since 1976, the Foreign Sovereign Immunities Act has codified U.S. practice regarding the immunities of foreign states.[42] In 1996, Congress created a new exception to immunity for states designated by the President as sponsors of

---

40 *Id.* ¶ 297. The dissent cited, in addition to *Armed Activities on the Territory of the Congo*, note 15 *supra*, Arrest Warrant (Democratic Republic of Congo v. Belgium), [2002] I.C.J. Rpt. 25. In the latter case, the Court ruled that an arrest warrant issued with respect to a sitting foreign minister violated the customary-international-law head-of-state immunity, even though the alleged crime was a violation of a peremptory norm of international law.

41 28 U.S.C. § 1605A.

42 28 U.S.C. §§ 1330, 1332(a), 1391(f), 1602–11.

terror. That provision allows a person suffering personal injury or death due to "an act of torture, extrajudicial killing, aircraft sabotage, [or] hostage taking" to sue a state, providing the state was covered by a presidential designation and its agent either carried out the act in question or provided material support for it.[43] Currently designated states include Cuba, Iran, Syria and Sudan. At various times the President also identified Iraq, Libya, North Korea and South Yemen as state sponsors of terrorism, but diplomatic rapprochements or regime changes led to their removal from the list.

The practical consequences of the U.S. terrorism exception are limited, but concrete. In most if not all cases, states refuse to recognize these suits as legitimate and thus allow default judgments to enter. In a handful of cases involving Cuba and Iran, the United States has paid judgments out of its own resources and then subrogated the claims, to date without any recovery.[44] In a few instances, however, states have had to appear in U.S. proceedings to fend off attachments of their assets.[45] Moreover, Libya made significant payments in accordance with a global settlement of outstanding civil suits, as part of its resumption of normal relations with the United States.[46]

Even if Italy had prevailed in establishing a *jus cogens* exception to sovereign immunity, it is unclear whether U.S. practice would fit. Torture generally is regarded as subject to a peremptory norm, but the other items on the list are more problematic. The (il)legality of extrajudicial killings in noninternational armed conflicts is deeply controversial.[47] That relatively recent multilateral conventions

---

[43] Pub. L. 104–132, § 221(a)(1) 109 Stat. 1214, 1242, *codified at* 28 U.S.C. § 1605(a)(7), *amended by* Pub. L. 105–11, § 1, 111 Stat. 22; Pub. L. 107–77, § 626(c), 115 Stat. 748, 803; *and* Pub. L. 107–117, Div. B, § 208, 115 Stat. 2230, 2299, *repealed and superseded by* Pub. L. 110–181, §§ 1083(a)(1), 1083(b)(1)(A)(iii), 122 Stat. 3, 338, *codified at* 28 U.S.C. § 1605A.

[44] Victims of Trafficking and Violence Protection Act of 2000, Pub. L. 106–386, § 2002, 114 Stat. 1464, 1541, *amended by* Terrorism Risk Insurance Act of 2002, Pub. L. 107–297, § 201(c), 116 Stat. 2322, 2337.

[45] *E.g.*, Ministry of Defense and Support for the Armed Forces of the Islamic Republic of Iran v. Elahi, 556 U.S. 366 (2009) (International Chamber of Commerce arbitral award not subject to attachment).

[46] *See* Jonathan B. Schwartz, *Dealing with a "Rogue" State: The Libya Precedent*, 101 Am. J. Int'l L. 553 (2007).

[47] The U.S. statute stipulates that an extrajudicial killing does not include any killing "that, under international law, is lawfully carried out under the authority of a foreign nation." 28 U.S.C. § 1605A(h)(7) (referencing Section 3(a) of the Torture Victim Protection Act of 1991, 28 U.S.C. § 1350 note). This definition invokes international humanitarian law, specifically the four Geneva Conventions and the customary international law of war. But in the case of noninternational armed conflicts, the lawfulness of targeting and killing persons not directly and immediately engaged in hostilities is deeply contested. *E.g.*, Public Committee Against Torture in Israel v. State of Israel, HCJ 769/02 (Israel High Ct. 2005) (describing Israeli understanding of doctrine), *available at* http://elyon1.court.gov.il/Files_ENG/02/690/007/A34/02007690.A34.pdf; Matar v. Dichter, 563 F.3d 9

address aircraft sabotage and hostage taking at least suggests that peremptory norms do not.[48] A further complication is the selectivity of the U.S. exception, which turns on specific designations by the government. Exposing Cuba to liability, for example, while leaving out other states credibly accused of extrajudicial killings and substantial support for terrorist organizations, such as Russian and Venezuela, smacks much more of realpolitik than of a commitment to principle.

Thanks to the *Jurisdictional Immunities* decision, however, this line of defense has collapsed. Even if one could characterize the U.S. exception as corresponding to one for violations of peremptory norms, the Court has made clear that, at a minimum, it regards such an exception as illegitimate. A defender of U.S. practice would have to maintain not only that it tracks a peremptory norm exception, but that the Court's conclusions on the right of a state to carve out such an exception to sovereign immunity are wrong.

In one respect, however, the U.S. approach might seem more defensible than Italy's. Italy's executive defended its exception but did not create it or have any role in managing it. Its approach thus failed to tie the sanction (loss of immunity) to a determination of a prior international law violation. Under international law, immunity from judicial process comprises the initiation of litigation, not only the outcome. A state that is sued in a domestic court but ultimately found to owe nothing nonetheless has suffered an injury under international law. Italy allowed courts to be the gatekeepers, which meant that states that objectively violated no international obligation still could be sued, subject to later dismissal by the court.

The U.S. exception, by contrast, involves a collaboration of all three branches, with management of its application shared by the executive and the judiciary. Structurally, it ties the suspension of sovereign immunity to a failure by the state in question to comply with international law, with the executive as arbiter as to the state's status as a law-breaker.[49] In other words, the U.S. approach, unlike Italy's, ensures that only states that an authoritative actor (the executive) has determined to have violated international law suffer a loss of immunity.

(2d Cir. 2009) (invoking sovereign immunity to avoid deciding lawfulness of Israeli missile attack on suspected terrorists); McCann v. United Kingdom (A/324) (1995), 21 E.H.H.R. 97 (1996) (ruling that British attack on terrorists used excessive force).

48 Convention for the Suppression of Unlawful Acts Against the Safety of Civilian Aviation, Jan. 26, 1973, 974 U.N.T.S. 178; Convention Against the Taking of Hostages, Dec. 18, 1979, 1316 U.N.T.S. 205. Neither of these Conventions expressly authorizes civil suits or the suspension of sovereign immunity.

49 This argument works, however, only if "material support" for a violation of the international obligations in question itself violates international law. If not, then the U.S. exception is over inclusive and thus indefensible as a lawful countermeasure, because it extends to states that do not themselves transgress any international legal obligation. *Cf.* Hamdan v. United States, 696 F.3d 1238 (D.C. Cir. 2012) (material support for terrorism is not an international-law war crime).

So structured, the U.S. immunity exception invites characterization as a lawful countermeasure against breaches of international law.[50]

For a countermeasure to satisfy the requirements of customary international law, it must meet both substantive and procedural standards.[51] Substantively, it must be proportional to the breach and not itself in violation of any peremptory norm. Procedurally, the state taking a countermeasure must first demand that the wrongful state rectify its breach and announce its intention to impose a countermeasure. The U.S. exception arguably satisfies the procedural requirements, but not the substantive ones.

The process of creating and applying the U.S. exception probably satisfies the procedural component of countermeasures law. Presidents do not designate a state as terrorist without some prior protest of particular conduct that violates international law (if not necessarily a peremptory norm) and a demand for reparation. The statute gives such states clear notice as to the legal risk that they face if they do not satisfy this demand. Unlike Italy's judicially created exception to immunity, the U.S. approach seems to work precisely as a tit-for-tat response to another state's breach of international law, with the executive having responsibility for calibrating the U.S. response.

The difficulty with the U.S. approach, however, is one shared with Italy's. Ultimate control over the countermeasure lies in the hands of private actors. Jurisdictional immunity under international law means not simply freedom from judgments, but freedom from judicial process *simpliciter*. As noted above, putting a state to the choice of defending itself in a foreign court or running the risk of a default judgment completes the violation of international law. Under the U.S. system, private actors can produce this outcome regardless of the merits of their individual claim. Exposing states to nonmeritorious claims arguably is a disproportionately broad response to the offending state's default in failing to make reparations for meritorious claims.

It is an open question whether customary international law allows the delegation of retaliatory power to private actors. An ancient precedent would be letters of marque and reprisal, enshrined in the U.S. Constitution and established in British practice for centuries at the time of the founding.[52] The letters were official licenses to engage in conduct that otherwise would violate the law of nations, conduct that the licensee undertook at its own expense and for its own reward. But

---

50 For the suggestion that the U.S. terrorism exception might be defended as a lawful countermeasure, see Kimberley N. Trapp & Alex Mills, note 9 *supra*, at 165–66.

51 International Law Commission, Draft Articles on Responsibility of States for Internationally Wrongful Acts, with Commentaries, 2001/53, INT'L L. COMM'N YBK. Vol. 2, Pt. 2, at 128–37, A/CN.4/SER.A/2001/Add.1 (Part 2). *See generally* John Norton Moore, *Enhancing Compliance with International Law: A Neglected Remedy*, 39 VA. J. INT'L L. 881 (1999).

52 U.S. Constitution, Art. I, sec. 8, cl. 11.

this device has disappeared from international practice for more than a century. Many now see the outsourcing of state violence as deeply problematic, given the profound differences in incentives that private actors and ongoing states face.

Moreover, the analogy to letters of marque and reprisal is inexact. Issuance of a letter required a determination by the political branches that a particular person appropriately could invoke the sovereign's rights of retaliation. A categorical withdrawal of immunity, by contrast, leaves the political branches out of the process of making particularized determinations about claimants. Anyone can trigger the judicial process by filing a complaint, whatever its merits and whether the executive approves of the claim or not.

Litigation, of course, is not violence as such. Historically, however, the law of nations regarded the subjection of a foreign sovereign to a domestic court's jurisdiction as a violation of that sovereign's "perfect rights" and thus as legitimating retaliation, up to and including war.[53] Opening up a state's courts to unscreened plaintiffs, who merely have to allege an injury from an international law violation to engage in a practice that constitutes a violation of a traditional international legal obligation, thus seems excessive and disproportionate relative to the international legal injury used to justify this action.

Assuming that other states will conclude that the U.S. exception does not meets the standards for countermeasures and otherwise violates customary international law, there will be some, admittedly modest, consequences for those who obtain judgments (presumably default) from U.S. courts. A host state wishing to protect assets held on its territory by any listed state could disregard the U.S. judgment as obtained in violation of international law. As a result, plaintiffs would have less of a chance of collecting from the defendant government, and would instead have to hope to persuade Congress to fund their enterprise. This would accentuate a trend already apparent in U.S. practice, namely victims of foreign terrorism recovering from the U.S. taxpayer, and not the wrongful government, for their injuries.[54]

B. *The Structure of International Lawmaking*

The clash of views between the Corte Suprema di Cassazione and the ICJ over sovereign immunity illustrates two competing approaches to the formation and recognition of customary international law. One method, used by the ICJ

---

[53] *See* Anthony J. Bellia Jr. & Bradford R. Clark, *The Federal Common Law of Nations*, 109 Colum. L. Rev. 1, 16–19 (2009); Anthony J. Bellia Jr. & Bradford R. Clark, *The Law of Nations as Constitutional Law*, 98 Va. L. Rev. 729, 822–28 (2012).

[54] For the most recent instance of this practice, see Iran Threat Reduction and Syria Human Rights Act of 2012, § 502, P.L. 112–158, 126 Stat. 1214, 1258–60 (2012) (authorizing attachment of specified Iranian assets to enforce judgments based on terrorism claims).

majority, attempts to elicit the state of the status quo, concentrating on governmental practice and the norms that states abide by. The other, exemplified by the Italian court as well as Cançado Trindade's dissent, seeks to promote the emergence of new norms justified by reason, moral imperative, and a refined vision of best practice.[55] The first is mostly empirical, the second more normative.

This paper is not the place to rehearse the desirability of these competing visions of international lawmaking.[56] Rather, I will sketch briefly the reasons why it is far less likely that the ICJ will be an innovator in creating international law—in the language of behavioral law and economics, acting as a norm entrepreneur—than will the courts of some individual state. More broadly, institutional characteristics, rather than particular normative commitments, provide a good explanation for the distinct behavior of the ICJ and the Corte Suprema di Cassazione.

By design, the ICJ incorporates representatives of a wide variety of legal systems. While the judges do not in any sense submit to the direction of their countries, the selection criteria puts great weight on nationality. Moreover, nominations come from governments, rather than from the broader public. These features make it highly likely that the judges will represent a diverse set of views and that the median vote on the Court will not depart too greatly from something like the mainstream perspective of the governments of the nominating states.

National courts, by contrast, invoke international law for a wide range of reasons. Given the diversity of national contexts, one would expect uniform outcomes in the interpretation of international law only if local conditions had no influence on judicial decisions. The evidence we have is manifestly to the contrary. The disparate decisions appear to reflect the particular circumstances in which national courts find themselves much more than a unifying vision of international law. Put simply, national courts have every incentive to invoke international law for reasons other than the construction of a uniform jurisprudence that will bind all states.[57]

---

55 *See* Anthea Roberts, *Comparative International Law? The Role of National Courts in Creating and Enforcing International Law*, 60 Int'l & Comp. L.Q. 57 (2011).

56 For a full throated defense of a contractarian approach to international lawmaking that highlights the central role of the state, see Robert E. Scott & Paul B. Stephan, The Limits of Leviathan—Contract Theory and the Enforcement of International Law (2006).

57 *See* André Nollkaemper, National Courts and the International Rule of Law (2011); Anthea Roberts, note 55 *supra*; Anu Bradford & Eric A. Posner, *Universal Exceptionalism in International Law*, 52 Harv. J. Int'l L. 1 (2011). For efforts to put variations in national claims about international law in the context of international relations theory, see Eyal Benvenisti, *Reclaiming Democracy: The Strategic Uses of Foreign and International Law by National Courts*, 102 Am. J. Int'l L. 241 (2008); Paul B. Stephan, *Symmetry and Selectivity: What Happens in International Law When the World Changes?* 10 Chi. J. Int'l L. 91 (2009).

To be clear, the argument is not that all or even most national courts will be idiosyncratically inventive in the recognition of claims about international law. Many, for example, will refuse to recognize even well-established international legal obligations for reasons of expediency and peculiar domestic institutional constraints. The point is that the forces producing greater diversity in outcomes make it more likely that some national courts also will deviate from general practice in favor of expansion. What a single national court says about international law is likely to vary around a mean more greatly than what a body such as the ICJ will do.

This argument about idiosyncratic approaches to international law also applies to the political branches of states, which have plenty of reasons to bend international law to their particular needs. But one crucial difference exists. A national government, when it makes a claim about international law, must face the consequences. Other states may use the argument opportunistically to thwart the claiming government's interests, or otherwise may impose costs on that government as punishment for its idiosyncrasy. To put it conceptually, executive branches are more likely to engage in iterative interactions with other governments, resulting in different incentives regarding cooperation and opportunism. Moreover, acquiring a reputation for idiosyncrasy might also reduce the set of opportunities such a government might have to achieve valuable cooperation with other states.[58]

Domestic courts, by contrast, engage in no direct interactions with foreign governments or, for that matter, foreign courts. In a limited number of instances involving transnational litigation, conduct by one national court might have some impact on other judicial bodies. These instances of joint management of a single proceeding, however, are unusual.[59] To a far greater extent than national governments, a domestic court cannot be rewarded or punished for the effect that its work has on foreign actors. As a result, its incentives to curb extravagant or innovative claims about binding international law are greatly reduced.

Given their diverse contexts and incentives, it is not surprising that some national courts would ascribe to international law rules and norms that states in general have not embraced. A consent requirement restricts the pool of rules and norms otherwise available. Opening up the pool to ideas that some prominent person has forwarded, without waiting for any government to agree, greatly expands the repertoire of the courts in question.

---

[58] On the function of reputation in encouraging compliance with international law, see ROBERT E. SCOTT & PAUL B. STEPHAN, note 56 *supra*, at 118–22.

[59] A strong claim for transnational judicial interdependence can be found in ANNE-MARIE SLAUGHTER, A NEW WORLD ORDER 65–103 (2004). For the most part, Slaughter's argument is aspirational rather than descriptive, and in particular fails to specify persuasively a mechanism that would cause domestic courts to internalize the foreign consequences of their actions.

The Greek and Italian courts' decision to create a new exception to sovereign immunity illuminates how the process works. The courts in both countries perceived a need to judicialize claims for reparations for war crimes, perhaps because they perceived that opportunities for diplomatic settlement had ended. Both faced a barrier in the ancient and well developed doctrine of sovereign immunity. Both recognized that the trend in international law since the collapse of the Soviet system was in the direction of greater and more direct enforcement of human rights, even though this trend had not yet entailed a breach of the barrier raised by immunity. Both seized the opportunity, looking more to the future of international law than the past.

Symmetrically, the caution of the ICJ in constructing a new rule of international law illustrates what happens when multinational participation constrains decisionmaking. As noted above, the judges of the ICJ, while completely independent, are selected to reflect certain national outlooks and state interests. It is unlikely that many states would send judges off to the Hague to create new rules that those states had not adopted or endorsed. While such judges may not be immune to normative imperatives, the diversity of their backgrounds and perspectives is likely to narrow the range of claims that they could agree compel adherence regardless of provenance. Nor is there likely to be much space for logrolling, where one coalition trades imperative norms that they prefer for adherence to those that another coalition advocates. Instead, we see a conservative methodology for norm formation that puts the onus for legal change on other institutions.

It is instructive, for example, to compare the one decision implicating international human rights that the ICJ has decided since *Jurisdictional Immunities.* In *Questions Relating to the Obligation to Prosecute or Extradite* (*Belgium v. Senegal*),[60] the court addressed the duty of a state under the Convention Against Torture to initiate a criminal prosecution against someone located in its own territory who was accused of violating the Convention. An ancillary question involved the temporal scope of the duty. The former dictator of Chad, who had found refuge in Senegal, was accused of crimes across a lengthy period, including the time between promulgation of the Convention and Senegal's joining it. The Court ruled that "nothing in the Convention . . . reveals an intention to require a State party to criminalize . . . acts of torture that took place prior to its entry into force for that State."[61] The principle of legality, in particular a prohibition of retroactive criminalization of conduct, applied even with respect to the most heinous international wrongs. Cançado Trindade, in turn, indicated that he would recognize a customary rule against torture to make the retroactivity problem go

60 Judgment (Jul. 20, 2012), *available at* http://www.icj-cij.org/docket/files/144/17064.pdf.
61 *Id.* ¶ 100.

away.[62] Again, the majority believed that an international obligation could not arise before a state had acted to accept it, while the most outspoken proponent of human rights among its members would sweep away such a concern to strengthen the protection of individuals against their state.

IV. Conclusion

In the last three decades, private civil litigation has become an increasingly attractive avenue for human rights advocates to advance their preferences and values. The move enjoys enormous support in the academic community, but attracts somewhat less enthusiasm in the foreign offices of many states, great powers in particular. Litigation shifts rulemaking authority from legislatures and executives to the judiciary. It also greatly augments the influence of private actors. While a few official actors are relieved to have the burden of policy formation in this area lifted, most prefer to hold on to the authority to formulate and enforce human rights norms.

The ICJ decision in *Jurisdictional Immunities* represents a setback for the private-civil-litigation trend. Most directly, it indicates that sovereign immunity remains available even in the most egregious cases. This defense removes from civil litigation an easily accessible defendant, leaving available only government officials who may not be susceptible to process and who may not have attachable assets, as well as private actors to whom liability might be imputed under various complicity theories.

More generally, the decision casts doubt on the entire concept of transcendent norms in international law. By bringing states back into the lawmaking process, the ICJ restores a veto that can limit the work that international law can do. Whether such veto points also allow international law to do the work that it does more effectively remains a matter of debate.

---

62 Cançado Trindade agreed with the court that the parties had not properly raised the question of whether Senegal had violated customary international. He nonetheless explained that he would have ruled that a rule of customary international law prohibiting torture had existed before the Convention, and then states could and perhaps had to punish torture that had occurred before any assumption of a treaty obligation. Continuing the theme of breaking the tie between international law and state consent, he proclaimed in closing:

> Last but not least, the emancipation of the individual from his own State is, in my understanding, the greatest legacy of the consolidation of the International Law of Human Rights—and indeed of international legal thinking—in the second half of the XXth century, amounting to a true and reassuring juridical revolution.

Id. ¶ 184 (Separate opinion of Cançado Trindade), available at http://www.icj-cij.org/docket/files/144/17072.pdf.

HUMAN RIGHTS LITIGATION

NON-STATE ACTORS AND THE ALIEN TORT CLAIMS ACT

Ralph Steinhardt*

One of the most powerful and controversial developments in international human rights law is the emergence of a body of norms regulating—or purporting to regulate—the conduct of multinational corporations. In part, the initiative to impose these obligations has grown out of the public reaction against certain high-profile cases of human rights abuses by particular companies, especially in the extractive or security industries, sometimes in concert with government actors. Typically, the reaction has taken the form of domestic legislation prohibiting corporations from doing business in specific countries—like Sudan or Burma—but other regulatory approaches including securities regulations, export controls, and ethical screens on public sector pension investments have also been used to serve human rights purposes.

Companies themselves have been the source of social responsibility standards at least as often as civil society and governments; indeed, it was the early adoption of corporate principles by companies like The Body Shop and Nike that gave impetus to broader statements of principle across industries.[1] Although these initiatives gave the resulting norms a voluntary or aspirational character, the marketplace has continued to put its own limited form of human rights pressure on corporations. In effect, human rights compliance has become one means of competing for consumers and investors. So for example, a Starbucks cup explicitly reassures those customers concerned that their coffee was raised and processed in ways that are in compliance with environmental and labor standards. Conflict diamonds and the Kimberley Certification Process offer a similar example, replicated to some extent in broader efforts at social accountability certification.

* Professor of Law and International Affairs, Arthur Selwyn Miller Research Professor of Law, The George Washington University.

[1] *See generally*, Ralph G. Steinhardt, "Corporate Responsibility and the International Law of Human Rights: The New *Lex Mercatoria*," *in* NON-STATE ACTORS AND HUMAN RIGHTS (Alston, ed., 2005).

John Norton Moore (ed.) Foreign Affairs Litigation in United States Courts, pp. 89–97
 ISBN 978-90-04-25727-6

Other than the need to improve its competitive public image—its "human rights entrepreneurialism"—what accounts for the fact that Royal Dutch Shell has prominently adopted the Universal Declaration of Human Rights as corporate policy?

In a parallel and reinforcing development, intergovernmental organizations, including the United Nations and the European Union, the OECD and the OSCE, have contributed to an increasingly dense regulatory environment explicitly linking governments' human rights obligations with their regulatory power over businesses. Most prominently, the United Nations Human Rights Council unanimously adopted what is now referred to as the "U.N. Framework," resting on three essential norms or "pillars:" *first*, the state duty to protect against human rights abuses by third parties, including business, through appropriate policies, regulation, and adjudication; *second*, the corporate responsibility to respect human rights, which means the obligation to act with due diligence to avoid infringing on the rights of others and to address adverse impacts that occur; and *third*, greater access by victims to effective remedies, both judicial and non-judicial. The Council's vote marks the first time that a U.N. body had taken a substantive policy position on this issue of business and human rights.[2] Other intergovernmental bodies have been somewhat more proactive.

If there were time in this presentation for a full analysis of corporate human rights responsibilities generally, we would need to pay considerable attention to these interlocking developments in domestic regulatory regimes, the marketplace regimes, and the intergovernmental regimes of hard and soft law governing corporate accountability. But I want to suggest that the more dramatic developments have taken more coercive form and—as these colloquium papers go to press—are *sub judice* before the United States Supreme Court in *Kiobel v. Royal Dutch Shell*.[3] So let me narrow our focus to a particularly coercive form of liability, namely the civil liability of multinational corporations under the Alien Tort Claims Act of 1789 (a.k.a. the Alien Tort Statute or the ATS or simply Section 1350).[4]

The ATS provides in its modern form that "[t]he district courts shall have original jurisdiction of any civil action by an alien for a tort only, committed in violation of the law of nations or a treaty of the United States." Since 1980, when the Second Circuit Court of Appeals decided *Filártiga v. Peña-Irala*,[5] the ATS has been used in a series of cases to assure a measure of civil redress for the victims

---

2 "The UN 'Protect, Respect and Remedy' Framework for Business and Human Rights," *available at* http://198.170.85.29/Ruggie-protect-respect-remedy-framework.pdf (visited 7 January 2013).

3 No. 10–1491.

4 *See generally* MICHAEL KOEBELE, CORPORATE RESPONSIBILITY UNDER THE ALIEN TORT STATUTE: ENFORCEMENT OF INTERNATIONAL LAW THROUGH U.S. TORTS LAW (2009).

5 630 F. 2d 876 (2d Cir. 1980).

of egregious human rights abuse when the abuser could be found in the United States. In fact, *Filartiga* spawned a small cottage-industry in international human rights litigation against human rights violators from a variety of countries. The bulk of these cases have been modestly successful to the extent that they conform to the *Filartiga* paradigm: individual plaintiffs suing an individual human rights violator, who is present in the United States, for a clear violation of customary international human rights law.

Defendants have typically been individuals like police officers, military commanders, concentration camp guards, and even former heads of state, but over the last decade several ATS cases have also been filed against multinational corporations for their alleged participation in, or direct responsibility for, human rights violations. The case now before the Supreme Court, *Kiobel v. Royal Dutch Shell,* is one of a series of cases arising from claims that Royal Dutch Petroleum was complicit in human rights abuses against the Ogoni people in Nigeria.[6] The case came to the Court after the Second Circuit ruled that corporations cannot in principle be sued under the Alien Tort Statute for violations of customary international law. That was somewhat peculiar *inter alia* because a number of corporate cases had gone forward in the Second Circuit on the assumption that corporations did not enjoy some immunity from liability under the ATS. So, for example, the Second Circuit had previously allowed ATS cases to go forward against Pfizer for allegedly testing an anti-meningitis drug on Nigerian children without informed consent. In any event, four courts of appeals have explicitly rejected the Second Circuit's blanket rule in *Kiobel,* including the DC Circuit, the Seventh Circuit (per Judge Posner), the Ninth Circuit, and the Eleventh Circuit. Three of those came after the Second Circuit's decision in *Kiobel.* The idiosyncracy of the Second Circuit's approach is marked by the fact that the government of the United States came into the Supreme Court to say that there was no basis in law for the absolute rule of immunity embraced by the Second Circuit.

At oral argument in February 2012, the Court seemed equally concerned about corporate liability and so-called "foreign-cubed cases" generally, in which foreign nationals sue other foreign nationals in U.S. court for claims arising in foreign countries. Just a week after oral argument in *Kiobel* (right after the conference in which one assumes the initial votes were taken on the case), the Court issued an order, restoring the case to the calendar for reargument. Evidently, there weren't five votes to affirm outright the Second Circuit's corporate immunity decision, and the parties were directed to file supplemental briefs addressing the following question: "Whether and under what circumstances the Alien Tort Statute, 28 U.S.C. § 1350, allows courts to recognize a cause of action for violations of the

---

6 Three related cases (the so-called *Wiwa* cases) settled on the eve of trial in June 2009 for a disclosed settlement of $15.5 million. *See* Ralph G. Steinhardt, "Settlement Agreement in *Wiwa v. Royal Dutch Petroleum Company,*" 48 INT'L LEGAL MATS. 969 (2009).

law of nations occurring within the territory of a sovereign other than the United States."[7]

The broad consequence of the reargument order in *Kiobel* is that, instead of being a decision strictly about corporate liability under the ATS, the issue is whether the ATS will recognize a cause of action for violations arising extraterritorially. Significant as the case was before the reargument, the stakes went up considerably with the new Order, because it put in question whether *Filartiga, Karadzic* and *Marcos*—all touchstones in ATS jurisprudence, all foreign-cubed cases, and all cited with apparent approval by the Supreme Court in 2004—were rightly decided in the first place.

The current controversy over corporate liability under the ATS is framed but not resolved by the Supreme Court's decision in *Sosa v. Alvarez-Machain.*[8] In *Sosa,* the Court concluded that the ATS allows the federal courts to enforce a limited class of international norms that are "specific, universal, and obligatory." Drawing on the historical record, especially the writings of William Blackstone, the Supreme Court ruled that the actionable norms included the "violation of safe conducts, infringement of the rights of ambassadors, and piracy." The *Sosa* court explicitly held that ATS actions are no longer limited to those three specific wrongs, citing *Filártiga* and similar cases with approval. But the eighteenth-century norms that were actionable when the ATS was adopted continue to be relevant, because they inform a rule of evidence that governs contemporary ATS claims:

[7] *Kiobel* was consolidated for argument with *Mohamad v. Palestinian Authority* (No. 11–88), testing whether non-state entities—in that case the PA—could face civil liability under a different statute, namely the Torture Victim Protection Act. The Supreme Court decided unanimously that the language of the TVPA—which is quite different from the language of the ATS—applies to human beings and not to corporations or other non-state actors. __ U.S. __, 132 S.Ct. 1702 (2012). Among other things, the TVPA assures that U.S. citizens who are tortured have at least analogous rights to those of aliens under section 1350. But there are limits imposed by the statute that are not in the ATS, including a 10-year statute of limitations and an obligation to exhaust local remedies before coming into U.S. court. After the TVPA, the central spirit of *Filartiga* became nationwide law and was not limited to the Second Circuit and at least with respect to torture is not limited to alien plaintiffs. In her opinion for the Court in *Mohamad,* Justice Sotomayor explicitly distinguished the language of the ATS, noting that the word "individual," which does appear in the TVPA, does not appear in the ATS. In consequence, according to Justice Sotomayor, the ATS "offers no comparative value here regardless of whether corporate entities can be held liable in a federal common law action brought under that statute." *Id.,* at 1709. The issue of corporate liability under the ATS was explicitly reserved in *Mohamad* even as it was resolved in the negative for the TVPA.

[8] 542 U.S. 692 (2004).

> [C]ourts should require any claim based on the present-day law of nations to rest on a norm of international character accepted by the civilized world and defined with a specificity comparable to the features of the 18th-century paradigms we have recognized.[9]

As Justice Scalia noted in his separate opinion in *Sosa*, the Supreme Court did not question a single case in which this standard had been found to be satisfied other than the arbitrary arrest claim advanced by Alvarez-Machain himself, with the effect that *Sosa* effectively put alien tort litigation essentially where it was after *Filártiga*. In the eight years since *Sosa* was decided, the lower courts have taken *Sosa*'s rhetoric of caution seriously, distinguishing human rights claims that fit the "eighteenth-century paradigms" (*e.g.*, torture under government auspices, crimes against humanity, war crimes, and genocide) from those that do not (*e.g.* failure of consular notification and certain environmental torts). Aside from the claim in *Sosa* itself however, it is difficult to imagine a claim that would have been actionable before *Sosa* that would be foreclosed after *Sosa*.

In addition, nothing in *Sosa* undermined the established law that non-state actors can in principle bear international legal obligations in at least two broad circumstances, both identified by the Second Circuit Court of Appeals in *Kadic v. Karadzic*. In that case, the Second Circuit concluded that "certain forms of conduct violate the law of nations whether undertaken by those acting under the auspices of a state or only as private individuals." Specifically, there is one category of wrongs that do not require state action to be wrongful: in addition to the customary law governing piracy and similar crimes, specific treaties of the United States establish that private actors may be punished for acts of genocide, slavery, and war crimes, *inter alia*. These regimes do not explicitly distinguish between natural and juridical individuals, suggesting that a handful of *per se* wrongs do not require state action to be illegal under international law. There is a second, broader category of wrongs that do require state action, and the *Karadzic* court determined that private actors might bear a measure of legal responsibility for this conduct by virtue of their relationship with state actors. It bears emphasis that *Karadzic* was decided nine years before *Sosa* and was cited with approval in *Sosa*.

Indeed, on precisely the question of whether a particular claim might be advanced under the ATS against corporations, the *Sosa* court determined that international law should be consulted on a case-by-case basis. Referring to the fundamental determination of "whether a norm is sufficiently definite to support a cause of action," the Court observed in footnote 20:

---

[9] 542 U.S. at 725 (2004).

> A related consideration is whether international law extends the scope of liability for a violation of a given norm to the perpetrator being sued, if the defendant is a private actor such as a corporation or individual. Compare *Tel-Oren v. Libyan Arab Republic,* 726 F. 2d 774, 791–795 (CADC 1984) (Edwards, J., concurring) (insufficient consensus in 1984 that torture by private actors violates international law), with *Kadic v. Karadzic,* 70 F. 3d 232, 239–241 (CA2 1995) (sufficient consensus in 1995 that genocide by private actors violates international law).

Until the Second Circuit's decision in *Kiobel,* not a single court of appeals had ruled that corporations are in principle immune from all liability under the ATS, although various courts—and various judges on those courts—have offered contrasting standards for aiding-and-abetting liability, and they have disagreed on whether international law or federal common law is the proper source of these standards. But until the Second Circuit's decision in *Kiobel,* no court (as distinct from a handful of individual judges) had embraced the extreme position that corporations were in principle immune under the ATS.

The key analytical point to be derived from footnote 20 is that the *Sosa* Court rightly distinguished *not* between corporate actors and human beings but between those wrongs that require state action to be wrongful and those that do not. The proper legal question is therefore whether the corporate defendants in *Kiobel* are alleged to have committed acts that fall into one category or the other and whether the complaint adequately pleads the factual elements of each legal claim. It will not suffice to prove that few other countries have explicitly allowed human rights tort actions against corporations. To draw that inference is in direct violation of the essential lesson from the *Lotus* decision in the Permanent Court of International Justice, namely that a sovereign like the United States need not look to international law for permission to act, and the absence of similar arrangements in other countries does not create a prohibitory rule. Other States' abstention from a practice is merely evidence of its rarity, not its illegality.

Judging from the initial argument in *Kiobel,* several members of the Supreme Court cannot get past the question of why the case is in a U.S. court in the first place. But that question actually has a straight-forward answer. The courts of the United States have long recognized a cause of action under the ATS for violations of the law of nations occurring within the territory of another sovereign state, subject of course to case-by-case considerations like personal jurisdiction, *forum non conveniens,* comity, and other limitations on the exercise of jurisdiction that may apply in *any* transnational case. So long as the underlying cause of action in an ATS case rests on specific, universal, and obligatory norms of international law, nothing in international law prohibits the exercise of remedial jurisdiction in so-called "extraterritorial" or "foreign-cubed" cases; indeed, as noted, the *Sosa* Court cited with apparent approval a line of cases that took precisely that approach.

Even more telling, the *Sosa* Court determined that the Alien Tort Statute is "purely jurisdictional." It imposes no substantive obligations and therefore must be distinguished from the substantive American laws denied extraterritorial effect in such cases as *Boureslan v. Arabian American Oil Co.* (anti-discrimination laws);[10] *Morrison v. National Australian Bank* (securities regulation);[11] and *Foley Brothers Inc. v. Filardo* (labor law).[12] These cases tested the projection of substantive U.S. law into foreign territories and held that U.S. standards could not govern foreign conduct by foreigners in the absence of a clear Congressional directive to the contrary. The contrast with ATS cases could not be starker: the very essence of the *Sosa* decision is that the cause of action in ATS cases—the applicable standard of *conduct*—is the law of nations, not U.S. law. Under *Sosa*, federal common law is the vehicle for inferring a cause of action, but *Sosa* only allows the enforcement of norms that meet the 18th-century paradigm case. In other words, the wrong is only actionable under the ATS if it violates a specific, universal, and obligatory norm of *international* law. From that perspective, ATS litigation does not involve the extraterritorial application of U.S. law at all. Rather it offers a local remedy for a violation of substantive international law—not the kind of prescriptive jurisdiction that involves the application of a State's substantive law to foreign persons or transactions. It is true of course that the ATS potentially provides a forum and a remedy for cases that arise in foreign territory. But that is neither new nor extraordinary. As noted by the *Filartiga* court,

> [c]ommon law courts of general jurisdiction regularly adjudicate transitory tort claims between individuals over whom they exercise personal jurisdiction, *wherever the tort occurred.* * * * Thus, Lord Mansfield in *Mostyn v. Fabrigas*, 1 Cowp. 161 (1774), *quoted in McKenna v. Fisk*, 42 U.S. (1 How.) 241, 248, 11 L.Ed. 117 (1843) said:
>
> > [I]f A becomes indebted to B, or commits a tort upon his person or upon his personal property in Paris, an action in either case may be maintained against A in England, if he is there found.... [A]s to transitory actions, there is not a colour of doubt but that any action which is transitory may be laid in any county in England, though the matter arises beyond the seas.[13]

In the thirty-two years since *Filartiga* was announced, not a single court has rejected this conclusion, and every court presented with the argument that the ATS does not apply to wrongs committed in foreign territory has rejected it.[14]

Even as cases have proliferated over the years naming different kinds of defendants and advancing different kinds of international claims arising within the territory of many different nations, Congress has done nothing to cut back on ATS

---

[10] 499 U.S. 244 (1991).

[11] 130 S. Ct. 2869 (2010).

[12] 336 U.S. 281 (1949).

[13] 630 F.2d at 885.

[14] *See, e.g., Trajano v. Marcos*, 978 F.2d at 500 (emphasis supplied) ("We are constrained by what § 1350 shows on its face: no limitations as to the citizenship of the defendant or *the locus of the injury*"). *See also Breach of Neutrality*, 1 Op. Att'y Gen. 57, 59 (1795) (acknowledging the applicability of the ATS to civil actions for violations of the law of nations in the territory of another state).

cases that arise "extraterritorally." To the contrary, in the Torture Victim Protection Act,[15] Congress extended *Filartiga*-like protections to U.S. citizens with the explicit understanding that it would apply to torture in foreign countries. And lest skeptics attempt to read some limitation on the ATS from the extension of the TVPA to foreign torture, it bears repeating that Congress explicitly clarified that nothing in the TVPA could be used to cut back on the ATS.

The argument to the contrary has been rejected by every court to which it has been presented. The reasons for that remarkable unanimity over three decades are neither obscure nor subtle: (i) the statute by its terms does not specify the citizenship of the defendant or the locus of the injury; (ii) *Sosa*-qualified norms cannot qualify as the kind of domestic law to which international limits on prescriptive jurisdiction apply; (iii) the transitory tort doctrine, on which *Filartiga* and its progeny partially rest, is fully consistent with the international norm that every state retains the sovereign authority to resolve disputes that are brought within its territory by the presence of the defendant; (iv) the ATS as interpreted and applied is consistent with the international obligation of the United States to provide a meaningful remedy for egregious violations of international human rights law and to prevent its territory from routinely becoming a safe haven for abusers; and (v) even if the ATS were an exercise in jurisdiction to prescribe, the restrictive international standards governing such jurisdiction do not apply when norms within each State's universal jurisdiction are involved.

The consequence is that a new judicially-created rule that the ATS does not extend to violations of the law of nations in foreign nations not only rewrites the statute and overturns *Filartiga* and its progeny, it is completely unnecessary: the courts of the United States have developed numerous case-specific doctrines to ensure respect for foreign sovereigns and international law, especially *forum non conveniens* and other prudential limitations on the exercise of jurisdiction in *any* transnational case. Nothing in international law takes these prudential tools out of the courts' hands, and they remain available to dispose of litigation with insufficient connections to the United States. In contrast to Constitutional limitations which might also derail ATS litigation—like the due process requirements of personal jurisdiction—these case-by-case considerations do not create *per se* barriers to ATS litigation and in my opinion should not be interpreted to do so without an indication from Congress even hinting that the *Filartiga-Sosa* line of cases is wrong.

I conclude by observing that the *Kiobel* case raises in pointed form the issue of private international law's domain. There are the obvious choice-of-law and extraterritoriality issues in the case, and these are the bread-and-butter of a course in private international law. There are also issues surrounding the obligations of multinational corporations and the source of those obligations such as

---

15 28 U.S.C. § 1350 Note.

might inhabit a course in "private international law" defined as international business transactions. The litigation also reflects a privatized law-making process—the rise of what Harold Koh has called "transnational norm entrepreneurs"[16] and which Paul Stephan has criticized.[17] The *Kiobel* briefs themselves reflect the public private distinction: Royal Dutch argues that human rights and international law generally cannot in principle apply to non-state actors, and the human rights plaintiffs argue that the public-private divide—whatever its original virtues may have been—has become an anachronism and no longer offers a defensible or accurate structure for approaching the contemporary evolution of international law in its many forms.

16 Harold Hongju Koh, "The 1998 Frankel Lecture: Bringing International Law Home," 35 Hous. L. Rev. 623 (1998).

17 Paul B. Stephan, "Privatizing International Law," 97 Va. L. Rev. 1573 (2011).

EQUITY, DAMAGES AND THE RULE OF LAW

Baher Azmy[1]

I. Introduction

This essay starts with a premise that, at least for the purposes of the of this Colloquium, I intend to assume, as a heuristic, rather than prove fully: that policies pursued by the Bush Administration, grounded in dramatic and arguably unprecedented assertions of Executive prerogative, represented a substantial departure from American constitutionalism and the rule of law. While some will no doubt protest that this premise is false or exaggerated, for the purposes of this essay its widespread acceptance matters nearly as much as its internal accuracy. The premise is, in fact, widely shared by the legal academy,[2] international bodies,

[1] Professor of Law, Seton Hall University School of Law (on leave); Legal Director, Center for Constitutional Rights. This paper is based on the author's presentation at the 2012 Sokol Colloquium at the University of Virginia School of Law.

[2] Legal scholarship deeply critical of legal positions taken the Bush Administration in its support of its "war on terror" is certainly too vast to catalog. For a small sample, *see, e.g.*, Jeremy Waldron, *Torture and Positive Law: Jurisprudence for the White House*, 105 Columbia L. Rev. 1681 (2005); Jordan Paust, Beyond the Law: The Bush Administration's Unlawful Responses in the "War on Terror" (2005); Peter Margulies, Law's Detour: Justice Displaced in the Bush Administration (2009); Jon Hafetz, Habeas Corpus after 9/11: Confronting America's New Global Detention System (2010); Nasser Hussain & Austin Surat, eds., When Governments Break the Law: The Rule of Law and the Prosecution of the Bush Administration (2009); Margaret Satterthwaite, *Rendered Meaningless: Extraordinary Rendition and the Rule of Law*, 75 George Washington Law Review 1333 (2007); David Cole, *Reviving the Nixon Doctrine: NSA Spying, the Commander-In-Chief, and Executive Power in the War On Terror*, 13 Wash. & Lee J. Civil Rts. & Soc. Just. 17–40 (2006); David D. Cole & James X. Dempsey, Terrorism And The Constitution: Sacrificing Civil Liberties In The Name Of National Security (2006). Clark Butler, ed., Guantanamo Bay and the Judicial-Moral Treatment of the Other (2007).

John Norton Moore (ed.) Foreign Affairs Litigation in United States Courts, pp. 99–115
 ISBN 978-90-04-25727-6

mainstream commentators,[3] newspaper editorial boards,[4] and a U.S. presidential candidate—Barack Obama.[5]

Those policies include, among many other serious things, (i) incommunicado indefinite detention of foreign nationals (and citizens) in offshore and, in some cases, secret prisons in order to avoid the jurisdiction of U.S. courts and application of law; (ii) the intentional disregard of human rights and humanitarian law treaties governing the treatment of wartime detainees; (iii) the approval of systematic forms of abusive interrogation, including techniques previously decried (and criminally prosecuted) by the U.S. government as torture; (iii) frequent use of extrajudicial transfers, called "extraordinary renditions," of terrorist suspects, for detention and interrogation by notorious human rights-abusing regimes; (iv) a nationwide program of warrantless wiretapping of U.S. citizens' phones.

Given a widespread perception that a number of early Bush Administration policies were grossly unlawful and excessive, this essay seeks to explore and understand the judiciary's apparent disinterest in employing a critical tool in remediating Executive wrongdoing—adjudication of damages cases brought against responsible Executive Branch officials. Indeed, one could say that the judiciary's role in responding to the Bush Administration's post-9/11 practices has been somewhat schizophrenic. On the one hand, equitable challenges in the habeas and FOIA contexts have seen some notable success, at least at the Supreme Court, revealing substantial judicial skepticism about the legal authority and Executive competence of the Administration to carry out detention and

---

[3] *See, e.g.*, Jane Mayer, THE DARK SIDE: THE INSIDE STORY OF HOW THE WAR ON TERROR TURNED INTO A WAR ON AMERICAN IDEALS (2006); Joe Margulies, GUANTANAMO AND THE ABUSE OF PRESIDENTIAL POWER (2006); Charlie Savage, TAKEOVER: THE RETURN OF THE IMPERIAL PRESIDENCY AND THE SUBVERSION OF AMERICAN DEMOCRACY; Anne-Marie Slaughter, THE IDEA THAT IS AMERICA: KEEPING FAITH WITH OUR VALUES IN A DANGEROUS WORLD (2008); Barton Gellman, ANGLER: THE CHENEY VICE PRESIDENCY (2006); Ron Suskind, THE ONE PERCENT DOCTRINE: DEEP INSIDE AMERICA'S PURSUIT OF ITS ENEMIES SINCE 9/11 (2003); Mark Danner, TORTURE AND TRUTH: AMERICA, ABU GHRAIB AND THE WAR ON TERROR (2004); Karen Greenberg, ed., The TORTURE DEBATE IN AMERICA (2005); Alfred W. McCoy, A QUESTION OF TORTURE: CIA INTERROGATION FROM THE COLD WAR TO THE WAR ON TERROR (2005).

[4] *See, e.g.*, Editorial, *A Victory for the Rule of Law*, N.Y. TIMES, June 30, 2006 (praising Hamdan decision).

[5] To be sure, as many commentators have noted, President Obama has continued some of the practices long associated with the Bush Administration, such as indefinite detention without trial and the targeted killing of terrorist suspects by unmanned drones, and courts have largely ratified those practices *See, e.g.*, Jack Goldsmith, POWER AND CONSTRAINT: THE ACCOUNTABLE PRESIDENCY AFTER 9/11 (2011). Yet, as far as we know, the worst excesses of the first few years of the Bush Presidency have not been continued by Obama—and in fact, were largely abandoned by the Bush Administration's second term. Still, as I question in this essay, there has been a surprisingly weak judicial response to cases challenging the early, since-abandoned practices that I suggest were widely considered unlawful.

classification decisions free of judicial review. On the other hand, cases seeking accountability and damages against individual government (or associated private) officials for egregious conduct such as torture, rendition, and religious discrimination, have been nearly categorical failures.

Among the myriad of legal challenges to Bush (and now Obama) policies, this proposed dichotomy is admittedly crude and, for a number of reasons, may not lend itself to simple comparative analysis. Nevertheless, it is worth investigating when one considers these counter-vailing factors. First, the Supreme Court repeatedly and resoundingly rejected in the habeas detention context, the theoretical premise upon which many of the damages cases were dismissed—that the judiciary is not competent to second guess Executive decisions in wartime, or that Executive officials should have near complete discretion to act in matters related to national security[6]—and did so in a manner that itself marked a conscious departure from the Court's regrettable World War II-era deference to the military.[7] Second, our foundational *Marbury* paradigm observes, judicial remediation of Executive wrongdoing is critical to the maintenance of the rule of law. As Chief Justice Marshall famously explained, "The very essence of civil liberty certainly consists in the right of every individual to claim the protection of the laws, whenever he receives an injury. One of the first duties of government is to afford that protection."[8] Likewise, the recognition that victims of federal government misconduct are entitled to monetary remediation formed the basis for the creation of the *Bivens* cause of action (at least in its earlier, more robust form),[9] as

6 *See* Rasul v. Bush, 542 U.S. 466 (2004); Hamdi v. Rumsfeld, 542 U.S. 507 (2004); Hamdan v. Rumsfeld, 548 U.S. 557 (2006); Boumediene v. Bush, 553 U.S. 723 (2008).

7 *See, e.g.*, Korematsu v. United States, 323 U.S. 214 (1944); *In re* Yamashita, 327 U.S. 1 (1946).

8 Marbury v. Madison, 5 U.S. (1 Cranch) 137 (1803). Naturally, Marbury envisions exceptions to this general principle, for "political acts" for which the Executive has full discretion, and some of the bases for denying damages to victims of government misconduct are fit into a broad conception of this modern political question doctrine.

9 As Justice Harlan's landmark concurrence in *Bivens* explains:

> The [government's] arguments for a more stringent test to govern the grant of damages in constitutional cases [than that governing a grant of equitable relief] seem to be adequately answered by the point that the judiciary has a particular responsibility to assure the vindication of constitutional interests.... But it must also be recognized that the Bill of Rights is particularly intended to vindicate the interests of the individual in the face of the popular will as expressed in legislative majorities....

Bivens v. Six Unknown Fed. Narcotics Agents, 403 U.S. 388 407 (1971) (Harlan, J., concurring) (citation and footnote omitted). *See also* Wilkins v. May, 872 F.2d 190, 194 (7th Cir. 1989), *cert. denied*, 493 U.S. 1026, (1990) (Posner, J.). Since *Bivens* remedy was created, of course, it has been progressively neutered by the Supreme Court. *See, e.g.*, Willkie v. Robins, 127 S. Ct. 2588 (2007).

is its goal of awarding damages in order to deter government misconduct.[10] Third, sister nations such as Canada and the United Kingdom have provided substantial damages awards (aided by, if not directly compelled by, judicial decree) for their role in abuses of some of the very same people denied relief in U.S. courts,[11] while international bodies have held foreign governments responsible for complicity with extra-legal U.S. practices, and have awarded damages to victims denied any relief in U.S. courts.

What can we make of this differential treatment? Is it simply that as a doctrinal matter the judiciary was overly solicitous of Executive discretion in rejecting the damages claims, and/or insufficiently solicitous in granting equitable relief as many on either side could credibly argue? Can it be explained by straightforward and context-neutral application of immunity and justiciability doctrines? After all, the *Bivens* remedy has been shrinking in recent years just qualified immunity doctrine has been expanding. Or, is there something distinctive and compelling about the exigent context of Executive responses to 9/11, an event the Supreme Court characterized in the *Ashcroft v. Iqbal* damages case, as "a national and international security emergency unprecedented in the history of the American republic"?[12]

Without discounting these or other possibilities, I wish also to consider the way in which these decisions may be explained by deeper political, cultural or social forces that preference the kinds of equitable relief guaranteed by the Court over retrospective monetary awards against government actors. Thus, despite the considerable hysteria (at least in legal circles), does this post-9/11 episode teach us about (or perhaps just confirm for us) the judiciary's conception of its limited

---

10 There is a wide body of literature identifying this as a prominent goal of Bivens liability, and almost as wide a body questioning whether such liability in fact advances it. *See, e.g.*, Joanna Schwartz, *Myths and Mechanics of Deterrence: The Role of Lawsuits in Law Enforcement Decisionmaking*, 57 UCLA L. Rev. 1023 (2010); James Park, *The Constitutional Tort Action as Individual Remedy*, 38 HARV. CIV. RTS-CIV. LIB. L. REV. 393 (2003); Peter Margulies, *Judging Myopia in Hindsight, Bivens Actions, National Security Decisions, and the Rule of Law*, 96 IOWA L. REV. 195 (2010); George D. Brown, *Counter-Counter Terrorism via Lawsuit: The Bivens Impasse*, 82 S. CAL. L. REV. 841 (2009); Alex Reinert, *Measuring the Success of Bivens Litigation and Its Consequences for the Individual Liability Model*, 62 STAN L. REV. 810 (2010).

11 The Canadian government issued a formal apology to Canadian citizen Maher Arar, for its secondary role in the U.S. government's decision to render him to torture in Syria and awarded him $10 million in compensation, while U.S. courts summarily dismissed his case and the U.S. government refuses to accept responsibility for its direct role in Arar's gruesome torture and imprisonment. The British government awarded U.K. citizen Binyam Mohammed a large monetary settlement for its role in cooperating with U.S. officials in Mohammed's rendition and torture, while the U.S. courts have refused to let Mohammed's case against a corporation complicit in his rendition to torture to proceed. *See infra* note 36.

12 556 U.S. 662, 670 (2009).

role in preserving the rule of law? Lessons from reflections on this episode, however, might instruct advocates how (or if) to pursue accountability of high-level government officials for past or future misconduct, as well illuminate for us all the limits of law to change government policy.

The first part of the essay will review the series of Supreme Court "enemy combatant" decisions, which as a doctrinal matter, reject the Executive's claimed preeminence in our separation-of-powers scheme even in a wartime setting, and more broadly, can be seen as a vigorous judicial response to the Bush Administration's illegal excesses. In the second part, the essay will examine several seemingly compelling cases seeking damages from government officials for egregious post-9/11 conduct, such as torture, which might have called for similarly strong judicial response. Quite to the contrary, these courts invoke, expand and, in some cases, contort immunity or *Bivens* doctrine—in a manner that uniformly provides great deference to Executive decision-making—to deny plaintiffs relief. The third part will explore possible reasons for the court's dismissive treatment of post-9/11 cases accountability, by asking if it is a product of the unique 9/11 context in which they were raised, or if it reflects a broader historical, cultural and legal ambivalence toward monetary relief by certain kinds of plaintiffs.

II. Judicial Review of Executive Judgments in the Equitable Context

There were some prominent judgments imposing judicial constraints on Executive post-9/11 decision-making. A series of Supreme Court cases including *Rasul v. Bush, Hamdi v. Rumsfeld, Hamdan v. Rumsfeld,* I refer to as the "Enemy Combatant Triad,"[13] rejected assertions by the Executive that proper regard for separation of powers, limitations on the competence of the judiciary, and the unique challenges presented by a this enemy, required broad deference to Executive decision-making in the wartime context.

In *Rasul,* the Court held that U.S. courts had jurisdiction under the habeas statute, 28 U.S.C. § 2241, to hear petitions filed by detainees held in Guantanamo, despite the government's protest that the United States did not exercise formal sovereignty over that territory.[14] In so doing, the Court rejected the Executive's demand for deference to an assertion of military exigency during wartime;[15] and held that the Executive's reliance on a World War II-era precedent, *Johnson v.*

---

13 Baher Azmy, *Executive Detention, Boumediene and the New Common Law of Habeas,* 95 Iowa L. Rev. 445 (2009).

14 *Rasul,* 542 U.S. at 480.

15 *See id.* at 488 (Kennedy, J., concurring) ("Indefinite detention without trial or other proceeding presents altogether different considerations.... It suggests a weaker case of military necessity and much greater alignment with the traditional function of habeas corpus.... as the period of detention stretches from months to years, the case for continued detention to meet military exigencies becomes weaker.").

Eisentrager,[16] which had held that federal courts have no jurisdiction to hear habeas petitions by enemy aliens held by U.S. forces outside the territorial United States, was unwarranted in this generation.[17]

In *Hamdi*, a plurality of the Court agreed in part with the Bush Administration in holding that the Congressional Authorization for the Use of Military Force of 2001, included the authority to detain "enemy combatants" captured on the battlefield, if conditioned upon compliance with "longstanding law-of-war principles"[18] Despite that limited grant of conditional detention authority, the Court held that a detainee must be provided a meaningful opportunity to challenge the factual basis of his "enemy combatant" designation.[19] Specifically, the Court rejected the Executive's argument that "individual process" or "factual exploration" by the judiciary into the Executive's proffered bases for detention was categorically impermissible in light of what it suggested was a "the limited institutional capabilities of courts in matters of military decision-making."[20] The Court explained that categorical deference to Executive fact-finding would *invert* our system of separation of powers because the Constitution, regardless of the marginal burden it might place on the Executive, requires there to be "a basic system of independent review."[21]

In the final case of the Triad, *Hamdan v. Rumsfeld*, the Court considered a challenge to the legality of President Bush's November 2001 Executive Order authorizing the trial of enemy combatants by military commissions. On the merits, the Court held that, while the AUMF may have "activated the President's war powers," it could not be read to displace the limited grant of authority to convene military commissions provided by Congress under the Uniform Code of Military Justice ("UCMJ")[22]—a statute which prohibits the use of military commissions if (as in *Hamdan*) their procedures are inconsistent with the laws of war or if such compliance would prove "impracticable."[23] It also concluded that Common Article 3 of the Geneva Conventions covered even Al Qaeda suspects, and thus prohibited the Executive Branch from continuing to use cruel, inhuman and degrading treatment in its treatment of detainees.

Boumediene went even further. By invalidating concerted action of both Congress and the President during wartime, *Boumediene* crossed a threshold never

---

16 339 U.S. 763 (1950).

17 *Rasul*, 542 U.S. at 475.

18 *Hamdi*, 542 U.S. at 518.

19 *Hamdi*, 542 U.S. at 535. *See also Hamdan v. Rumsfeld*, 548 U.S. 557, 646 (2006) (Breyer, J., concurring) ("Congress has not issued the Executive a 'blank check.' ").

20 542 U.S. at 527.

21 *Id.* at 535.

22 *Hamdan*, 548 U.S. at 594.

23 *See* 10 U.S.C. §§ 801–946 (2000); *Hamdan*, 548 U.S. at 594–97.

before traversed in Supreme Court history.[24] Specifically, first, the Court held that the Suspension Clause of the Constitution (and potentially other fundamental constitutional provisions) have extraterritorial reach to Guantanamo and beyond.[25] The Court rejected the bright-line jurisdictional rule proffered by the Executive, because any such rule might ultimately "be subject to manipulation by those whose power it is designed to restrain,"[26] and permit the Executive "to govern without legal constraint."[27] I have argued that this deep skepticism over the Bush Administration's motives—and the aggressive assertion of jurisdiction—was animated precisely by the Court's undoubted awareness of repeated abuses of legal process described above.[28]

In addition, the Court held that the alternative review procedures Congress created—which placed in the Court of Appeals extremely truncated reviews of "enemy combatant" findings by *ad hoc* administrative review boards in Guantanamo (called Combatant Status Review Tribunals)—fell short of core guarantees of habeas, even in a "wartime" setting. As in *Hamdi, Boumediene* rejected the Executive's generalized assertions that individualized judicial review of lawfulness of the detentions would categorically interfere with core military functions or unduly hamper the military's ability to wage war.[29] Rather, it emphasized the "expertise and competence" to make on a case-by-case basis to protect the military's sensitive "sources and methods of intelligence gathering" or otherwise to make "certain accommodations," of the military as of specific circumstances may require.[30] Judicial review, therefore, is necessary to maintain the " 'delicate balance of governance' that is itself the surest safeguard of liberty."[31]

I by no means wish to impart an overly-triumphalist narrative for evaluating the judiciary's role in the context of checking Executive detention practices. Following the Supreme Court's decision in Boumediene, district courts attempted faithfully to carry out the Supreme Court's mandate and, in several dozen habeas cases, issued decisions constraining the scope of the government's detention authority pursuant to international law, dismissed evidence against detainees procured by torture and abuse, and scrutinized the frequently over-general and

24 Azmy, *Common Law of Habeas, supra* note 13.

25 *Boumediene*, 128 S. Ct. at 2243.

26 *Boumediene*, 128 S. Ct. at 2259.

27 *Boumediene*, 128 S. Ct. at 2259. To thereby permit the political branches the latitude to "switch the Constitution on and off at will" would produce a "striking anomaly in our tripartite system of government, leading to a regime in which Congress and the President, not this Court, say 'what the law is.' " *Id.* (quoting Marbury v. Madison, 1 Cranch 137, 177, 2 L.Ed. 60 (1803)).

28 *See* Azmy, *Common Law of Habeas, supra* note 13.

29 *See Boumediene*, 128 S. Ct. at 2261.

30 *Id.* at 2276.

31 *Id.* at 2247.

vague factual allegations against detainees.[32] Since then, however, the D.C. Circuit has revealed that it does not share the Supreme Court's articulation of the judiciary's role in scrutinizing Executive Branch detention decisions. In summary, the D.C. Circuit has repeatedly reversed the decisions of the district courts granting the writ, at times simply disagreeing with the trial court's factual findings, expanding the scope of the government's detention power beyond that accepted by the district courts, suggested (in contradiction to the Hamdi plurality's clear command) that international law or laws of war have no role in constraining wartime detention power, and in other respects offering the government more leniency in defending detentions than government lawyers sought.[33] The D.C. Circuit Court has reversed every district court decision granting the writ, and affirmed nearly every decision denying the writ.[34]

Still, the decisions of the Supreme Court bolstering judiciary's role in checking Executive discretion during wartime provide a useful contrast to the categorical abdication of the judicial role occurring in the damages and accountability context.

III. Damages Claims in the Post-9/11 Context: Ambivalence about the Marbury Paradigm

In this section I will briefly describe subset of cases brought by plaintiffs seeking accountability—in the form of a damages remedy—against government officials for a variety of practices associated with the worst excesses of the Bush Administration, cases challenging extraordinary rendition, torture and supervisory responsibility for a subordinate's wrongdoing in an effort to highlight the variety of ways the judiciary has declined to second guess, retrospectively, judgments of the Executive Branch in implementing post-9/11 policies. In this section, I intend to be critical of these decisions first, because I cannot help myself, but also to

32 Azmy, *Common Law of Habeas, supra* note 13.

33 *See* Mark Denbeaux & Jonathan Hafetz, No Hearing Habeas: D.C. Circuit Restricts Meaningful Review, http://papers.ssrn.com/sol3/papers.cfm?abstract_id=2145554 (cataloguing myriad ways in which D.C. Circuit decisions have restricted scope of habeas review contemplated by *Boumediene*).

34 *Id.* The D.C. Circuit also reversed a district court opinions: (i) extending the court's jurisdiction over habeas corpus petitions filed by individuals transferred to Bagram Air Force base from countries outside the battlefield, *see Al-Maqaleh v. Gates*, 605 F.3d 84 (2010); (ii) requiring the Administration to bring concededly non-enemy combatants into the territorial United States in order to effectuate the traditional habeas remedy of release, *Kiyemba v. Obama*, 555 F.3d 1022 (2009) ("Kiyemba I"); (iii) requiring the (Bush, then Obama) Administration to give the court and detainees advance notice of any proposed transfer from Guantanamo to another country, in order to afford detainees an opportunity to challenge a transfer into a risk of torture, *Kiyemba v. Obama*, 569 F.3d 509 (2009) ("Kiyemba II").

show that the results in the cases were by no means doctrinally obvious or inevitable and thus underscore the possibility something deeper may be animating the rulings.

A. *Extraordinary Rendition:* Bivens *Special Factors and State Secrets*

Maher Arar, a Canadian citizen, sued a variety of U.S. government officials under *Bivens* for their respective roles in subjecting him to the Bush Administration's "extraordinary rendition" program. U.S. officials apprehended Arar at JFK Airport en route home to Canada, detained and abused him for days there and thereafter in a Brooklyn detention facility, and over his vociferous objections, and through a deliberate evasion of judicial process, rendered him to Syria, where he was tortured as part of an allegedly joint Syrian-U.S. interrogation plan.[35] The Canadian government acknowledged Arar's innocence, apologized to him, and paid him over $10 million for its role in his rendition, which included providing Americans patently false information about Arar's connections to terrorist groups.[36] The Second Circuit, however, sitting en banc dismissed the suit in its entirety, foreclosing any accountability from the American side of this travesty.[37] The Court concluded that a number of "special factors"—most general among them, the national security context in which the case arose—counseled against providing a *Bivens* remedy for Arar.[38] The court's concern about its limited institutional capacity and the broad prerogatives of the Executive Branch in making discretionary decisions regarding the treatment are in some tension with separation of powers theories endorsed in the enemy combatant cases and, as Judge Calabrese powerfully explained, the judiciary's core function is to remediate harm done to individuals when it unambiguously errs.[39]

Suits were also brought against the CIA Director for the government's tragically misguided role in kidnapping and rendering Khaled El Masri, a German citizen, from Macedonia to detention, torture and abuse in the "Salt Pit" prison in Afganistan,[40] and by a number of torture victims, including British citizen Binyam Mohamed, against a private corporation that knowingly supported the CIA's extraordinary rendition program by providing aircraft to transfer CIA prisoners to third countries for torture.[41] Notably, the European Court of Human Rights found the Macedonian government acted unlawfully in conspiring with U.S. officials to effectuate El-Masri's rendition, and ordered payment of damages to El-Masri.[42]

---

35 Arar v. Ashcroft, 414 F.Supp.2d 250, 252–56 (2006).
36 *Canada Reaches Settlement with Torture Victim*, NY Times, Jan. 26, 2007.
37 Arar v. Ashcroft, 585 F.3d 559 (2d Cir. 2009) (en banc).
38 *Id.* at 573–78.
39 *Arar*, 585 F.3d at 638 (Calabresi, J., dissenting).
40 El-Masri v. United States, 479 F.3d 296 (4th Cir. 2007).
41 Mohamed v. Jeppesen Dataplan, 614 F.3d 1070 (9th Cir. 2010) (en banc).
42 El-Masri v. Macedonia, No. 39630-09, Judgment, E. Ct. Hum. Rts (Dec. 12, 2012).

The British government paid Mohamed and other British citizens millions of dollars in compensation for the British government's role in the rendition, unlawful detention and torture at the hands of the Americans.[43] In U.S. courts, El-Masri's and Mohamed's cases got nowhere. The Fourth Circuit (in El-Masri's case) and the Ninth Circuit (in Mohamed's case) each ruled that the "state secrets" doctrine required dismissal of the torture and rendition claims against the CIA on the pleadings, even assuming that the plaintiffs could prove all facts necessary to prevail based on already-public information.[44] The U.S. courts' refusal to consider the case is in obvious tension with assessments by other courts and countries that responsibility can and should be imposed for the human rights abuses in these cases; and, the courts' concern about an unacceptable risk of disclosure of classified information seems overblown given the judiciary's notable success in adjudicating numerous detention cases without unauthorized disclosures of classified information.

B. *Torture: Qualified Immunity and Battlefield Immunity*

In the torture context, in *Rasul v. Myers*, the D.C. Circuit ruled that government officials allegedly responsible for the torture and abuse of Guantanamo detainees, were entitled to qualified immunity because the detainees' constitutional right to be free from torture and abuse outside the territorial United States was not "clearly established," and because military personnel alleged to have engaged in torture were acting "within the scope of their employment."[45]

Even U.S. citizens fared no better. In *Vance v. Rumsfeld*, the Seventh Circuit, sitting en banc dismissed a *Bivens* suit brought by a U.S. citizen against the former Defense Secretary for authorizing interrogation techniques that resulted in Vance's torture while in U.S. custody in Iraq.[46] The court stretched a line of cases denying military personnel a right to pursue a *Bivens* against the military, to hold that no individual can use *Bivens* to challenge the legality of military decisions across the board.[47] In *Padilla v. Yoo*, the Ninth Circuit dismissed Jose Padilla's suit

---

43 *See* Patrick Wintour, *Guantanamo Bay Detainees to be Paid Compensation by UK Government*, The Guardian, Nov. 15, 2010.

44 *El-Masri v. United States*, 479 F.3d 296 (4th Cir. 2007); *Mohamed v. Jeppesen Dataplan*, 614 F.3d 1070 (9th Cir. 2010) (en banc).

45 512 F.3d 644 (D.C. Cir. 2008). *See also* Al Zahrani v. Rodriguez, 669 F.3d 315 (D.C. Cir. 2012) (dismissing *Bivens* suit brought by families of individuals who died in Guantanamo); Ali v. Rumsfeld, 649 F. 3d 762 (D.C. Cir. 2011) (dismissing torture suit brought by Afghan and Iraqi citizens); Doe v. Rumsfeld, 683 F. 3d 390 (D.C. Cir. 2012) (dismissing suit brought by U.S. citizen alleging arbitrary detention by U.S. officials while serving as private military contractor in Iraq).

46 Vance v. Rumsfeld, 701 F.3d 193 (7th Cir. 2012) (en banc).

47 See Susan Hu, *Vance v. Rumsfeld: An Erosion of Torture Protection*, Jurist, Dec. 13, 2012, available at: http://jurist.org/hotline/2012/12/susan-hu-vance-torture.php.

against John Yoo for authorizing interrogation techniques constituting torture, which resulted in years of Padilla's torment as an "enemy combatant" detained in a U.S. brig. The court reasoned that, while it was clearly established that convicted U.S. prisoners have a right to be free from torture, it was "not beyond debate" that U.S. citizens held as uncharged enemy combatants have such rights.[48] Perversely thus, the court absolved Yoo from responsibility for torture where the only reason the legality of torture of a U.S. citizen could conceivably be "not beyond debate" was Yoo's own corrupt authorship of the Torture Memos which authorized the illegal torture in the first instance.

Even Abu Ghraib victims have encountered difficulties in obtaining justice in U.S. courts. For example, in *Saleh v. Titan*,[49] the D.C. Circuit appeared dismissive of claims of torture brought by civilians detained in Abu Ghraib against private military contractors for their role in the abuse while acting as translators and interrogators. After questioning the severity of their harms even at the motion-to-dismiss stage, and incorrectly referring to them as "enemy combatants," the court created a broad doctrine of "battlefield immunity," to insulate military officials and private military contractors from any suits arising from human rights abuses occurring "on the battlefield." Parallel cases brought outside the D.C. Circuit have fared better. In *Al Quraishi v. Nakhla*,[50] and *Al-Shimari v. CACI, Premier Tech, Inc.*,[51] district courts rejected the D.C. Circuit's "battlefield immunity" doctrine, and denied private military contractors' motions to dismiss the suits. After an unsuccessful attempt to appeal those rulings,[52] the 71 Iraqi torture victims in *Al Quraishi* reached a financial settlement with L-3—the first monetary settlement of a torture case in the post-9/11 era.[53] The *Al-Shimari* case is, at the time of this writing, on course for trial on the question of CACI corporation's complicity in torture in Abu Ghraib.[54]

C. *Supervisory Liability: The Ineluctable Lesson of* Iqbal

The Supreme Court in *Ashcroft v. Iqbal* added another significant obstacle in front of individuals seeking to hold high level government officials liable for allegedly unlawful policies. The suit, brought by Muslims detained after 9/11 named various prison personnel for abusive treatment during their incarceration and also sued Attorney General John Ashcroft and FBI Director Robert Mueller for creating a special "hold until cleared" policy that applied only to Muslims and Arabs in an

48 Padilla v. Yoo, 678 F.3d 748 (9th Cir. 2012).
49 500 F.3d 1 (D.C. Cir. 2009).
50 728 F. Supp. 702 (D. Md. 2010).
51 657 F. Supp.2d 700 (E.D. Va. 2009).
52 Al-Shimari v. CACI, Int'l, Inc. 679 F.3d 205 (4th Cir. 2012) (en banc) (dismissing interlocutory appeals).
53 Pete Yost, *$5M Paid Iraqis Over Abu Ghraib Abuse*, Associated Press, January 8, 2013.
54 CCR is counsel to the Plaintiffs in *Saleh, Al Quraishi* and *Al-Shimari*.

intentionally discriminatory manner.[55] The Court held that a plaintiff must present non-conclusory allegations plausibly supporting the "personal involvement" of high-level officials. In dismissing the suit against Ashcroft and Mueller, the Court concluded that the plaintiff's allegations that the officials acted with the required discriminatory animus in creating the special hold policy for Muslim detainees were conclusory and "implausible," particularly in light of an "obvious alternative" explanation—*i.e.*, valid law enforcement goals in pursuing suspected terrorists following the calamity of 9/11.[56]

The decision makes it difficult, prior to discovery, to allege that a high-level policy-maker had the requisite personal involvement in alleged illegal activity and otherwise provides significant insulation to government policy decisions that, down the line, result in even gross constitutional rights abuses.[57] Indeed, the decision may make it ultimately impossible for any plaintiff to succeed in holding high level government officials accountable via damages, for decisions made or policies implemented post-9/11. The Court claim it is implausible to believe Ashcroft and Mueller harbored anti-Muslim animus in promulgating a special detention policy following 9/11 is a conclusion that creeps suspiciously close in my mind to Justice Black's rejection of charges of racism as in part motivating Japanese internment. It may well be ultimately implausible—or not. Typically, that kind of plausibility determination would go to a jury. But, by making the plausibility determination at the motion-to-dismiss threshold, the Court may well have ensured that no jury in this case and others, will have the chance to apply any hindsight bias and find, years after-the-fact, that these government officials acted unreasonably.

IV. Some Explanatory Theories

This section suggests some serious, some slightly whimsical, political and cultural explanations for the judiciary's apparent ambivalence to the foregoing damages claims—explanations that deserve fuller attention in later work. Many of these explanations are context neutral, *i.e.*, they would hold force even independent of the calamity of 9/11. Others take on far greater weight in the 9/11 context. Indeed, that the dichotomy could persist despite claims of egregious government actions and in a milieu that plausibly charged the Bush Administration with widespread lawless conduct, may well underscore the broader social and political ambiva-

---

55 129 S. Ct. 1937 (2009).

56 *See also* Ashcroft v. Al-Kidd, 131 S. Ct. 2074 (2011) (granting Ashcroft qualified immunity for allegedly pretextual use of material witness warrant process to detain plaintiff).

57 For example, in *Vance v. Rumsfeld*, the Seventh Circuit, as an alternative basis for dismissal, stressed that plaintiffs could not plausibly allege that the Secretary of Defense personally authorized the actual torture and abuse of Vance himself, and thus failed to meet *Iqbal*'s "personal involvement" threshold. *Vance*, 701 F.3d at 203.

lence we have toward holding high-level officials monetarily responsible for their misdeeds.

A. *Narratives: Liberty versus Greed, or Worthy versus Unworthy Plaintiffs*

One of the most powerful narrative tropes about American law in particular is its power to recognize and then free an innocent man. The image of a gavel-smashing decree delivered from the bench that this man has been wrongly imprisoned and may walk out a free man populates high and low art, and has the power to change otherwise static public opinion—consider, for example, the demonstrable effect of creditable claims of actual innocence ushered by DNA evidence on decreasing public approval of the death penalty. *Hamdi* guarantee of judicial examination of the factual basis of detention is animated by the possibility of an erroneous guilt determination by the Executive, and expressly raised the possibility of an innocent war correspondent or humanitarian reporter being captured in the fog of war—a concern that was repeatedly borne out in the profile of great number of Guantanamo detainees. Similarly, *Boumediene*'s broad sweep, in particular, is largely a function of the sinking recognition that the prison housed many innocent men swept up by bounty, as well as paradigmatic chicken farmers or detainees like Murat Kurnaz—as well as the related recognition of the Executive's apparent incompetence in exercising their discretion. Popular discourse among critics of prison seemed to shift from criticizing Executive arrogance to sympathy for the wrongly imprisoned. The strength of the American narrative of law also explains in part the failure of attempts by individuals inside of the Bush Administration—such as Cully Simpson and Lynne Cheney—to demonize lawyers representing Guantanamo detainees; the Bar, journalists and the public at large recognized that lawyers were upholding the highest traditions by fighting for elementary due process for their clients.

Claims for money, on the other hand, look to some a tad dirtier. In political circles, they often are linked to abuses of the tort system, trial lawyers and greedy plaintiffs. To many in America, liberty is sublimely different in its purity and aspirational function; it is thus more worthy of the judiciary's attention (and more consistent with the traditional virtues and competencies of the court).

But what of innocent victims of torture and abuse like El Masri or Maher Arar? Surely we should want a court and a society to be sympathetic enough to compensate them for blatant and catastrophic Executive Branch error; or, in the words of law and economics, to internalize the costs of their egregious (or willful) errors. In his majority en banc opinion in *Arar*, Judge Cabranes put his finger on a lingering, if often muted, concern of certain members of the judicial branch. It is not just that arguably *innocent* folks like Maher Arar will sue in U.S. courts; permitting his case to proceed may at some point make courts complicit in awarding damages to genuine terrorists. It's one thing to let the goat farmer go back to his village in Afghanistan, it's quite another to award Khaled Sheik Mohamed a million dollars from the U.S. government's coffers. In *In re Iraq & Afghanistan*

Detentions, the district court, dismissing damages claims by individuals wrongly detained and torture in U.S. detentions, that "there is no getting around the fact that authorizing damages remedies against military officials engaged in an active war would invite enemies to use our own federal courts to obstruct the Armed Forces ability to act decisively and without hesitation in defense of liberty and national interests." To lawyers for these clients, including myself, these concerns seem unrealistic, bordering on hysterical, and serve to elide the genuine harm done to individuals actually before the court.

B. *Go West Young Man*

The American political and legal system, premised as it is on economic and social progress, tends to prefer to look forward, rather than backward. This frame of reference was the central feature of President Obama's stated position against the criminal prosecution of Bush Administration officials. Equitable claims for prospective relief may remedy ongoing wrongs; in theory, they advance social welfare. Damages claims force us literally to litigate the past, and only in order to effectuate a private wealth transfer.

In legal doctrine, this preference is present in the distinction between injunctive and damages claims in the sovereign immunity context and even in the affirmative action context—Justice Stevens long ago stressed that remedial justifications for affirmative action (in the employment context) are not as compelling as forward-looking ones (in the educational context), and this perspective is reflected in current doctrine.

C. *The Thin Blue Line, or Mistakes Were Made*

Qualified immunity uncontroversially protects discretionary decisions of government officials acting in good faith. The decisions dismissing damages claims seem to take one step farther and conclude, unpersuasively in my view, that special exigencies of 9/11 required additional space for government officials to respond—and respond more aggressively than we would otherwise tolerate. Judge Cabranes' opinion in *Arar* is replete with highly charitable interpretations of the Executive officials' discretionary decisions, characterizing them as requiring split-second, life-and-death choices, a characterization which the dissenters strongly reject when they correctly stress the amount of time and deliberation available to government decision-makers, and their willful refusal to consider facts contrary to their predisposed view of Mr. Arar.

In *Iqbal*, the Supreme Court twice observed that the plaintiff's complaints arise out of "a national and international security emergency unprecedented in the history of the American Republic." And, in reaching out to decide a question about the scope of supervisory liability which had not been briefed by the parties and, as noted earlier, in concluding that the "plausibility" of allegations of high-level officials' discriminatory motives could not go to a jury, *Iqbal* all but ensured that high level officials would face no trial or even discovery related to their post-9/11 actions.

In *Rasul v. Myers*, Judge Henderson all but states that prisoner abuse is an expected and sometimes necessary part of our military's conduct of warfare. Similarly, the state secrets decisions also appear to fall on the other side of the Thin Blue Line. The Obama Administration had strenuously criticized the breadth of the Bush Administrations' state secrets position, but essentially ratified it and defended it in the Ninth Circuit immediately upon entering office. No doubt Obama faced substantial pressure from the CIA to squelch any investigation of CIA practices at the threshold, perhaps reflecting Jack Nicholson's trenchant observation that Americans "can't handle the truth"—and, two courts of appeal agreed.

D. *A Few Bad Apples*

Secretary of Defense Rumsfeld famously characterized the astonishing abuses at Abu Ghraib as the work of "a few bad apples on the night shift." In so arguing, he meant to deflect properly directed blame away from high level government officials who made a number of policy decisions that contributed to a ghastly culture of abuse lawlessness in Guantanamo and Iraq. To this day, only low-level officers from Bagram and Abu Ghraib have been prosecuted for abuses they committed with their own hands, while policy makers have been free from accountability.

Here, too, *Iqbal*'s surprising limitation of "supervisory liability"—which in subsequent cases the government has interpreted as categorically eliminating liability for any conduct short of direct and immediate participation in the underlying constitutional tort—appears to accept the "few bad apples" theory of responsibility. *Iqbal* makes plain that the thugs who actually beat Javid Iqbal can and perhaps should be held responsible, but is unwilling to permit a plaintiff to examine whether policy decisions by supervisory government officials contribute to underlying wrongs. *Iqbal* may well be limited to the particular claims at issue in the case, but I'm not so sure. I suspect *Iqbal* will more broadly stand for the proposition that law—or at least courts—have little power to deter policymakers conduct.

E. *No Right to Have Rights*

Some deeper criticisms of the judiciary's response would challenge even the premise that there is much distance between equitable and damages claims—*i.e.*, they would contend that the equitable remedies provided by the Court cannot really be classified as a "success." They would argue that in the detention cases the Supreme Court fetishized procedural rights, while consistently rejecting opportunities to recognize that detainees might have enforceable substantive rights under humanitarian, human rights or U.S. constitutional law. The decisions, after all, were largely framed in terms of separation of powers and protecting the narrow institutional prerogatives of the Court from the persistent disrespect of the Executive Branch. According to this view, the treatment of equitable claims and damages claims are quite similar: in both cases, the courts are largely unwilling to rule that an individual had rights that were violated.[58]

This critique would continue by observing that, despite his harsh campaign rhetoric, President Obama has continued nearly all of the policies of the Bush Administration's second term. And, more to the point, no one really cares anymore. Public outrage about languishing detainees in Guantanamo and the harm to America's image in the world has faded as the Obama Administration keeps the camp open and defends a number of Bush Administration policies in court.

This view would suggest that I'm asking completely the wrong question or only a marginally relevant question, as what courts do is dependent on far more fundamental considerations than I'm even prepared to see: the possibility that for some populations, rights are suspended not just during wartime, as in the traditional cyclical account, but indefinitely. Under this theory, not only should we be unsurprised that courts failed to seriously remediate substantial rights violations in the midst of wartime fervor, we should be unsurprised that it continues.

V. Implications—Narrow and Broad

If it is true that persons damaged by actions taken by high level officials, particularly in a national security context, will not get relief from a U.S. court, what implications lie? For human rights lawyers, it might suggest being even more circumspect in pursuing certain kinds of cases, in certain forums; it might suggest trying alternative forums. One potential irony of these cases is that the next time around, lawyers might pursue accountability in the international forums—rather than domestic courts that U.S. government officials are most resistant to (which is not at all to say there'd be any success in those forums). It might mean that lawyers should still bring damages cases, but only to accomplish strategic ends independent from getting a judgment for their client, such as raising public awareness of a morally problematic—if ultimately unjusticiable—controversy.

More broadly, as much as our national character reveals about these cases, these cases may reveal something about our national character. Perhaps this episode underscores the Tocquevillian notion that in America, all political questions are transformed into legal ones. In these cases, it appears that we choose to mediate problems through a litany of Dickensian legalisms that mask substantive policy preferences, rather than make open and considered moral choices. Perhaps we (*i.e.*, the political branches) could just publicly declare that we will immunize government officials for past misconduct arising out of 9/11 responses. (Along

---

[58] *See, e.g.*, Muneer I. Ahmad, *Resisting Guantanamo: Rights at the Brink of Dehumanization*, 103 Northwestern L. Rev. 1683 (2009).

this line, President Obama started such a conversation by declaring he would not pursue criminal prosecutions, and the Military Commissions Act prohibited damages suits by persons found to be "enemy combatants"). But would we be willing to take so broad a step, to formally admit as much to ourselves and to the world? To do so would be to invite charges that we have abandoned a central part of our commitment to the rule of law. Yet, apparently we have little or no problem charging courts—through opaque and hyper-technical legal doctrine—to get us to the same place. In contrast to the democracy-enhancing effects of the Supreme Court's habeas decisions, it appears that courts prefer to sweep other concerns about past unlawful conduct under the judicial rug.

THE ACT OF STATE DOCTRINE IN RECENT "LOOTED" ART LITIGATION

Allan Gerson[1]

The inherent tension between the twin imperatives of avoiding judicial interference in the smooth functioning of diplomatic relations, and on the other hand, protecting human rights, including the right to cultural property recently came to the fore in two cases currently before the courts, *Konowaloff v. the Metropolitan Museum of Art* (the *MET* case) and *Konowaloff v. Yale University* (the *Yale* case). I am involved as co-counsel for the plaintiff in both cases. Seen in context, they illustrate the difficulty in reconciling these competing tugs and pulls that affect the conduct of U.S. foreign relations and the rights of museums and public institutions to profit from the larcenous acts of foreign states. I am therefore grateful to this Colloquium for the opportunity to deal more comprehensively with these issues than is possible in an eight minute Court of Appeals argument, or even in the confines of a brief before the court.

The MET case was heard on April 20, 2012 in Manhattan. The U.S. Court of Appeals for the Second Circuit affirmed, on the basis of the so-called "act of state doctrine," the dismissal of a civil complaint for the restoration of expropriated art.[2] The plaintiff, who was heir to the original owner, sought the return of a painting—Cézanne's exquisite work, *Lady in the Conservatory*—confiscated by the Bolshevik regime in Russia in 1918. The heir argued that his claim for the return of the painting, framed as a writ of replevin under New York law, was not barred by act of state, because the confiscation was not a legitimate official act.

---

[1] Allan Gerson is chairman of AG-International Law which specializes in complex issues of international law and policy. This paper is based upon a presentation given at the 24th Sokol Colloquium at the University of Virginia, April 19, 2012. I am enormously indebted to my good friend Professor John Norton Moore for his friendship and for his wisdom over decades. I also welcome the timeliness of his convening this colloquium "Foreign Affairs Litigation in US Courts," centering on the twin objects of his professional concerns, national security and the advancement of human rights.

[2] Docket No. 11-4338-cv, decided December 18, 2012.

John Norton Moore (ed.) Foreign Affairs Litigation in United States Courts, pp. 117–125

The Soviet regime's sale of the painting to an American collector, via an allegedly corrupt European intermediary or mid-level Soviet official, was also said to be pertinent to whether the act of state defense should apply to thwart return of the painting.

Although the Yale case involved nearly the same set of facts: the Bolshevik confiscation in 1918 of its prized acquisition, Van Gogh's iconic *The Night Café*, together with Cézanne's *Lady in the Conservatory* and their joint sale in 1933 to the same American buyer, the New Haven federal court took a markedly different approach. Where the district court in the *MET* case summarily rejected the plaintiff's claim, the New Haven court refused to dismiss the Yale case. Instead, it allowed limited discovery, especially as to the circumstances of the sale by the Soviet Union to Mr. Stephen Clark in July 1933, four months before the United States recognized the Soviet Union, and permitted normal economic transactions to resume. Late in his life, in 1962, Clark bequeathed the Cézanne and van Gogh paintings to the MET and Yale University, respectively, and both institutions took possession, without any notification to, or even any effort to ascertain the identity of, the heir of the original owner.[3]

The MET decision is now the subject of a petition for rehearsing, *en banc*; and a petition for certiorari to the Supreme Court seems likely. The Yale case has not yet been decided. Nevertheless, several observations, based on the record, seem in order.

(1) The act of state doctrine, like its statutory relative—the law of foreign sovereign immunity—both aim at avoiding unwarranted judicial interference in the Executive Branch's management of foreign affairs. Both shield from judicial scrutiny the sovereign acts of a foreign state. Act of state extends that privilege to private claimants, the latter reserves it to the state. But because the act of state doctrine is not statutory but created by judges, it should provide courts with more discretion than accorded to them in interpreting foreign sovereign immunity as codified by Congress. Yet, some courts, most especially the Second Circuit in the MET decision, have needlessly imposed strait-jackets on judicial discretion and flexibility.

(2) The modern revulsion at shielding governmental seizure of private cultural property, now regularly incorporated in museum guidelines applicable to Nazi looted art, should be applied equally to art looted by the Bolsheviks.

I.

It is useful at the outset to re-examine why U.S. courts first accorded foreign states immunity from scrutiny of even their most heinous acts, especially where

[3] The estimated value of the Van Gogh painting is $150 million or more; the estimated value of the Cezanne is $70 million or more.

the effects of those acts could be felt in the United States. In the Supreme Court's landmark opinion in *The Schooner Exchange v. McFaddon*,[4] Chief Justice John Marshall made clear that according sovereign immunity stems from the need to avoid giving offense to other nations, so that this nation will be treated with the same respect when its agents are haled before foreign courts. His view mirrored the classic exposition by one of the "fathers" of international law, Hugo Grotius, who pronounced that international law is a pact among "like-minded" sovereign states based on reciprocal commitments to non-interference in each others' internal affairs.

In contemporary public international law, the same principle is embedded in the first article of the UN Charter (Article 1:1) which obliges respect for "the sovereign equality" of all Member States regardless of their economic or political systems. Article 2:7 of the UN Charter amplifies that commitment by requiring all states to eschew interference in the internal affairs of others. But that presumption of sovereign spheres—as if kings still sat on thrones, scepters in hand, obligated and accountable to no one but themselves—has been severely challenged with the advent of international human rights law, most importantly in the international insistence that South Africa's apartheid policy not be treated as a purely internal affair. Further erosion of the rigid rule of non-interference in internal affairs where acts repugnant to international law and morality are at issue can be seen in UN-authorized military intervention to prevent wholesale slaughter in Kosovo, and more recently in the Security Council's authorization of military intervention in Libya to protect the citizens of Benghazi.

As concerns the courts, even as far back as 1812 Chief Justice Marshall in *McFaddon* foresaw the erosion of absolute sovereignty as a bar to judicial inquiry. "The jurisdiction of the nation within its own territory is necessarily exclusive and absolute ... the world being composed of distinct sovereigns, possessing equal rights and equal independence," said the Chief Justice.[5] But absolute sovereign immunity also stopped, Marshall said, at a state's borders where acts in one state spill over into another state's sovereign territory. Chief Justice Marshall looked also to the views of another founder of international law, Emmerich Vattel: "Now, the laws of nature being no less obligatory on nations than on individuals (Prelim. § 5), whatever duties each man owes to other men, the same does each nation, in its way, owe to other nations (Prelim. § 10, &c)."[6] On examination of international law's underpinnings in the regard to the state sovereignty, Marshall concluded that an absolutist view must occasionally yield to pragmatism: "All sovereigns have consented to a *relaxation in practice*, in cases under certain

[4] *The Schooner Exchange v. McFaddon*, 11 U.S. 116 (1812).

[5] *The Schooner Exchange*, 11 U.S. at 136.

[6] Vattel, Section 4 Book 1, The Law of the Nations, Chapter One of Nations and Sovereign States, available at: http://www.constitution.org/vattel/vattel_01.htm.

peculiar circumstances of that absolute and complete jurisdiction within their respective territories which sovereignty confers" (emphasis added).[7]

In codifying the law of sovereign immunity in 1976, Congress provided a number of exceptions, which deprive foreign states of the prerogative. States may not claim immunity from the scrutiny of U.S. courts when, for example, they engage in commercial activities causing effects in this country: in such circumstances, they are seen as traders entitled to no privileges denied to other traders. Although the specifics of the 1976 statute are far more complex than what Chief Justice Marshall contemplated, they demonstrate the vitality of his view that immunity derives from, and can be overridden by, the context in which it is asserted.

Marshall's call to heed pragmatism in the application of sovereign immunity foreshadowed what another Supreme Court Justice, Antonin Scalia, would pronounce many decades later in the landmark ruling on act of state, *W.S. Kirkpatrick Co. v. Environmental Tectonics Corp.*, 493 U.S. 400 (1990). There, Justice Scalia warned that "[T]he *policies* underlying the act of state doctrine should be considered in deciding whether, *despite the doctrine's technical availability*, it should nonetheless *not* be invoked. *Id.* at 409 (emphasis added).

Yet even as Justice Scalia pointed out in *Kirkpatrick* that there is ample room for judicial discretion in applying the doctrine, some courts have seen fit to treat such discretion as beyond their reach. That is surprising, as the Supreme Court has consistently called for a *balancing* of policy considerations in determining whether to apply the act of state doctrine on a case by case basis, particularly to whether foreign relations would in fact be threatened by adjudication.

A decade ago, in representing Pan Am 103 families in their claim against Libya for its downing of a civilian aircraft, I argued that blowing up an airplane with 259 people on board should be treated as an implicit waiver, or forfeiture, of sovereign immunity. But the U.S. District Court ruled that even implicit waiver under the 1976 Foreign Sovereign Immunities Act required a finding of intent to waive immunity—as if state bent on terrorism could be expected execute a document or the like signaling its intent to accept being sued by victims in foreign courts.

With their claim for damages dismissed, the Pan Am 103 families charted a legislative route to amend the 1976 Federal Sovereign Immunities Act, resulting in passage of the 1996 Antiterrorism and Effective Death Penalty Act (AEDPA). That act explicitly recognized that a nation engaging in state-sponsored terrorism forfeit their right to sovereign immunity, provided that the State Department has listed that nation as a "state sponsor of terrorism." Ultimately, after the constitutionality of the AEDPA provision was upheld—establishing that the Executive Branch, and not the courts can make that determination—the families entered into a $2.7 billion settlement with Libya. Yet, had it not been for the legislative revision (forged by a collaboration between the families of Pan Am 103 and the

[7] The Schooner Exchange v. McFaddon, 11 US 116, 136 (1812).

1995 Oklahoma bombing victims), there would be no remedy today for victims of state sponsored terrorism insofar as the courts declined to endorse the idea that even the deliberate bombing of a foreign state's civilian aircraft could be construed as an implicit waiver of sovereign immunity.

That exercise in judicial rigidity can be forgiven in the case of the Pan Am 103 litigation because the courts were operating within the confines of a statute. But the act of state doctrine is purely judge-made law, envisioned as a tool for determining whether to defer adjudication of a case. It is thus within the capacity of the judiciary to interpret and revise. Indeed the U.S. Supreme Court has repeatedly spoken in these terms.

Nevertheless, in the lower court decision in September 2011 in *Konowaloff v. MET*, Judge Shira Scheindlin of the U.S. District Court for the Southern District of New York ruled that the act of state doctrine necessarily barred adjudication of the illegality of the Bolsheviks' confiscation of a work of art. This ruling came despite the clear American connection, insofar as the Bolshevik regime's successor, the Soviet Union, later sold that painting to an American buyer, and a prominent American museum has displayed the work for six decades and claims legitimate title.

Judge Scheindlin stated that "the Supreme Court, the Second Circuit, and this Court have consistently held Bolshevik/Soviet nationalization decrees to be official acts accepted as valid for the purpose of invoking the act of state doctrine." She further claimed that "I accept that the Soviet government took ownership of the Painting in 1918 through an official act of state, and accordingly, the Painting's sale abroad in 1933—whether legal or illegal, act of a party or an act of state—becomes irrelevant, as [the plaintiff] lacks any ownership stake in the Painting."

The Supreme Court cases cited by the district court—*U.S. v. Belmont*[8] and *U.S. v. Pink*[9]—hardly support the sweeping proposition that the validity of all Bolshevik/Soviet nationalization decrees are off-limits to scrutiny by U.S. courts. Those cases, adjudicated in 1937 and 1942, were decided on particular facts of an assignment pursuant to the Roosevelt-Litvinov Accord recognizing the Soviet Union. They involved Soviet assets in a New York bank transferred to the federal government pursuant to that agreement. Obviously, enforcement of that key diplomatic accord was of supreme concern to the Soviet Union. But Judge Scheindlin was hardly presented with an analogous set of facts in the MET controversy. Nevertheless, the Second Circuit Court of Appeals affirmed Judge Scheindlin. In doing so, the Court adopted an unprecedented requirement that plaintiffs must establish specific repudiation of the acts in question by a successor state (here the Soviet Union as successor to the Bolsheviks) before those acts can be reviewable and a case may proceed to trial.

---

8 301 U.S. 324 (1937).
9 315 U.S. 203 (1942).

The matter of the Soviets' subsequent sale of the painting was thus never factored into the analysis of whether to accord immunity. Instead, the Court of Appeals ruled that the district court had properly concluded "in light of the Soviet government's appropriation of the painting in 1918," that the plaintiff had "no standing to complain of any sale or other treatment of the painting after 1918." But is "standing" really obtained or denied by invocation of act of state to *abstain* from a judicial ruling? Does not such abstention necessarily avoid any endorsement of a claim of title? And if there is no such affirmative endorsement, but only a recognition that the courts will not wade in those waters, should lack of plaintiff's "standing" determine whether a U.S. court would be stepping on another state's toes by passing judgment on title to a painting held in the United States?

Yet, even assuming that if abstractly act of state is not only a policy of abstention but one that includes the presumptive recognition of the challenged act as legitimate, there remains the requirement that its application be tempered by a balancing of all pertinent interests. Key among these surely is that it is clear beyond doubt that international law forbids state expropriation of private property without compensation. And even if such acts may not be questioned as to their consequences within the expropriating state's own borders, our courts need not validate foreign confiscatory decrees affecting property on our shores. Thus—while there is no case-law directly on point—it surely is inconsistent with international law and with the laws of this country not to recognize the title of someone claiming ownership of an artwork when he knowingly bought it from a thief, especially where (as here) the thief was hiding behind the sovereignty of a state.

In 1964 in *Banco Nacional de Cuba v. Sabbatino*,[10] the Supreme Court prescribed a balancing test for answering these questions. The Court held, "the greater degree of codification or consensus concerning a particular area of international law, the more appropriate it is for the judiciary to render decisions regarding it."[11] To this holding, Justice Scalia added on behalf of the majority in *Kirkpatrick*: "Act of state issues only arise when a court *must decide*—that is, when the outcome of the case turns upon—the effect of official action by a foreign sovereign."[12] Thus by focusing on whether the sale was an unofficial act—the approach favored by the Yale district court—there would have been no reason to compel examination of act of state issues.

Balancing means paying due attention to the context of any controversy. Whether U.S. foreign relations will be impaired must be assessed, *Kirkpatrick* teaches, with due attention to all relevant factors so that "even though the validity of the act of a foreign sovereign within its territory is called into question,

10 376 US 398, 428 (1964).
11 *Id.*
12 *Kirkpatrick* at 406 (emphasis in original).

the policies underlying the doctrine may not justify its application."[13] Surely one relevant policy factor is that the Van Gogh and Cézanne paintings in question here—alone among several hundred paintings confiscated by the Soviets from the Morozov estate to which Konowoloff was the heir—were sold by the Soviet Union, and to an American buyer at that. Although ostensibly nationalized for the public good of making them accessible to view by the Russian public, by virtue of the sale the paintings ended up in New York and Connecticut for over sixty years. Moreover, unlike the massive sales, in the tens of millions of dollars of Tsarist-held art, to Paul Mellon and J.P. Morgan, authorized at the highest levels of the Soviet Union, in the 1930s, these two paintings were sold for a relatively small amount of money, raising the question whether the sale itself was even authorized.

But these questions were never given their day in court, quashed by the act of state doctrine before the legitimacy of the sale under Soviet law could be questioned. Indeed, had Russia and not Yale or the MET been the defendant, a challenge to the sale would have been permitted under the statutory sovereign immunity doctrine, in which immunity is waived when a state engages in commercial activity. This then is a tale of how a judicial doctrine of abstention, conceived as a flexible discretionary tool, has been construed as iron-clad and inflexible.

The outcome of the MET case is especially surprising in light of the 2000 Second Circuit ruling in *Bigio v. Coca-Cola.* There, the Court recognized the "substantial gloss" to the act of state doctrine: "The function of the court in applying the act of state doctrine is to *weigh in balance* the foreign policy interests that favor or disfavor [its] application."[14] [E]ach case [must] be analyzed individually to determine [whether there is] the need for a separation of powers."[15] One of the individual factors prominent in *Bigio* was a change in government: the fact that the new government in Egypt would never have confiscated all Jewish-owned property as Nasser's regime had done. The court pointed out that once a new foreign government repudiates its predecessor's practices, there is virtually no chance that adjudication would interfere with U.S. foreign policy, since the government whose acts would be under review is no longer in existence.[16] Yet in the MET case the Second Circuit simply assumed that the Soviet Union was the successor government to the Bolshevik regime and imposed upon the plaintiff the responsibility for demonstrating such repudiation in order to avoid summary dismissal.

---

[13] *Id.* at 409.

[14] *Bigio v. Coca-Cola Company*, 239 F.3d 440, 452 (2d Cir. 2000)(citing *Republic of the Philippines v. Marcos*, 806 F.2d 344, 359 (2d Cir. 1986)).

[15] *Id.* (citing *Braka Bancomer, S.N.C.*, 762 F.2d 222, 224 (2d Cir. 1985)), (quoting *Sabbatino*, 376 U.S. at 428).

[16] *Id.* at 453.

Most egregiously, the Second Circuit Court of Appeals merely assumed without any hearing on the facts the likely impairment of U.S. foreign relations. In sharp contrast, the District of Columbia Circuit in *Agudas Chasidei Chabad v. Russian Federation* 528 F. 3d 934 (D.C. Cir. 2008) rejected such an approach in an analogous cultural property confiscation case brought under the Foreign Sovereign Immunities Act, even over the strenuous protests of the Russian Federation. Indeed, on January 16, 2013, Chief Judge Royce Lamberth of the U.S. District Court for the District of Columbia issued an order fining Russia $50,000 a day until it complies with his earlier order to return Bolshevik-seized books and documents to their proper owners. The MET case, however, resulted in summary dismissal without a single protest from Russia, and without even a solicitation of the views of the U.S. government.

Overall, the MET case marks a departure from the trend in current judicial decisions toward the considered balancing of sovereign rights where significant human rights are affected. Indeed, there is no longer a knee-jerk deference by courts to even the Executive Branch's own requests not to adjudicate a case because foreign affairs may be implicated. *See Khulumani v. Barclay National Bank*, 504 F.3d 254 (2d Cir. 2007), where the federal court in New York determined that it could assess any claimed adverse impact to U.S. bilateral relations as one factor among many when evaluating demands for dismissal by the Executive Branch and the government of South Africa.

II.

Finally, I wish to raise the question of whether Nazi "looted art" and the museum guidelines that pertain to it should be treated as limited to the takings of the Third Reich.[17]

U.S. courts have consistently held that the act of state doctrine does not bar recovery of cultural property confiscated by the Nazi regime. But they have not been presented, until the MET and Yale cases, with the opportunity to draw parallels to Bolshevik looted art.

The approach of the Holocaust Memorial Museum is instructive. Its mission statement makes clear that although the Museum focuses on the Nazi era, the Holocaust is treated as generating lessons applicable to other genocides. The Museum is intended to serve as an "an inspiration to citizens and leaders worldwide to confront hatred, prevent genocide, and promote human dignity," and to "teach millions of people each year about the dangers of unchecked hatred and the need to prevent genocide... and encourage them to act, cultivating a sense

[17] American Association of Museums, Guidelines Concerning the Unlawful Appropriation of Objects during the Nazi Era, available at: http://www.aam-us.org/museumresources/ethics/nazi_guidelines.cfm.

of moral responsibility among our citizens so that they will respond to the monumental challenges that confront our world."[18]

By this rationale, what justifies differentiating Bolshevik thugs from Nazi storm-troopers stripping paintings off the walls of the homes of their legitimate owners? Why is there accountability to the victims of Nazi looted art, but not to the victims of Bolshevik looted art?

Rendering justice in cases of stolen art requires the intelligent application of law to different historical contexts. Respect for the principles underlying the act of state doctrine does not require the judicial strait-jacket of a long-discredited absolutist view of sovereignty.

When a foreign state decides to sell looted goods abroad it should be deemed to have forfeited the privilege of getting a pass from adjudication by U.S. courts insofar as such an act of comity, or deference to the Executive Branch's conduct of foreign relations, is no longer justified by the need to respect foreign economic and political systems whose wanton confiscation of cultural property is repugnant to our national values. Otherwise, by treating looted art, laundered to our shores and to our museums, as beyond the reach of the law, American judges become Lenin's enforcers: awarding the imprimatur of good title to American institutions that benefit from foreign confiscations of cherished works of art.

Such an odious result, at odds with sound U.S. policy, is hardly required by the intelligent application of the act of state doctrine.

---

18 *Id.*

FOREIGN AFFAIRS TAKINGS ACTIONS IN THE COURT OF FEDERAL CLAIMS

FOREIGN AFFAIRS TAKINGS: THE QUESTION OF FOREIGN PLAINTIFF STANDING

Douglas J. Pepe*

Do noncitizen plaintiffs have a right to sue the Federal government for the taking of property on foreign soil? This seemingly fundamental Constitutional question has no clear answer. In the lower courts, the settled answer used to be yes. Now it is a clear maybe. And the doctrinal ground underlying prior decisions has shifted in a manner that renders the Takings Clause jurisprudence incoherent.[1] This paper analyzes the question in light of the text, history and judicial interpretations of the Takings Clause and concludes that foreign plaintiffs should have no entitlement to sue for foreign "takings" in the United States courts.

Background

The text of the Takings Clause is as follows: "[N]or shall private property be taken for public use, without just compensation."[2] Unlike other Constitutional proscriptions, the Takings Clause does not say *who* it applies to. The First, Second and Fourth Amendments speak to rights of "the people."[3] The Third Amendment protects "the Owner" of "any house."[4] The Sixth Amendment applies to "the accused" in criminal cases.[5] The other clauses of the Fifth Amendment apply to any "person."[6]

---

* Douglas J. Pepe is a partner at Gregory P. Joseph Law Offices LLC in New York City.

1 For a comprehensive discussion of the problem, *see* Jeffrey Kahn, *Zoya's Standing Problem, Or, When Should the Constitution Follow the Flag?*, 108 Mich. L. Rev. 673, 709–13 (2010).
2 U.S. Const. amend. V.
3 U.S. Const. amend. I, II, IV.
4 U.S. Const. amend. III.
5 U.S. Const. amend. VI.
6 U.S. Const. amend. V.

John Norton Moore (ed.) Foreign Affairs Litigation in United States Courts, pp. 129–143
©2013 Koninklijke Brill NV, The Netherlands. ISBN 978-90-04-25727-6

Who does the Takings Clause protect? The text is silent. Nor does the clause specify where the property must be located. Must it be in the United States? Does it have to be somewhere within the Government's sovereign reach? Can it be anywhere at all? These fundamental questions are unaddressed in the language of the Takings Clause itself, leaving the matter for judicial resolution.[7]

Takings Clause precedents can be divided into four categories:

Category 1: Citizen Plaintiff/Domestic Property. A United States citizen whose property is taken on U.S. soil clearly has standing to bring a Takings Claim.[8]

Category 2: Citizen Plaintiff/Foreign Property. It has been the decisional law of the lower courts since at least the 1867 Court of Claims decision in *The Wiggins Case*—involving the authorized destruction by a U.S. Navy commander of gunpowder stored in Punta Arenas, Costa Rica—that U.S. citizens have standing to bring Takings Clause claims for the taking of their property outside the United States.[9]

---

[7] *See, e.g., El-Shifa Pharm. Indus. Co. v. United States*, 378 F.3d 1346, 1351 (Fed. Cir. 2004) ("To be sure, the text of the Takings Clause does not qualify what is meant by 'private property' or indicate that it must be located in this country. Nor does the text say that only American citizens may receive just compensation.").

[8] *Portsmouth Harbor Land & Hotel Co. v. United States*, 260 U.S. 327 (1922) (Holmes, J.); *United States v. Russell*, 80 U.S. 623 (1871). This rule has also been applied to United States territories. *See, e.g., Grant v. United States*, 1 Ct. Cl. 41, 49 (Ct. Cl. 1863).

[9] *Wiggins v. United States*, 3 Ct. Cl. 412 (Ct. Cl. 1867); *see also Seery v. United States*, 127 F. Supp. 601 (Ct. Cl. 1955) (confiscation of U.S. citizen's property in Austria for use as officer's club during WWII); *Langenegger v. United States*, 756 F.2d 1565, 1570 (Fed. Cir. 1985) ("It is settled law that the United States is bound by our Constitution when it takes actions that affect citizens outside our territory; therefore the government must provide just compensation for takings by its forces which occur abroad, when not acts of war.") (citations omitted). *Mitchell v. Harmony*, 13 How. 115, 14 L.Ed. 75 (1851), is often incorrectly cited as a Takings Clause case involving seizure of citizen property abroad, but *Mitchell* was not a Takings Clause case, it was an action for trespass. *Id.* at 128. The defendant, a United States Colonel, was held individually liable for *damages* arising from his confiscation of a nationalized citizen's property in Mexican territory during a military expedition. *Id.* at 129–30. Dictum in *Mitchell* does, however, imply an early understanding of the Takings Clause as operating outside the United States in situations involving the confiscation of United States citizens' property. *See id.* at 134 (An officer's "distance from home, and the duties in which he is engaged, cannot enlarge his power over the property of a citizen, nor give to him, in that respect, any authority which he would not, under similar circumstances, possess at home. And where the owner has done nothing to forfeit his rights, every public officer is bound to respect them, whether he finds the property in a foreign or hostile country, or in his own. There are, without doubt, occasions in which private property may be lawfully taken possession of or destroyed to prevent it from falling into the hands of the public enemy; and also where a military officer, charged with a particular duty, may impress private property into the public service or take it for public use. *Unquestionably, in such cases, the government is bound to make full compensation to the owner*; but the officer is not a trespasser.") (emphasis added).

Category 3: Foreign Plaintiff/Domestic Property. Foreign plaintiffs also have clear standing to sue for domestic takings. The Supreme Court so held in the 1931 *Russian Volunteer Fleet* case.[10] In *Russian Volunteer Fleet,* the U.S. government requisitioned partially constructed ships owned by a Russian corporation and docked in New York harbor, as well as the corporation's contracts to build those ships.[11] The Supreme Court had little difficulty applying the Takings Clause to the requisition, and awarding compensation, despite the corporation's "alien" status:

> The petitioner was an alien friend, and as such was entitled to the protection of the Fifth Amendment of the Federal Constitution.... Exerting by its authorizing agent the power of eminent domain in taking the petitioner's property, the United States became bound to pay just compensation.[12]

Category 4: Foreign Plaintiff/Foreign Property. The more difficult—and more interesting—cases arise when a foreign plaintiff sues for just compensation for a taking of property located outside the United States. Does the foreign plaintiff have standing? The settled answer in the Court of Federal Claims and Federal Circuit[13] used to be yes. Now, the answer is not so clear.

---

[10] *See Russian Volunteer Fleet v. United States,* 282 U.S. 481 (1931).

[11] *Id.* at 487.

[12] *Id.* at 489. The plaintiff in *Russian Volunteer Fleet* was an "alien friend." *See id.* Enemies of the United States, by contrast, may be divested of any recourse against the United States for confiscation of their property. *See, e.g., United States v. Chemical Foundation,* 272 U.S. 1, 11 (1926) ("Congress [is] untrammelled and free to authorize the seizure, use or appropriation of [enemy] property without any compensation to the owners. There is no constitutional prohibition against confiscation of enemy properties.") (citations omitted); *Cummings v. Deutsche Bank,* 300 U.S. 115, 120 (1937) (Congressional enactment "directing seizure, use and disposition of property in this country belonging to subjects of the enemy" is "untrammeled by the due process or just compensation clause"). *See also Brown v. United States,* 12 U.S. 110, 122–23 (1814) (Marshall, C. J.) ("That war gives to the sovereign full right to take the persons and confiscate the property of the enemy wherever found, is conceded. The mitigations of this rigid rule, which the humane and wise policy of modern times has introduced into practice, will more or less affect the exercise of this right, but cannot impair the right itself. That remains undiminished, and when the sovereign authority shall choose to bring it into operation, the judicial department must give effect to its will.... [T]he power of confiscating enemy property is in the legislature."); *Miller v. United States,* 78 U.S. 268, 305 (1870) ("The Constitution confers upon Congress expressly power to declare war, grant letters of marque and reprisal, and make rules respecting captures on land and water. Upon the exercise of these powers no restrictions are imposed. Of course the power to declare war involves the power to prosecute it by all means and in any manner in which war may be legitimately prosecuted. It therefore includes the right to seize and confiscate all property of an enemy and to dispose of it at the will of the captor. This is and always has been an undoubted belligerent right.").

[13] The Federal Circuit has adopted the precedent of the Court of Federal Claims as its own. *See S. Corp. v. United States,* 690 F.2d 1368, 1369 (Fed. Cir. 1982) (en banc).

I. Doctrinal Foundations: From Turney to Atamirzayeva

A. *Turney*

For more than a half-century following the Court of Federal Claims' 1953 decision in *Turney v. United States*,[14] the law was settled that foreign plaintiffs could sue for foreign takings. *Turney* involved the post-WWII sale by the U.S. government of bulk surplus property at a U.S. air depot in the Philippines to two former U.S. pilots, who transferred the property to a foreign corporation in which they had a minority stake (the majority stake was held by the Chinese citizens who funded the acquisition).[15] Following the transfer, certain classified radar equipment was discovered in the surplus that had been sold, and the U.S. government requested that the newly-constituted Philippine government issue an embargo.[16] The Philippine government gladly obliged, and the U.S. Army officially took possession of the radar equipment.[17]

Under these facts, the Court of Claims held that the seizure by the U.S. government constituted a compensable taking, despite the fact that both the plaintiff corporation and the situs of the property were foreign.[18] In a short analysis containing almost no discussion of the doctrinal basis for its holding, *Turney* extended precedents from the "foreign plaintiff/domestic property" and "citizen plaintiff/foreign property" categories, and applied those precedents whole cloth to the very distinct context of "foreign plaintiff/foreign property" takings:

> The Government urges that the just compensation provision of the Fifth Amendment does not apply in foreign countries. The plaintiff points out that the Fifth Amendment has been applied to the taking of the property belonging to a resident alien and situated in the United States. *Russian Volunteer Fleet v. United States*, 282 U.S. 481, 51 S.Ct. 229, 75 L.Ed. 473; and to the property, located abroad, of an American citizen. *Wiggings* [sic] *v. United States*, 3 Ct.Cl. 412. He urges that cases such as *Ross v. McIntyre*, 140 U.S. 453, 11 S.Ct. 897, 35 L.Ed. 581, in which it [sic] held that an American convicted by a consular court in Japan could not complain that he had been denied a constitutional right to trial by jury, do not mean that other constitutional rights, such as the right to just compensation for property taken, which can, without

---

14 *Turney v. United States*, 115 F. Supp. 457 (Ct. Cl. 1953).

15 *Id.* at 458–59.

16 *Id.* at 460.

17 *Id.* at 464. The unique nature of the relationship between the U.S. and Philippine governments in the immediate aftermath of the Japanese liberation underlay the Court of Claims' holding that a Constitutional taking occurred when the U.S. Army took possession of the property after the Philippine government's embargo. *Id.* at 463–64. Subsequent cases involving governments with different relationships to the United States have distinguished *Turney*'s holding on this issue. *See, e.g., Langenegger v. United States*, 756 F.2d 1565, 1572 (Fed. Cir. 1985) (no taking when U.S. government engages in "friendly" persuasion of foreign government).

18 *Turney*, 115 F. Supp. at 464.

> inconvenience or practical difficulty, be applied to a taking abroad, should not be so applied. There is no decision directly in point. We think the plaintiff's contention is sound.[19]

From its inception, the *Turney* decision was on shaky ground. *Turney* made no effort to address the Supreme Court's statement in *United States v. Curtiss-Wright Export Corporation* almost 17 years earlier that "[n]either the constitution nor the laws passed in pursuance of it have any force in foreign territory unless in respect of our own citizens...."[20] Nor did the *Turney* court grapple with the Supreme Court's decision just three years earlier in *Johnson v. Einsentrager* refusing to extend the writ of habeas corpus and Fifth Amendment protections to German enemy nationals abroad.[21] Nevertheless, *Turney* remained the settled law of foreign plaintiff standing in the takings context for over 50 years.[22]

B. Verdugo-Urquidez

In 1990, however, *Turney's* foundation was shaken by the Supreme Court's decision in *U.S. v. Verdugo-Urquidez*.[23] That case involved the very different question

---

19 *Id.*

20 *See United States v. Curtiss-Wright Export Corp.*, 299 U.S. 304, 318 (1936); *see also United States v. Belmont*, 301 U.S. 324, 332 (1937).

21 *See Johnson v. Eisentrager*, 339 U.S. 763, 784–85 (1950) ("If the Fifth Amendment confers its rights on all the world except Americans engaged in defending it, the same must be true of the companion civil-rights Amendments, for none of them is limited by its express terms, territorially or as to persons. Such a construction would mean that during military occupation irreconcilable enemy elements, guerrilla fighters, and 'werewolves' could require the American Judiciary to assure them freedoms of speech, press, and assembly as in the First Amendment, right to bear arms as in the Second, security against 'unreasonable' searches and seizures as in the Fourth, as well as rights to jury trial as in the Fifth and Sixth Amendments. Such extraterritorial application of organic law would have been so significant an innovation in the practice of governments that, if intended or apprehended, it could scarcely have failed to excite contemporary comment. Not one word can be cited. No decision of this Court supports such a view. None of the learned commentators on our Constitution has ever hinted at it. The practice of every modern government is opposed to it.") (citation omitted); *see also United States v. Verdugo-Urquidez*, 494 U.S. 259, 269 (1990) (*Eisentrager* "rejected the claim that aliens are entitled to Fifth Amendment rights outside the sovereign territory of the United States.") (citation omitted).

22 *See, e.g., Atamirzayeva v. United States*, 524 F.3d 1320, 1327 (Fed. Cir. 2008) (recognizing *Turney* as binding on the Federal Circuit); *El-Shifa Pharm. Indus. Co. v. United States*, 378 F.3d 1346, 1352 (Fed. Cir. 2004) (holding that *Turney* can be overruled only by the Federal Circuit sitting *en banc*); *Porter v. United States*, 496 F.2d 583, 591 (Ct. Cl. 1974) (noting, in the context of takings claim by foreign plaintiff corporation, that "[t]he just compensation clause of the Fifth Amendment has, in fact, been applied to takings of property located outside the United States, even in the absence of Congressional extension of the Constitution to such foreign soil") (citing *Turney*).

23 *Verdugo-Urquidez*, 494 U.S. 259.

whether the search and seizure clause of the Fourth Amendment applied to a search by American authorities of a Mexican citizen's house in Mexico.[24] The Supreme Court held that it did not.[25]

Then-Chief Justice Rehnquist's Opinion for the Court placed particular emphasis on the textual usage of the phrase "the people" in the search and seizure clause of the Fourth Amendment, as referring to "a class of persons who are part of a national community or who have otherwise developed sufficient connection with this country to be considered part of that community."[26] The opinion contrasted this language with provisions of the Fifth and Sixth Amendments, which are not so limited textually.[27] Justice Kennedy joined the Court's opinion in its entirety, but in a separate concurrence refused to adopt the Court's textual exegesis, making clear that he did not place "any weight on the reference to 'the people' in the Fourth Amendment as a source of restricting its protections."[28]

This textual distinction having failed to persuade at least five justices left behind the key element of the majority opinion in *Verdugo-Urquidez*: the Court's citation to, and distinction of, cases in which Constitutional protections had been previously extended to aliens, including the *Russian Volunteer Fleet* case in the takings context. In distinguishing the *Russian Volunteer Fleet* and other cases, the Court held:

> These cases ... establish only that aliens receive constitutional protections when they have come within the territory of the United States and developed substantial connections with this country.... Respondent is an alien who has had no previous significant voluntary connection with the United States, so these cases avail him not.[29]

So sounded the death knell of *Turney*.

C. El-Shifa

The Federal Circuit took some time to reach and directly address the question of foreign plaintiff standing under the Takings Clause following *Verdugo-Urquidez*.

In the 2004 *El-Shifa* case,[30] the Federal Circuit was squarely confronted with the continuing validity of *Turney* in light of *Verdugo-Urquidez*. The plaintiffs in *El-Shifa* were a corporation that owned and operated a pharmaceutical plant in Khartoum, Sudan, and the corporation's principal owner.[31] The plant was destroyed by a 1998 cruise missile strike directed by President Clinton, and the

---

24 *Id.* at 259.
25 *Id.*
26 *Id.* at 265.
27 *Id.* at 265–66.
28 *Id.* at 276 (opinion of Kennedy, J., concurring).
29 *Id.* at 271.
30 *El-Shifa Pharm. Indus. Co. v. United States*, 378 F.3d 1346 (Fed. Cir. 2004).
31 *Id.* at 1349.

plaintiffs brought claims under the Tucker Act[32] for compensation under the Takings Clause.[33] The Court of Federal Claims recognized that "the strength of *Turney* as a precedent for the application of the 'takings' clause to foreign-situated, foreign-owned property has been eroded by" *Verdugo-Urquidez*, but followed *Turney* on the basis of *stare decisis*, inviting the Federal Circuit to revisit the issue on appeal.[34]

On appeal, the Federal Circuit declined the invitation. After raising the question of *Turney's* validity directly, the Federal Circuit concluded that it was reluctant to apply the Supreme Court's "significant voluntary connection" test without hearing the matter *en banc*.[35] Because the *El-Shifa* panel had other bases to sustain dismissal, the court "decline[d] to hold, as the government asks, that the Takings Clause does not protect the interests of nonresident aliens whose property is located in a foreign country unless they can demonstrate substantial voluntary connections to the United States."[36]

D. Atamirzayeva

The law in the Federal Circuit and Court of Federal Claims remained in limbo for the next four years, until 2008. The Federal Circuit addressed the issue again in *Atamirzayeva v. United States*, a Tucker Act case brought by a citizen of Uzbekistan seeking compensation for the destruction of her property adjacent to the United States embassy in Uzbekistan.[37] In *Atamirzayeva*, the Federal Circuit paid lip service to the notion that "*Turney* is binding" on that court, but went on to limit *Turney* to its precise facts:

> To be sure, the court in *Turney* did not state that the plaintiff was required to demonstrate any connection with the United States [as would be required by *Verdugo-Urquidez*]. In light of the facts of the case, however, we do not interpret the decision in *Turney* to have established a blanket rule that the Fifth Amendment protects the foreign property of citizens of every foreign country without regard to their connections with the United States. Such a rule would be far broader than any rule previously adopted by the Supreme Court for extraterritorial application of any constitutional provision. Indeed, reading *Turney* in the manner that Ms. Atamirzayeva suggests would require us to infer from a single, brief paragraph of analysis a remarkable holding that would far exceed what the facts of the case required the court to decide and would be in tension with the Supreme Court's decision in *Verdugo-Urquidez*. The sounder approach is to treat the holding in *Turney* as limited to the

---

32 28 U.S.C. § 1491(a)(1) ("The United States Court of Federal Claims shall have jurisdiction to render judgment upon any claim against the United States founded upon either the Constitution or any Act of Congress … in cases not sounding in tort.").

33 *El-Shifa*, 378 F.3d at 1349.

34 *See El-Shifa Pharm. Indus. Co. v. United States*, 55 Fed. Cl. 751, 763–64 (Fed. Cl. 2003).

35 *El-Shifa*, 378 F.3d at 1352.

36 *Id.*

37 *Atamirzayeva v. United States*, 524 F.3d 1320, 1320 (Fed. Cir. 2008).

> proposition that providing a right to seek just compensation was appropriate under the facts of that case.[38]

The Federal Circuit went on to import the "significant voluntary connection" test from *Verdugo-Urquidez* to the Takings Clause context, and rejected the *Atamirzayeva* plaintiffs' claims for failure to establish any connection.[39]

E. *Current State of the Law*

Atamirzayeva reflects the current state of the law in the Federal Circuit. While *Turney* remains technically on the books, it is a precedential dead letter. For now, a foreign plaintiff has no standing unless the *Verdugo-Urquidez* test is satisfied: the property taken must be within the United States, or the plaintiff must have

---

[38] *Id.* at 1327–28. In distinguishing *Turney*, the *Atamirzayeva* panel emphasized "three significant connections" of the plaintiff in *Turney* to the United States: "First, the corporation had been formed by two United States citizens. Second, the corporation received its ownership interest in the surplus property by assignment from those United States citizens. Third, after liquidation of the corporation, a United States Citizen was appointed as the liquidating trustee and the plaintiff in the Court of Claims action." *Id.* at 1328. These fine factual distinctions, while correct, are irrelevant. There is no question that the corporate plaintiff in Turney was a foreign corporation, majority owned by a Chinese citizen at the relevant time—*i.e., the time of the taking. See Turney*, 115 F. Supp. at 463–64 ("[I]n our opinion, [the property] was repossessed from the corporation in whose shoes the plaintiff stands.... We think that the taking occurred on October 13, 1947, when the Army officially took possession of the property. The plaintiff is entitled to recover its fair value as of that date...."); *see generally Am. Pelagic Fishing Co. v. United States*, 379 F.3d 1363, 1372 (Fed. Cir. 2004) ("It is axiomatic that only persons with a valid property interest at the time of the taking are entitled to compensation.") (citation omitted). The *Atamirzayeva* panel, like the panel in *El-Shifa*, felt constrained to conclude that *Turney* was binding precedent, requiring hearing *en banc* to overrule the decision. *Atamirzayeva*, 524 F.3d at 1327 (citing *El-Shifa*, 378 F.3d at 1352). Because the basis for overturning *Turney* is an intervening decision of the Supreme Court, however, the Federal Circuit may unnecessarily have taken an overly-restrictive view of *stare decisis. See, e.g., Teva Pharm. USA, Inc. v. Novartis Pharm. Corp.*, 482 F.3d 1330, 1338 (Fec. Cir. 2007) ("intervening... Supreme Court decision" is sound basis to reject prior Circuit precedent); *see generally* CHARLES ALAN WRIGHT ET AL., FEDERAL PRACTICE AND PROCEDURE § 3506 (3d ed. 1998) ("The courts of appeals generally follow the practice that one panel is bound by the previous decision of another panel of that court. This rule does not apply if an intervening decision of the Supreme Court or by the court of appeals *en banc* casts doubt on the prior ruling....") (citations omitted). Nevertheless, to the extent *Turney* no longer remains good law in light of *Verdugo-Urquidez*, the Federal Circuit—sitting either in panel or *en banc*, to the extent such a procedure is believed required—should say so in the next case, rather than maintain a fiction that *Turney* said what it did not say, or remains viable in some limited factual sphere. It is important for litigants to know what the law is.

[39] *See Atamirzayeva*, 524 F.3d at 1329.

a "significant voluntary connection" with the United States when the property is abroad.[40]

Standing jurisprudence in the takings context has thus become unmoored. *Verdugo-Urquidez* adopted the "significant voluntary connection" test in the context of the Fourth Amendment, not the Takings Clause. These two Constitutional clauses are very different, each with a different text, meaning, history and purpose. In *Atamirzayeva*, the Federal Circuit adhered to the *Verdugo-Urquidez* precedent blindly, importing the "significant voluntary connection" test into takings jurisprudence with no discussion of its validity in the context of Constitutional takings, perhaps because the alternative—maintaining *Turney's* cursory analysis and conclusion that foreign plaintiffs can sue for foreign takings, as the *El-Shifa* panel had done—would have been equally unappealing. In all events, there is very little reason to believe that the Supreme Court would consider its string-cite distinction of Fifth Amendment and other cases in *Verdugo-Urquidez*, or any other aspect of that opinion, as having set the bar for extraterritorial takings jurisprudence for all time.

II. The Impact of *Boumediene*

Significantly, neither the Federal Circuit nor the Supreme Court has had an opportunity to consider *Atamirzayeva*'s use of the "significant voluntary connection" test in light of the Supreme Court's decision one month later in *Boumediene v. Bush*.[41] In *Boumediene*, the Supreme Court held that the Suspension Clause of the Constitution[42] "has full effect at Guantanamo Bay" Cuba—despite the fact that the United States has no *de jure* sovereignty in Guantanamo Bay—and extended what the Court described as the "constitutional privilege of habeas corpus" to non-citizen detainees imprisoned there.[43] Critically, those detainees had no significant and voluntary connection with the United States as a factual matter, and therefore would have failed to meet the requirements of *Verdugo-Urquidez*.

Boumediene thus eliminates any notion that *Verdugo-Urquidez* set forth the proper—and certainly not the exclusive—test for Constitutional extraterritoriality.[44]

---

40 *See Doe v. United States*, 95 Fed. Cl. 546, 567 (Fed. Cl. 2010) (citing *Russian Volunteer Fleet*, 282 U.S. at 489 and *Atamirzayeva*, 524 F.3d at 1329); *see also Al-Qaisi v. United States*, 103 Fed. Cl. 439, 444 n.5 (Fed. Cl. 2012).

41 *Boumediene v. Bush*, 553 U.S. 723 (2008).

42 U.S. Const. art. I, § 9, cl. 2.

43 *Boumediene*, 553 U.S. at 732, 771.

44 *See* Gerald L. Neuman, *The Extraterritorial Constitution After Boumediene v. Bush*, 82 S. Cal. L. Rev. 259, 259 (2009) (*Boumediene* "repudiates the stance of the plurality in *United States v. Verdugo-Urquidez*. . . .); Andrea Paraud, *Foreign Nationals and Principles of Extraterritoriality: Why Atamirzayeva v. United States Was Decided Incorrectly*, 59 Cath. U. L. Rev. 559, 561 (2010) ("Although both the Court of Federal Claims and the Federal

In *Boumediene*, the Supreme Court established an entirely different functional approach, grounded in "objective factors and practical concerns" that looked to "at least three factors" deemed "relevant in determining the reach of the Suspension Clause: (1) the citizenship and status of the detainee and the adequacy of the process through which that status determination was made; (2) the nature of the sites where apprehension and then detention took place; and (3) the practical obstacles inherent in resolving the prisoner's entitlement to the writ."[45] *Boumediene* does not even mention the *Verdugo-Urquidez* test.[46]

Should the Federal Circuit adopt a similar functional test in the takings context, or maintain a rigid doctrinal adherence to *Verdugo-Urquidez*? In *Doe*, the Court of Federal Claims maintained allegiance to *Verdugo-Urquidez*, distinguishing *Boumediene* on the basis that "[n]othing in *Boumediene* suggests that the Court intended its holding to broadly apply to the Bill of Rights or to the takings clause, in particular."[47] The same, however, can be said of *Verdugo-Urquidez*, where the Supreme Court majority thought it "significant to note that [the Fourth Amendment] operates in a different manner than the Fifth Amendment, which is not at issue in this case."[48] *Boumediene* in fact covered far more ground than the *Doe* court was willing to recognize. While *Boumediene*'s non-exhaustive list of three "relevant" factors has specific application to the Suspension Clause, the Supreme Court grounded those factors in a functional approach with general applicability.[49] Following *Boumediene*, the continuing validity of *Atamirzayeva's* reliance on *Verdugo-Urquidez* is substantially in doubt,[50] calling for a rethinking of the question of standing in modern takings jurisprudence.

III. Toward a Coherent View of Foreign Plaintiff Takings

In order to rationalize the question of foreign plaintiff takings, it is worthwhile to step back to first principles. Does application of the Takings Clause properly

---

Circuit relied on the substantial-connection test in ruling against Ms. Atamirzayeva, new developments show that *Verdugo-Urquidez*'s substantial-connection test is not the appropriate approach for courts to follow.") (citations omitted).

45 *Boumediene*, 553 U.S. at 764, 766.

46 The *Boumediene* majority opinion, authored by Justice Kennedy, cited to Justice Kennedy's concurrence in *Verdugo-Urquidez* twice, but declined to cite to the opinion of the *Verdugo-Urquidez* court or its "substantial connection" test at all. *See id.* at 760, 762.

47 *See Doe v. United States*, 95 Fed. Cl. 546, 570 (Fed. Cl. 2010).

48 *See Verdugo-Urquidez*, 494 U.S. at 264.

49 *Boumediene*, 553 U.S. at 764.

50 *See* Erin Creegan, *The Extraterritorial Constitutional Rights of Aliens in the Federal Circuit*, 19 Fed. Cir. B.J. 273, 274, 299 (2009) (noting that "[t]he Supreme Court's recent holding in *Boumediene* may suggest a changing tide in extraterritorial constitutional law").

turn on the status of the plaintiff whose property is taken? If so, the connection between the plaintiff and the United States would prove to be the paramount consideration, counseling in favor of a test similar to the *Verdugo-Urquidez* test employed in *Atamirzayeva*. Or, conversely, is the Takings Clause properly viewed as a Constitutional constraint on the exercise of inherent sovereign or governmental authority? Under this construct, the *Verdugo-Urquidez/Atamirzayeva* emphasis on a plaintiff's connections to the United States is at best incomplete. The status of the plaintiff cedes importance to the more fundamental question whether the United States is exercising its inherent sovereign or governmental authority at all when it confiscates alien property abroad. The relevant question is not, "who is the plaintiff?" It becomes, "are we really dealing with a taking?"

In choosing between these two competing interpretations, an approach more in line with the spirit of *Boumediene* would look to the basic function served by the Takings Clause, as elucidated by its text, history and purpose, and identify the circumstances under which it is correctly applied in furtherance of that function.

Text and Drafting History. The text and drafting history of the clause provide some minimal, but inconclusive, guidance in resolving these questions. Madison's original formulation stated: "No person shall be... obliged to relinquish his property, where it may be necessary for public use, without just compensation."[51] This language emphasizes protection of the individual: its focus is on the "*person*" "*obliged*" to "*relinquish*" property. Madison's proposed language, however, is not the Fifth Amendment. The language ultimately adopted—"nor shall private property *be taken*... without just compensation"[52]—reads more like a condition on the exercise of sovereign power. It is unclear whether this shift in focus is a mere drafting anomaly, devoid of substantive import, or a significant change in focus. Unfortunately, as other commentators have noted, no historical record explains the change in language.[53]

Historical Commentary. Early authoritative interpretations of the Takings Clause, however, begin to tilt the scale in favor of a reading of the Takings Clause as a condition on the exercise of inherent sovereign or governmental authority. Chancellor Kent expressed this view clearly in his COMMENTARIES:

> The right of eminent domain, or *inherent sovereign power*, it is admitted by all publicists, gives to the legislature the control of private property for public uses, and for public uses only.... [T]he interests of the public is deemed paramount to that of any private individual; and yet, even here, the constitution[] of the United States... ha[s] imposed *a great and valuable check upon the exercise of legislative power*, by declaring,

---

[51] *See* James Madison, Speech Proposing Bill of Rights (June 8, 1789), in 1 ANNALS OF CONG. 451–52, *available at* http://memory.loc.gov/cgi-bin/ampage?collId=llac&fileName=001/llac001.db&recNum=226. *See also* William M. Treanor, *The Original Understanding of the Takings Clause and the Political Process*, 95 COLUM. L. REV. 782, 836 (1995).

[52] U.S. CONST. amend. V.

[53] *See* William M. Treanor, *Take-Ings*, 45 SAN DIEGO L. REV. 633, 641 (2008).

> that private property should not be taken for public use without just compensation. A provision for compensation is a necessary attendant on the due and constitutional exercise of *the power of the lawgiver* to deprive an individual of his property without his consent; and this principle in American constitutional jurisprudence, is founded in natural equity, and is lain down by jurists as an acknowledged principle of universal law.[54]

Supreme Court Precedent. Dating at least to the latter half of the 1800s, the Supreme Court has repeatedly the power reflected in the Takings Clause as "inseparable from sovereignty,"[55] and an unbroken line of Supreme Court cases holds that the Takings Clause itself is a condition to the exercise of sovereignty.[56]

---

54 2 J. James Kent, Commentaries on American Law 275–76 (New York, O. Halsted 1827) (citation omitted) (emphasis added); *see generally* Thomas McIntyre Cooley, A Treatise on the Constitutional Limitations Which Rest Upon The Legislative Power of the States of the American Union 528 n. 1 (Boston, Little, Brown & Co. 1868) ("Whatever may be the theoretical foundation for the right of eminent domain, it is certain that it attaches as an incident to every sovereignty, and constitutes a condition upon which all property is holden. When the public necessity requires it, private rights to property must yield to the paramount right of the sovereign power.").

55 *Kohl v. United States*, 91 U.S. 367, 368–72 (1875); *see also United States v. Jones*, 109 U.S. 513, 518–19 (1883) (describing the power to appropriate private property for public uses as one of the "sovereign attributes" of the general government); *Searl v. Sch. Dist. No. 2, of Lake Cnty.*, 133 U.S. 553, 562 (1890); *City of Cincinnati v. Louisville & Nashville R.R. Co.*, 223 U.S. 390, 404 (1912) ("This right of appropriating private property to a public use is one of the powers vital to the public welfare of every self-governing community. It is a power which this court has described as an 'incident to sovereignty,'-a power which 'belongs to every independent government.' ") (citation omitted); *State of Ga. v. City of Chattanooga*, 264 U.S. 472, 480 (1924) ("The power of eminent domain is an attribute of sovereignty, and inheres in every independent state."); *Youngstown Sheet & Tube Co. v. Sawyer*, 343 U.S. 579, 680 (1952) (Frankfurter, J., concurring) ("The power of eminent domain ... is an essential attribute of sovereignty and has long been recognized as a power of the Federal Government.") (citation omitted).

56 *See Jones*, 109 U.S. at 518–19 ("The power to take private property for public uses, generally termed the right of eminent domain, belongs to every independent government. It is an incident of sovereignty, and ... requires no constitutional recognition. The provision found in the fifth amendment to the federal constitution, and in the constitutions of the several states, for just compensation for the property taken, is merely a limitation upon the use of the power. It is no part of the power itself, but a condition upon which the power may be exercised.") (citation omitted); *Bauman v. Ross*, 167 U.S. 548, 574 (1897) ("The right of eminent domain ... is the offspring of political necessity, and is inseparable from sovereignty unless denied to it by its fundamental law. It cannot be exercised except upon condition that just compensation shall be made to the owner....") (citation omitted); *W. Union Tel. Co. v. Pa. R.R. Co.*, 195 U.S. 540, 583 (1904) (same, citing *Jones*); *Albert Hanson Lumber Co. v. United States*, 261 U.S. 581, 587 (1923) ("The power of eminent domain is not dependent upon any specific grant; it is an attribute of sovereignty, limited and conditioned by the just compensation clause of the Fifth Amendment."); *United States v. Gen. Motors Corp.*, 323 U.S. 373, 377 (1945) ("[T]he constitutional provision: 'nor shall private property be taken for public use, without just compensation', ... conditions the otherwise unrestrained power of the

These sources all point toward a consistent view of the function of the Takings Clause as a condition placed on the government's exercise of inherent sovereign or governmental authority. When viewed in this light, the relevant touchstone is not simply the relation between the plaintiff and the United States, as in *Verdugo-Urquidez/Atamirzayeva*. More fundamentally, a functional approach suggests that if the plaintiff's claim does not arise from an exercise by the United States of its inherent sovereign or governmental authority in the first instance, there is no right to just compensation under the Takings Clause at all, because the predicate to application of that Constitutional condition is absent.

As used here, the notion of inherent sovereign or governmental authority has both territorial *and* relational aspects. To be sure, when the United States takes property within the *territorial* sovereignty of the United States, the Government is constrained by the Takings Clause to compensate the owner as a condition on the exercise of that power. This is true notwithstanding whether the plaintiff is a citizen (as in the garden-variety takings case) or non-citizen (as in, for example, the *Russian Volunteer Fleet* case).[57] In both situations, the government's assertion of inherent sovereign or governmental authority within its territory gives rise to the Constitutional obligation to provide just compensation.

Outside the United States, however, the government exercises a degree of inherent sovereign or governmental authority only in respect of its own citizens.[58]

---

sovereign to expropriate, without compensation, whatever it needs."); *United States v. Carmack*, 329 U.S. 230, 241 (1946) ("The Fifth Amendment to the Constitution says 'nor shall private property be taken for public use, without just compensation.' This is a tacit recognition of a preexisting power to take private property for public use, rather than a grant of new power. It imposes on the Federal Government the obligation to pay just compensation when it takes another's property for public use in accordance with the federal sovereign power to appropriate it.") (citation omitted); *First English Evangelical Lutheran Church of Glendale v. L.A. Cnty., Cal.*, 482 U.S. 304, 314 (1987) ("Consideration of the compensation question must begin with direct reference to the language of the Fifth Amendment, which provides in relevant part that 'private property [shall not] be taken for public use, without just compensation.' As its language indicates, and as the Court has frequently noted, this provision does not prohibit the taking of private property, but instead places a condition on the exercise of that power."); *Lingle v. Chevron U.S.A. Inc.*, 544 U.S. 528, 536 (2005) (same); *Kelo v. City of New London, Conn.*, 545 U.S. 469, 487 n. 19 (2005) ("The Takings Clause… 'operates as a conditional limitation, permitting the government to do what it wants so long as it pays the charge.'") (citing *Eastern Enters. v. Apfel*, 524 U.S. 498, 545 (1998) (Kennedy, J., concurring in judgment and dissenting in part)).

57 With respect to foreign nationals on United States soil, this Constitutional guarantee of just compensation is also mandated by, and in accord with, modern notions of international law. *See* Restatement (Third) of Foreign Relations Law of the United States § 712(1) (2012) ("Restatement").

58 *Cf. United States v. Verdugo-Urquidez*, 494 U.S. 259, 275, 110 S. Ct. 1056, 1066, 108 L. Ed. 2d 222 (1990) (Kennedy, J. concurring) ("The distinction between citizens and aliens follows from the undoubted proposition that the Constitution does not create, nor do

United States citizens are bound to abide the United States government's commands abroad.[59] Foreign nationals generally are not.[60] When the United States government seizes, confiscates, appropriates or destroys the property of foreign nationals on foreign soil, it may be an act of war, or an act subject to whatever

---

general principles of law create, any juridical relation between our country and some undefined, limitless class of noncitizens who are beyond our territory.").

59 *See, e.g., Steele v. Bulova Watch Co.*, 344 U.S. 280, 285–86 (1952) ("[T]he United States is not debarred by any rule of international law from governing the conduct of *its own citizens* upon the high seas or even in foreign countries when the rights of other nations or their nationals are not infringed. With respect to such an exercise of authority there is no question of international law, but solely of the purport of the municipal law which establishes *the duty of the citizen in relation to his own government.*") (citing *Skiriotes v. State of Florida*, 313 U.S. 69, 73, 61 S.Ct. 924, 927 (1941)) (emphasis added); *Blackmer v. United States*, 284 U.S. 421, 436–38 (1932) ("While it appears that the petitioner removed his residence to France in the year 1924, it is undisputed that he was, and continued to be, a citizen of the United States. He continued to owe allegiance to the United States. By virtue of the obligations of citizenship, the United States retained its authority over him, and he was bound by its laws made applicable to him in a foreign country.... *Nor can it be doubted that the United States possesses the power inherent in sovereignty to require the return to this country of a citizen, resident elsewhere, whenever the public interest requires it, and to penalize him in case of refusal....* What in England was the prerogative of the sovereign in this respect pertains under our constitutional system to the national authority which may be exercised by the Congress by virtue of the legislative power to prescribe the duties of the citizens of the United States.") (emphasis added). *See generally* Paraud, *supra* note 44, at 564 ("[T]he Constitution is applicable to the U.S. government any time and at any place it exercises its power.... In other words, the Constitution and its provisions are applicable to those who are required to obey the laws of the United States.").

60 With limited exceptions, states have extraterritorial jurisdiction to prescribe only in respect of their own nationals as a matter of international law. *See, e.g.*, RESTATEMENT § 402(2) (state has jurisdiction to prescribe "the activities, interests, status, or relations of *its nationals* outside as well as within its territory") (emphasis added); *see also Blackmer*, 284 U.S. at 438 n. 2 ("The law of Nations does not prevent a State from exercising jurisdiction *over its subjects* traveling or residing abroad, since they remain under its *personal supremacy*.") (emphasis added; citations omitted); *compare* RESTATEMENT § 402(3) and cmt. f (recognizing extraterritorial jurisdiction to prescribe with respect to foreign nationals under the "protective principle" in strictly limited circumstances implicating state security or offenses threatening the integrity of a governmental function); *Hartford Fire Ins. Co. v. California*, 509 U.S. 764, 795 (1993) (recognizing jurisdiction to prescribe under Sherman Act where conduct abroad "was meant to produce and did in fact produce some substantial effect in the United States"). United States laws are to be interpreted consistent with this principle. *See Murray v. Schooner Charming Betsy*, 2 Cranch 64, 118, 2 L.Ed. 208 (1804) (Marshall, C.J.) ("[A]n act of congress ought never to be construed to violate the law of nations if any other possible construction remains."); *see also F. Hoffman-La Roche Ltd. v. Empagran S.A.*, 542 U.S. 155, 164 (2004) ("Prescriptive comity" is a "rule of statutory construction [that] cautions courts to assume that legislators take account of the legitimate sovereign interests of other nations when they write American laws.") (citations omitted).

rights and remedies may exist under international law or local municipal law, but it is not a "taking" in the Constitutional sense because it is in no way an exercise of inherent sovereign or governmental authority of the kind the Takings Clause serves to constrain.

If this view is correct, it follows that if the Takings Clause is to be given any extraterritorial effect—in the sense that it operates outside the territorial sovereignty of the United States—it should have that effect only with respect to United States citizens.

IV. Conclusion

The question of foreign plaintiff standing in takings jurisprudence currently lacks any coherent foundational principle. In *Atamirzayeva*, a decades-long era of dogmatic allegiance to *Turney* was cast aside, only to be replaced by an equally rigid doctrinal fidelity to *Verdugo-Urquidez*. *Verdugo-Urquidez*, however, is a blunt and inapt instrument in the Takings Clause context. This article advocates for an approach that focuses on the function of the Takings Clause in determining its scope and application. When the Takings Clause is viewed as a Constitutional constraint imposed on the United States government's exercise of its inherent sovereign or governmental authority, it follows that this just compensation constraint is properly imposed only when an exercise of inherent sovereign and governmental authority is at issue. Within the territorial sovereignty of the United States, the government exercises this authority with respect to citizens and aliens alike. When the United States confiscates or seizes foreign property outside its territorial sovereignty, however, it does so in the exercise of inherent sovereign or governmental authority only in respect of United States citizens. Under this approach, foreign nationals suing for foreign seizures may or may not have remedies under other sources of law, but they have no basis to assert claims under the Takings Clause of the Fifth Amendment.

THE FOREIGN CLAIMS SETTLEMENT COMMISSION

THE WORK OF THE FOREIGN CLAIMS SETTLEMENT COMMISSION OF THE UNITED STATES

Timothy J. Feighery[1]

I. Introduction

I have now served as Chairman of the Foreign Claims Settlement Commission ("FCSC" or "Commission") for a little over a year, and the more I learn the more respect I have for this institution. The Commission's work is, I believe, fundamentally important to the values we hold as a society. I believe that it is right and just that we come together as a society, through our government, to assist fellow citizens who have suffered loss or injury at the hands of foreign states. All branches

[1] Partner, Arent Fox LLP, Washington D.C.; Chairman, Foreign Claims Settlement Commission (March 2011–February 2013). I would like to thank Avin Sharma for his able assistance in preparing these remarks. My thanks also to the University of Virginia School of Law, the Virginia Journal of International law, and in particular Professor Moore for inviting me to participate in this esteemed colloquium [April 19, 2012]. It is an honor for me to be here, following in the footsteps of so many renowned scholars and practitioners in international law.

I first became aware of the Sokol Colloquium back in early 1995, when I began work at the United Nations Compensation Commission in Geneva. A couple of months prior to my arrival there, the Thirteenth Sokol Colloquium had taken place, and all of the senior people at the UNCC at that time had participated, including Carlos Alzamora, the Executive Secretary, Michael Raboin, the Deputy Executive Secretary, and Norbert Wühler, Chief of the Commission's Legal Service. Looking recently at the volume that was the product of that conference, I was struck by how prescient and insightful those contributions were, and how relevant they continue to be.

Unfortunately, I am also struck by the loss to the international legal community of three participants in that colloquium who are no longer with us—Richard Lillich, a giant of international claims law, David Bederman, who in many ways followed in Professor Lillich's footsteps, and Michael Raboin, who was a good friend, in addition to being my boss at the UNCC. What impressed me most about Mike, perhaps, was the fact that he never seemed to lose sight of the human factor inherent in claims work. He was incredibly thorough as a lawyer, and never cynical, qualities that I think are particularly important in this field.

John Norton Moore (ed.) Foreign Affairs Litigation in United States Courts, pp. 147–164

of our government have recognized this since the founding of our Republic. And the work of the Commission is as a critical part of that commitment we make to each other as citizens.

I would like to share with you some aspects of the Commission's work, about which I have formed a much deeper understanding and appreciation over these past 14 months or so. I do so mindful that the Commission has before it an active program for claims against Libya. Consequently, my remarks here are my own thoughts and impressions, and do not represent the views of the Commission, the Department of Justice, or indeed the Executive. Furthermore, I will not discuss issues that relate to claims still pending, and request understanding for that.

The Commission has begun what I believe will be viewed as another distinct phase in its history. The end of World War II, which prompted the founding of the Commission to address claims of U.S. citizens directly arising out of that conflict, marked the first phase. The subsequent confiscation of private property by post-war Communist regimes marked another distinct phase in the Commission's work. Most recently, the referral by the State Department of categories of claims arising out of injuries suffered at the hands of Libya as a state sponsor of international terrorism marks a new phase in the Commission's work. For the reasons I will discuss, the unique attributes of the Commission—including its independence, transparent processes, and reliance on the rule of law—make it a vital part of the Executive's ability to discharge properly its constitutional power to settle international claims.

I will review briefly the historical context that is relevant, I believe, to where the Commission is today, and the question of where lies its future. Second, I will discuss the Commission's jurisdiction and its applicable law. Third, I will address certain issues of legitimacy surrounding the jurisprudential value of claims settlements and claim settlement commissions. Here, my intention is to add to the defense of these commissions that was mounted by Professor Lillich, later joined by Professor Bederman, in their volumes on this subject, published from the 1960s through the 1990s. Fourth, I want to give some general remarks on the Libya program. Finally, I will leave you with a list of factors that I see as primarily relevant to the decision of whether the Foreign Claims Settlement Commission should be charged with the responsibility of adjudicating claims under state-to-state settlements that do not involve expropriation or other taking of property.

II. The FCSC in Historical Context

The FCSC was created to perform an essential element of the Executive's foreign affairs authority to settle international claims;[2] namely, to adjudicate and render

---

[2] The Supreme Court most recently reaffirmed this authority in *Medellin v. Texas*, 552 U.S. 491 (2008).

final decisions on such claims. It was established in 1954 as the successor to the War Claims Commission ("WCC") and the International Claims Commission ("ICC"), both of which were established to address claims arising out of World War II.

Congress granted the WCC and the ICC distinct jurisdictional mandates. The WCC, established in 1948, was granted jurisdiction over claims of the United States and of U.S. nationals against World War II enemy states of the United States.[3] The ICC, established in 1949 as an independent agency within the Department of State, was given two distinct jurisdictional grants.[4] The first was jurisdiction over claims included within the terms of the Yugoslavian Claims Agreement of 1948. The second was jurisdiction over claims included within the terms of any claims agreement thereafter concluded between the United States and a foreign government, "similarly providing for the settlement and discharge of claims."[5]

There were two express and significant limitations to this second jurisdictional prong of the ICC. First, the ICC's jurisdiction excluded claims over which the WCC had jurisdiction; that is, it excluded claims between the United States and its nationals on the one hand, and governments against which the United States declared the existence of a state of war during World War II on the other.[6] Second, and most significantly for the future work of the ICC and its successor, the FCSC, this jurisdiction was limited to claims "arising out of the nationalization or other taking of property."[7]

Pursuant to President Eisenhower's Reorganization Plan Number 1 of 1954, the WCC and the ICC were abolished, and in their place was established, as a separate agency, the FCSC.[8] The FCSC assumed the jurisdiction and functions of these predecessor Commissions; it completed the Yugoslavian program on the statutory termination date of December 31, 1954 and completed the War Claims programs by its statutory termination date of March 31, 1955.[9] With the conclusion of these programs by the FCSC, the jurisdiction of the Commission was limited to jurisdiction over claims included within the terms of any claims agreement

---

3 The War Claims Commission was established pursuant to the War Claims Act of 1948, Pub. L. No. 80-896, 62 Stat. 1240; Pub. L. No. 82–303, 66 Stat. 47 (codified at 50 U.S.C. app. §§ 2001 *et. seq.* (1964)).

4 The International Claims Commission was established pursuant to the International Claims Settlement Act of 1949, Pub. L. No. 81–455, 64 Stat. 12 (codified at 22 U.S.C. §§ 1621 *et. seq.* (1955)).

5 22 U.S.C. § 1623(a)(1)(B).

6 *Id.*

7 *Id.*

8 19 Fed. Reg. 3985, 68 Stat. 1279 (July 1, 1954) (codified at 22 U.S.C. §§ 1621 *et. seq.* (19XX)).

9 *See* Settlement of Claims by the Foreign Claims Settlement Commission of the United States and its Predecessors from September 14, 1949 to March 31, 1955, Government Printing Office 3–4 (1955).

concluded by the United States after March 10, 1954 arising out of the nationalization of property.[10]

The relative narrowness of the Commission's jurisdiction at this time is apparent from the way the United States handled claims under its 1950 settlement agreement with Panama.[11] The Panama agreement included two categories of claims of the United States against Panama: first, the claims of six members of the U.S. Army for personal injuries sustained during disturbances in the city of Panama in 1915; and (2) claims for the nationalization by Panama of property located in Panama that was owned by U.S. nationals.[12] The nationalization claims came under the jurisdiction of the Commission (the ICC at the time), but the personal injury claims were paid directly by the State Department. As I will discuss, there are echoes of this bifurcated approach to the distribution of compensation for international claims more than 60 years later in the Libya program.

The State Department could distribute these funds because its authority to receive and distribute settlement monies was already long established by the time of the Panama settlement. In the State Department Act of 1896, Congress authorized the Secretary of State to receive funds received from foreign governments "in trust for citizens of the United States," and to determine the amounts due to claimants and to certify those amounts to the Secretary of the Treasury for payment.[13] The text of this Act, codified at 22 U.S.C. section 2668a, is as follows:

> All monies received by the Secretary of States from foreign governments and other sources, in trust for citizens of the United States or others, shall be deposited and covered into the Treasury.
>
> The Secretary of State shall determine the amounts due claimants, respectively, from each of such trust funds, and certify the same to the Secretary of the Treasury, who shall, upon presentation of the certificates of the Secretary of State, pay the amounts so found to be due.
>
> Each of the trust funds covered into the Treasury as aforesaid is appropriated for the payment to be ascertained beneficiaries thereof of the certificates provided for in this section.

The existence of this very broad statutory authority prompts the question of why the State Department pushed, after World War II, for the establishment by Congress of a separate and independent claims commission—even if organized under the Department of State—to adjudicate claims; and indeed, why Congress

10 *See* 22 USC § 1623(a)(1)(C). In March 1980, the FCSC was transferred to the Department of Justice as a separate agency within that Department. 22 USC § 1622a.

11 Claims Convention Between the United States of American and Panama, U.S.-Pan., Jan. 26, 1950, 1 U.S.T. 685; 132 U.N.T.S. 233.

12 Claims Convention Between the United States of American and Panama, U.S.-Pan., art. I(b), (c), Jan. 26, 1950, 1 U.S.T. 685.

13 22 U.S.C. 2668a (Feb. 27, 1896) c. 34, 29 Stat. 32.

acquiesced by establishing such a Commission. What can be gleaned from the debates on the proposed legislation that led to the establishment of the ICC in 1949, which also included provisions for the lump-sum settlement of claims of U.S. nationals against Yugoslavia, suggests that a number of factors were at play. These factors included concern with the sheer volume of anticipated claims to be adjudicated; recognition by the Department of State itself that it was not part of its mission to adjudicate large numbers of claims pursuant to the settlement agreements it had successfully negotiated, and that it did not want to make it part of its mission; a perceived need for the independent adjudication of claims, subject to express procedural and legal standards that certain members of Congress felt could not be guaranteed under the State Department Act; and the understanding of the State Department, conveyed to the Congress, that there would be a significant number of claims programs requiring adjudication over the years ahead, and the concomitant need to establish an organization that would develop a specific expertise to address these anticipated claims.[14]

The main congressional proponent of the bill to establish the ICC was Connecticut Representative Abraham Ribicoff, whose opening argument was that the proposed legislation represented no expansion of the power of the State Department. Congressman Ribicoff stated that the "bill does not add in any way to the power already vested in the Secretary of State by law," and went on to quote the language of the 1896 act.[15] He then explained that "the Secretary of State can do by law now what this bill would permit him to do. But the Secretary cannot do that job alone... It can best be done by an agency specially created for that purpose, an agency which can be discontinued when the task is done. That is far better than attempting to do it by adding to the permanent strength of the Department the many dozens of employees needed for this task."[16] Congressman Ribicoff also cited the need to give the new agency the "power to get evidence," as well as the need to "make explicit procedural standards for the adjudications."[17]

Congressman John Vorys of Ohio was the most vociferous opponent of the bill. He expressed concern with the independence of the proposed institution vis-à-vis the State Department, charging that "[i]t has a very fancy title, International Claims Commission of the United States, but it is nothing but a vest-pocket agency of the Department of State."[18] He further charged that the proposed bill, including the Yugoslavian settlement, was "strictly an inside job by departmental lawyers."[19] This hostility to the new commission appears to have been due, at least in part, to a hostility to the Yugoslavian Claims Settlement Agreement itself—

14 *See generally* XX CONG. REC. 8836, 8844, 8845 (July 5, 1949).
15 XX CONG. REC. 8836 (July 5, 1949).
16 Ibid.
17 Ibid.
18 XX CONG. REC. 8844 (July 5, 1949).
19 XX CONG. REC. 8845 (July 5, 1949).

as an inadequate settlement of American claims—rather than to the formation of a new commission that was part and parcel of the same legislative proposal. Thus, Congressman Vorys, in the same debate, asserted that "[t]his is called an International Claims Settlement bill and deals with claims of Americans against foreign countries; it might better be called an International Claims Surrender bill."[20] Vorys was, overall, mistrustful of the State Department: with regard to the State Department's existing statutory authority to distribute settlement monies, Congressman Vorys also alluded to the need for explicit procedural standards, stating that "I have been told that the State Department has under an 1896 statute the right simply to pass this money if they want to. However, they are properly scared to go about it in that cavalier way."[21] Indeed, it was Vorys' position (one also expressed by Senators during the debates), that distribution of settlement funds should be delegated to the already-established Court of Claims.[22]

The State Department expressed its views during Senate Foreign Relations Committee hearings on the proposed Bill. Acting Legal Adviser at the time, Jack Tate, testified that the creation of a permanent commission would enable it to "acquire certain competency, and we would hope that by the time they got into the work we would have some settlement with Czechoslovakia and Poland that would require the same type of Commission."[23] Specifically, and in response to a question about the adjudication of claims under a settlement agreement by the Court of Claims, Mr. Tate also stated that with the new bill, "you have an opportunity to get three men who are familiar with international law and practice more than the judges of the Court of Claims."[24] Tate explained his rationale for the need for this expertise as follows: "Since we settled on the basis of international law, we feel that the distribution ought to be consistent with international law, so a special tribunal, equivalent somewhat to the Mexican Claims Commission which was set up for the same purpose a few years ago, is set up for this particular job."[25]

---

20 XX Cong. Rec. 8844 (July 5, 1949). Congressman Vorys calculated that the claims of Americans against Yugoslavia amounted to between $40 and $42 million, while the State Department settlement provided for payment of only $17 million. *Id.*

21 XX Cong. Rec. 8845 (July 5, 1949).

22 *See, e.g.*, United States Senate, Committee on Foreign Relations, Hearings on H.R. 4406, p. 70 (July 26, 1949) ("Senator Lodge: I would like to ask him one question. If, as you say, the principal argument against having the Court of Claims handle it is that the Court of Claims is behind on its docket, doesn't that indicate that the thing to do is to beef up the Court of Claims so they can go a little faster, rather than to set up a new Court?") On the other hand, a number of Senators noted that the Court of Claims did not have jurisdiction over these kinds of claims.

23 United States Senate, Committee on Foreign Relations, Hearings on H.R. 4406, p. 96 (July 26, 1949).

24 United States Senate, Committee on Foreign Relations, Hearings on H.R. 4406, pp. 70–71 (July 26, 1949).

25 United States Senate, Committee on Foreign Relations, Hearings on H.R. 4406, p. 71 (July 26, 1949).

Notwithstanding the time and effort spent debating the issues surrounding the establishment of an independent Commission to adjudicate claims under the Yugoslavia—and possible subsequent—settlement agreements, one consideration was ever present in the background: the strategic importance, for national security reasons, of securing and concluding the Yugoslavia agreement itself. As recounted by Representative Ribicoff, in the previous year Russian forces blockaded Berlin, and this blockade was "foiled by two developments": the airlift to relieve the city, and the defection of Yugoslavia from the Cominform. According to Ribicoff, "[t]hat defection left the left flank of the Soviet position in central Europe exposed. Its effect in putting the brakes on the exercise of Russian power was tremendous—as great in its way as was to air lift itself."[26] Ribicoff concluded by stating:

> I think we need not press further the matter of the strategic importance of this settlement in midsummer 1948. Those who think we might have made something more of this settlement by compelling a few more millions out of Yugoslavia have simply lost their sense of proportion about the stakes of international life.[27]

For all of the above reasons—concern about the size of the anticipated programs; a corresponding concern about permanently expanding the State Department coupled with the Department's own reluctance to enter the field of claims adjudication; concern about process and transparency; the desire to establish an entity to build the requisite international law and claims expertise; and the strategic importance of the Yugoslavia Claims Settlement Agreement—the Congress passed the International Claims Settlement Act of 1949, which brought into existence the FCSC's predecessor, the ICC. When considering the role of the FCSC in the adjudication and claims settlement funds, these factors, which were so heavily debated in 1949, are as important today as they were sixty years ago. As I will discuss in more detail, the FCSC continues to fulfill the promises made by the proponents of the ICC six decades ago by employing open and transparent procedures and building upon its institutional knowledge as it continues to provide a mechanism for the efficient and independent adjudication of claims.

III. Post-ICC: The Continuing Need for Enabling Legislation

Notwithstanding the State Department's success in gaining passage of the International Claims Settlement Act, including approval of the Yugoslavia settlement and the establishment of the ICC, the State Department continued to find itself before Congress. In general, it came before Congress to gain approval either for specific aspects of subsequent claims settlement agreements, like the Yugoslavian

---

[26] XX Cong. Rec. 8838–89 (July 5, 1949).
[27] XX Cong. Rec. 8839 (July 5, 1949).

agreement, which provided for the lump-sum settlement of expropriation claims between U.S. nationals and foreign governments, or to broaden the Commission's authority in certain, specified circumstances. In the former situation, while the basic statutory authorities were in place for the ICC, and later the FCSC, to receive and adjudicate claims arising out of the nationalization of U.S. nationals' property abroad, certain peculiarities of subsequent agreements required Congressional approval. In the latter scenario, the State Department requested alterations to the Commission's authority for special purposes and in specific circumstances.

Thus, the State Department was back on the Hill in relation to the 1955 Bulgarian, Hungarian, and Romanian programs because it needed authority to vest and liquidate the assets of those states that had been blocked during WWII.[28] It again was before Congress in 1974 to seek approval for the settlement agreement with Czechoslovakia because part of the agreement reached with Czechoslovakia was that the U.S. would grant it "most-favored nation" status and other economic benefits, which required Congressional approval. When Congress became seized of the matter, it took the opportunity to reject the initial 1974 agreement, which provided for the payment of $20 million by Czechoslovakia, as inadequate compensation. According to the Conference Report, Congress urged the President, through "officials other than those who negotiated the unreasonable first tentative agreement," to renegotiate a more equitable claims settlement as a condition precedent to the granting of most-favored-nation treatment, the extension of other economic benefits, and the release of the Czech gold."[29] Thus, Congress not only rejected the initial deal as providing too little money to the U.S. for the settlement of claims, but it also ordered the State Department to renegotiate the deal, and it reserved the right to approve any future agreement. This was an extraordinary occurrence, and naturally was captured by Professor Lillich at the time.[30] In the end, it took the United States seven more years to negotiate a new agreement, and in 1981 Czechoslovakia agreed to pay approximately $80 million. The agreement received the approval of Congress in the Czechoslovakian Claims Settlement Act of 1981.[31]

Given the relatively narrow jurisdiction of the Commission in the decades following 1949 (*i.e.*, limited to the adjudication of claims by U.S. nationals for the nationalization or other taking of property), the State Department was also required to go to the Hill for approval to broaden the Commission's authorities as needs arose. In a series of situations beginning in the mid-1960s, the Department

---

28 Pub. L. No. 84_285, Titles II, III, 69 Stat. 562 (22 U.S.C §§ 1631a, 1641a (1955)).

29 Conference Report, Trade Act of 1974, H.R. Rep. No. 93–1644, 93rd Cong., 2nd Sess. 49 (1974).

30 For a detailed exposition of the background to the Czechoslovakian claims settlement agreement, see Lillich, R. *The Gravel Amendment to the Trade Reform Act of 1974: Congress Checkmates a Presidential Lump Sum Agreement*, 69 Am. J. Intl. L. 837 (1975).

31 Pub. L. No. 97–127, 95 Stat. 1675 (Dec. 29, 1981).

needed help in determining, for negotiation purposes or anticipated negotiation purposes, the approximate lump-sum amount of money that would be required of foreign governments to settle the claims of U.S. nationals. Thus, it sought and received Congressional approval to permit the Commission to conduct pre-settlement adjudications of claims in the cases of Cuba and China (codified at Title V of the ICSA, passed in 1964), the former German Democratic Republic (Title VI of ICSA, passed in 1974), and Vietnam (Title VII of ICSA, passed in 1980).

A review of the debates that led to the enactment of these various pieces of legislation gives the clear impression that the State Department probably did not relish going to the Hill for action relating to claims agreements. When seized of a matter, Congress could involve itself in matters that were otherwise within the authority of the Executive, as the Czechoslovakian experience showed most dramatically. Whether as a consequence of this or not, the Department sought, beginning in 1997, a permanent statutory fix for what it apparently saw then as the most pressing need: permanent authority for the FCSC to conduct pre-settlement adjudication of claims.

The requested authority was put forward as a proposed amendment to the Commission's enabling statute, 22 U.S.C. § 1623. The conference report provides the explanation of both Houses for the proposed amendment:

> The House bill (sec. 1205) amends section 4 of the International Claims Settlement Act to permit the Foreign Claims Settlement Commission to preadjudicate claims by U.S. citizens. Preadjudication would provide the Department with important information on the value and validity of claims by the U.S. public in advance of the negotiations and conclusion of an agreement. The Committee understands that in the event of preadjudication, the Secretary of State will make every effort to inform affected people.
>
> The Senate amendment (sec. 1122) amends section 4 of the International Claims Settlement Act to permit the Foreign Claims Settlement Commission to preadjudicate claims by the U.S. citizens in a category determined by the Secretary of State. Currently the Commission only has general authority to adjudicate claims after settlement has been reached by the Department with a foreign government. This section is designed to facilitate claims settlement practices by providing a mechanism for obtaining further information from U.S. citizens about their claims in advance of actual negotiation.[32]

---

[32] H.R. Rep. No. 105–432, pg. 26 (1998). This specific amendment became part of H.R. 1757, which President Clinton vetoed on October 21, 1998 for reasons unrelated to the amendment of 22 U.S.C. § 1623. H.R. Doc. No. 105–329, p. 1 (1998). The amendment was reintroduced as "Division G" of H.R. 4328, which was signed into law on October 22, 1998. During the debate on the passage of the conference report, Rep. Gilman stated "Accordingly, as chairman of the Committee on International Relations, with jurisdiction over H.R. 1757, I can state that for the purposes of legislative history, the legislative history of Division G is the legislative history of H.R. 1757." 144 Cong. Rec. H11667 (Daily Ed., Oct. 20, 1998).

However, the language of the amendment eventually passed is, on its face, far broader than the pre-settlement adjudication of claims. What is now 22 U.S.C. section 1623(a)(1)(C) provides that the Commission has jurisdiction over any claim "included in a category of claims against a foreign government which is referred to the Commission by the Secretary of State." There is neither a restriction to pre-settlement adjudication nor any restriction as to the kinds of claims the Commission may adjudicate when referred by the Secretary of State.

The amendment thus achieves two things, among others. First, it significantly increases the State Department's flexibility in ensuring the appropriate distribution of international settlement funds, without having continually to seek additional legislative authorizations from the Congress. Second, it greatly expands the jurisdiction of the Commission, well beyond the already-existing authority to adjudicate claims relating to the nationalization or other taking of property.

It is pursuant to this provision that the FCSC is currently adjudicating claims under the Libyan Claims Settlement Agreement; absent this amendment, the Commission would not have had the statutory authority to adjudicate terrorism claims. This is no small matter. The Libya Program is the Commission's first program addressing the claims of victims of international terrorism. Through its work on this program, the Commission has developed expertise in this distinct and expanding area of claims resolution.

IV. The Commission Today

Having effectively concluded its post-Communist-era programs based on the nationalization and other taking of property, it is appropriate to ask whether these kinds of programs are a thing of the past, and whether the Commission's future lies in referrals by the State Department of claims under *ad hoc* claims settlements, such as the Libya program. As is usually the case, the answer is probably not one or the other, but in all likelihood some combination of both.

With respect to claims for the nationalization and other takings of property, there is an argument that the proliferation of private causes of action against States—in the form, for example, of bilateral investment treaties with mandatory arbitration provisions—has done away with the need for diplomatic protection of nationals, especially with respect to property confiscation claims. There may or may not be merit to this. However, I will point out a few things which suggest to me that notwithstanding the increased ability of individuals to enforce their rights internationally on their own behalf, the need for diplomatic protection persists.

First, it is interesting to note that one of the arguments raised in 1949 against establishing the International Claims Commission as a permanent claims body was based on part of the post-World War II Marshall Plan, the Economic Cooperation Act of 1948. Under a provision of that Act, states that received U.S. aid were required to pledge to arbitrate any disputes relating to the investments of

U.S. citizens in those states. On the basis of this provision, Congressman Vorys argued as follows:

> There is general agreement as to the importance of encouraging private investment in foreign lands as a postwar policy. In the ECA law steps were taken towards encouraging such investment by requiring protection of United States investors. In section 115b(10) each participating country must agree to submit for the decision of an international tribunal mutually agreed upon case—"involving compensation of a national of the United States for governmental measures affecting his property rights, including contracts with or concessions from such country." This bill heads in the opposite direction; instead of our Government's insisting upon impartial arbitration of claims for seizure and nationalization of American property, our Government is to make a practice of wholesale diplomatic 'settlements' of such claims, with the proceeds to be parceled out to American claimants by a State Department agency without giving the claimant a chance to be heard in court either in the foreign country or here at home. This may encourage nationalization in foreign countries; it will certainly not encourage American investment abroad.[33]

So it is clear that we have been anticipating the demise of diplomatic protection in favor of private rights of action in international law for a long time.

Second, it is worth reflecting on what is happening now in the investment treaty world, with more and more States either failing to adhere to their obligations under investment treaties or withdrawing from those treaties. For example, a question that is relevant today is what happens when a State persistently refuses to pay an arbitration award due to a U.S. national under an investment treaty? We are seeing this very situation in a number of cases right now. The result is that private entities and individuals are being left without a tangible remedy. If this conduct of foreign states persists, it is foreseeable that the only recourse for a disappointed national in this situation will be, at some point, to turn to their State to seek protection to secure the award or some portion of it. In April 2012 the *New York Times* reported the threat by a Spanish oil company to sue Argentina for over $10 billion if it nationalizes, as Argentina announced that it would, foreign-owned oil industry assets in that country. The article also reported the Spanish government's support of its national via a threat of retaliatory measures.[34]

For all of these reasons, it seems to me that it is still a little early to write the obituary for the role of diplomatic protection in the expropriation area.

In the non-expropriation world, the U.S. 2008 settlement with Libya and the 2010 settlement with Iraq suggest that lump-sum settlements relating to the responsibility of foreign states for other kinds of internationally-wrongful acts are part of the future of claims settlements. The Arab Spring has reminded us that world events can move with breathtaking speed. We do not yet know where this particular wave of change will end, but certainly as we gather here today Syria is

[33] Minority Views to Accompany H.R. 4406, 81st Cong., 2nd Sess., Rept. 770, Part 2, p. 3 (June 30, 1949).

[34] *See Spain Weighs Response to Nationalization of YPF*, N.Y. TIMES, Apr. 18, 2012, p. B3.

in flux, and, in light of the events of the past year, who would predict with any certainty what may occur in Iran. Syria and Iran alone have been the cause of so much harm and loss to American citizens. Given the sheer scale of damages sought in our domestic courts as well as in foreign courts from these two countries (and a number of other states such as, for example, Sudan), it seems highly unlikely that the bulk of these claims can be resolved at anywhere near their asserted value, and ultimately lump-sum settlements are likely to be required. Indeed, the State Department will have to bring all of its skill and expertise, in additional to flexibility, if it is to be able to bring about tangible relief for U.S. victims from these states.

In any event, we cannot know whether the recent claims settlements with state sponsors of terrorism mark the beginning of a trend, but we do know that it is certainly the present state of affairs in regard to Libya and Iraq. Because of the very practical reason that the Commission is presently adjudicating claims against Libya under the Libya settlement, and may have a similar role in future claims settlements, I would like to say a few words about the "legitimacy" and jurisprudential value of the Commission's work, before concluding with some final observations about the Commission's Libya program.

V. Legitimacy

In addressing the question of legitimacy or jurisprudential legacy as these concepts relate to the adjudication of claims under state-to-state settlement agreements, I will begin by recalling a statement of Professor Bederman from the volume recording the proceedings of the Thirteenth Sokol Colloquium. Referring to the UNCC, Professor Bederman stated:

> At worst, the [UNCC] may be a jurisdictional shell, an elaborate scheme deciding cases under an exquisitely developed *lex specialis*. There is, of course, nothing wrong with that. It may even contribute to an orderly disposition of claims. Nonetheless, such a system can cause mischief. First, there may be a perception that the UNCC is not applying legally objective rules of decision. Second, there will be a concern that both the [UNCC's] decisions and Awards will not be worthy of precedential value in the subsequent development of the International Law of State Responsibility and claims settlement.[35]

With respect to the UNCC, Professor Bederman's point was, as usual, extremely insightful. But if you substituted the FCSC, or indeed any other national claims commission, for UNCC, you would have the kind of criticism that has been levied over the years against adjudications under lump-sum settlements.

[35] The United Nations Compensation Commission [Thirteenth Sokol Colloquium] (R. Lillich ed. 1995), pp. 286–87.

Before going further, let me stress that at the FCSC, I am not concerned about the development of the International Law of State Responsibility and claims settlement as ends in and of themselves. I am concerned, however, about the orderly and efficient disposition of the claims before us, about adhering to the Commission's enabling statute, and about applying the legally objective rules of decision specified there, whether those rules are found in the terms of the underlying settlement agreement or in the "applicable principles of international law, justice, and equity."[36] Indeed, these are the very rules that provide the *raison d'etre* for the Commission and ensure its legitimacy.

Ultimately, those who criticize state-to-state settlements as political, not legal, acts, ignore the reality of the settlement process, including the distribution of settlement funds. Again, it is useful to refer back to the debates of 1949 for elucidation of the inextricable link between international law and state-to-state claims settlements. Mr. Samuel Herman, Assistant to the State Department's Legal Adviser for International Claims, explained the process to the Senate Foreign Affairs Committee as follows:

> [W]hat should be borne in mind is that when we sit down with representatives of foreign governments to negotiate these agreements, we are faced with a barrage of matters of international law, and all matters that we present to them are either contested or accepted on the basis of the principles of international law. Of course we may be in a very anomalous position, because when we go to a foreign government to try and settle these claims we state that these were international wrongs committed by the foreign government.... Basically, this is how we approach them. Their reply, of course, is that if you allege a wrong under international law, the relief you get should be under international law.[37]

I would expect that this is not terribly unlike the approach followed today by the State Department. The point is that in interpreting state-to-state claims settlement agreements, it is appropriate, as the Commission's applicable law provision requires, to apply relevant principles of international law where the claims agreement is silent, because generally speaking the agreement itself was concluded between two States on the basis of international law. What I am expressing here is my belief that the merits decisions of the FCSC are based directly—or indirectly, through a claims settlement agreement—on international law, and therefore form part of the fabric of international law. They are legally-objective rules of decision. They may be relied upon by any national or international claims commission or court, and indeed have been throughout its history.

I recognize of course that States can agree between themselves to compromise in a way not required by international law. But these instances are the exception rather than the rule, and in any event are readily apparent.

---

36 22 U.S.C. § 1623(a)(2)(B).

37 United States Senate, Committee on Foreign Relations, Hearings on H.R. 4406, pp. 18–19 (July 19, 1949).

I would not, however, necessarily say the same thing about the quantum of compensation awarded for death, personal injury, hostage taking, etc. For one thing, there are no international "standards" or even uniformly accepted methods of calculating compensation for these kinds of harms. Even within our domestic system, there is no unified metric for awarding specific dollars to plaintiffs who suffered these kinds of harms. There are not even unified disability ratings—there are different systems for calculating ratings, of course, the American Medical Association, state workers compensation boards, etc.,—but these differ from one another, sometimes fairly dramatically. As Judge Lamberth explains in his paper in this volume, there is always an element of arbitrariness to the assessment of these kinds of damages, particularly, of course, with respect to pain and suffering.

From my experience at the FCSC, the UNCC, and the 9/11 Compensation Fund, it seems that the precise quantum to be awarded for these kinds of injuries depends in part upon the willingness or ability of the respondent—or, in the case of the 9/11 Fund, the U.S. taxpayer—to pay. For this reason alone, the amount of compensation to be awarded in one program is not necessarily precedent for another. The quantum of awards are typically unique to the particular program, and the result of negotiations based more on practical considerations rather than purely legal ones.

VI. Final Reflections on the FCSC's Libya Program

I would like to turn now to some observations on the Commission's Libya claims program. The biggest difference between the Libya program and prior FCSC programs is apparent, in my view, from the complexity of the referral itself. As discussed earlier, the FCSC received this program by referral from the State Department. Altogether in the Libya program, the State Department transmitted to the FCSC three separate referral letters, which together define the Commission's jurisdiction over claims submitted in this program.[38] These letters are public documents, available on the FCSC's website. It seems to me that the referral letters reflect the extraordinarily difficult task the State Department faced in reaching this settlement.

The referral letters contain far more detailed instructions than the traditional mandate to the Commission to "receive, examine, adjudicate, and render a final decision with respect to any claim ... included within the terms of any claims agreement."[39] Rather, the referrals specify in great detail the jurisdiction of the Commission for the various categories of claims. There are a number of defined terms, including "Pending Litigation," which specifies identified suits against

[38] *See* 2011 FCSC Ann. Rep. pp. 8–20 (available at www.justice.gov/fcsc/annrep11.pdf).
[39] *See* 22 U.S.C. § 1623(a)(1) and (a)(1)(A).

Libya in U.S. federal court that were required to be dismissed as part of the settlement agreement, and the term "Covered Incidents," which identifies specific terrorist attacks that are included within the referral. The referrals also include recommended amounts of compensation on a category-by-category basis.

Let me give you my sense of what the referrals are, and what the referrals are not. Primarily, the referrals provide the jurisdictional underpinning for the Commission's program. They define the claims over which the Commission has jurisdiction. Claims that do not meet the definitions established in the referral may not be the subject of Commission awards in the program. On occasion, for administrative efficiency and also to ensure that claimants are not unfairly prejudiced, the Commission will proceed to address the merits of a claim even where the Commission preliminarily determines that the claim falls outside its jurisdiction. These situations are, however, rare, and never result in an award to a claimant over which the Commission does not have jurisdiction.

The referrals are not a statement of the substantive law to be applied by the Commission, although, as I will explain, they do inform that law. The law to be applied by the Commission has been determined by Congress, and is set forth in the Commission's enabling statute, 22 U.S.C. 1623(a)(2). That provision states that "[i]n the decision of claims under this subchapter, the Commission shall apply the following in the following order: (A) the provisions of the applicable claims agreement; and (B) the applicable principles of international law, justice, and equity." Thus, by statute, the Commission's first stop in deciding the claims under a referral is the applicable agreement, which, in the Libya program is the 2008 Claims Settlement Agreement between Libya and the United States.

The referrals, however, provide interpretative assistance in reading and applying this Agreement. In general, lump-sum settlements are relatively simple and straightforward because the party that is paying money to settle claims typically does not care how the money is distributed so long as it gets the benefit of its bargain—settlement of the claims, normalization of relations, legal peace, etc. This is especially true where the settlement agreement does not provide for a reversionary interest in the Fund, if there are funds left after all distributions are made. Libya does not have a reversionary interest in the funds deposited with the United States as part of the 2008 Agreement, and thus, it is not likely to be concerned with how the fund deposited with the United States is distributed, so long as it gets the benefits of the bargain it struck by paying that lump sum amount. With that in mind, it should not be surprising that the Claims Settlement Agreement between the U.S. and Libya itself is relatively simple and straightforward. Where detail is lacking, the referrals can serve as an important interpretive aid to the intent of the state parties in reaching the agreement. In this way, the referrals also inform the substantive law to be applied.

This distinction—between the primary purpose of the referrals as establishing the Commission's jurisdiction over claims and its use as informing the applicable law—is fundamentally important to the Commission's decision-making. Where the referrals define the specific elements that must be met by claimants seeking compensation, these are typically issues that go to the Commission's jurisdiction. If a claimant does not meet these criteria, the Commission is not competent to expand its jurisdiction to include them.

For example, if the referral requires that a claimant in a particular category have been a "Pending Litigant," as a number of categories in the Libya referrals do, then claimants who were not Pending Litigants—that is, claimants who did not have a pending litigation in U.S. federal court at the time of the settlement—cannot have their claims adjudicated by the Commission under that category. Those claimants and their claims fall outside the Commission's authority. The question is very clear: the referral defines and enumerates the Pending Litigations in an Annex. There is no room to go behind the very explicit text of the referral.

This can lead to seemingly harsh or inequitable results. For example, imagine two American citizens sitting next to each other on Pan Am Flight 76 when it was hijacked in Pakistan in 1986. Neither was injured, but both endured the terrifying ordeal in extraordinarily difficult conditions for the approximately 16 hours of the hijacking. After the hijacking, one of these passengers filed a claim in U.S. federal court against Libya for hostage taking or unlawful detention. The other did not. Pursuant to the Claims Settlement Agreement, the victim with the federal court claim dismissed that claim against Libya so that she could participate in the compensation fund. Assume also that because this victim filed her claim and then dismissed it, she meets the jurisdictional criteria, set forth in the referral letter, to have her claim adjudicated by the FCSC, and to qualify for an award of $1 million. The other victim does not, and receives nothing from the Libya claims settlement.

Now there are arguments for and against this result in terms of policy and fairness, including the contention that the victim who filed a suit gave up that suit to participate in the Libya claims settlement program, while the claimant who did not file a suit gave up nothing. On the other hand, both American citizens suffered the same harm, side by side, at the hands of the same foreign government. The point is not to debate here the equities of the situation I have described, but rather to highlight the unforgiving nature of the jurisdictional aspect of the referral process. If, instead of a jurisdictional question, the Commission were faced with an issue that went to the merits of the claims of these two hypothetical claimants, then the Commission is empowered—indeed mandated—to invoke applicable principles of international law, justice, and equity to ensure as far as possible that similarly-situated claimants are treated equitably.

Let me conclude by giving you my list of factors that I see as primarily relevant to the decision of whether the FCSC should be charged with the responsibility of distributing claims funds under a state-to-state settlement that does not involve expropriation or other taking of property. I do not intend to place a qualitative judgment on any of these factors but merely to identify them. Necessarily, these factors require comparison with another entity that might distribute the funds, such as the State Department, or for example an entirely new entity, such as a Special Master in the 9/11 Fund mold.

1. The FCSC's statutory framework is already in place. No new authorities need be granted by Congress.
2. By statute, the FCSC's final awards are final and binding, and not subject to appeal.
3. The FCSC provides a forum for victims of terrorism themselves to make their case as witnesses. My experience at the 9/11 Fund was that the hearing process was as important, certainly in emotional terms, to many claimants as was the outcome. My experience at the FCSC is the same. The value of process in these kinds of claims is, in my view, of particular importance.
4. The FCSC's processes and procedures are, by statute and regulation, open and transparent. It issues detailed and reasoned opinions on each claim.
5. The FCSC has a statutory cap on attorney fees. Whether this is a plus or a minus, of course, depends on your perspective. However, what I will say is that so long as the State Department can distribute claim funds without a cap on attorney fees, this factor, whether it is a good one or a bad one, simply must be an issue in the decision of whether to refer claims to the FCSC.
6. Time. It takes significantly longer for a claimant to get its award monies if the award is made through the FCSC than if the award is made through the State Department. There are a number of reasons for this, most of which have to do with the very fact that the FCSC process is open and transparent. That process requires, for example, public notice periods, which necessarily delay claims processing. Also, the statutory payment process permits the Treasury Department to pay claimants only in ratable proportions, which means, in practice, that claimants can only expect to receive their full awards when an entire program is completed. On the other hand, the State Department can pay immediately upon its determination that a claimant merits payment.
7. Finally, the Commission can provide needed flexibility in appropriate circumstances. Consider the complexity of the negotiations with Libya. Obviously, they involved direct negotiations between the United States and Libya. Underlying these negotiations were a number of complicating factors. First, the fact that Libya was the subject of damage claims in U.S. courts in which U.S. claimants were seeking billions of dollars. Libya had also been engaged directly in settlement discussions with certain of those U.S. claimants, thereby involving the claimant community deeply in the overall process. In addition, the U.S. Congress became involved at the behest of constituent-claimants, and had specific expectations in terms of the adequacy of the settlement.[40]

[40] Section 5(a)(2) of the LCRA required a certification by the Secretary of State to "the appropriate congressional committees" that the U.S. government had received from

In negotiations of this complexity, some measure of flexibility to conclude the agreement to the satisfaction not only of the parties to the settlement agreement itself, but also to the satisfaction of closely-related interested parties, *i.e.*, the U.S. Congress and the claimant community, is required. In my view, in these situations, the FCSC can provide needed flexibility: where express or explicit promises cannot be made or demanded—by the State Department, by Congress, or by the claimant community—referring claims to the FCSC, an impartial adjudicatory body that decides claims on the basis of a statutorily-mandated applicable law via clear rules and procedures, with written and reasoned opinions, can be an important tool in enabling the attainment of a final agreement.

Libya "funds pursuant to the claims agreement that are sufficient to ensure—. . . (ii) fair compensation of claims of nationals of the United States for wrongful death or physical injury in cases pending on the date of enactment of this Act. . . ."

LAWSUITS BY FOREIGNERS IN THE U.S. COURTS AND IN THE FOREIGN CLAIMS SETTLEMENT COMMISSION

Allan I. Mendelsohn[1]

I. Introduction

The subject of this symposium is "Foreign Affairs Litigation in the courts of the United States." In these times, there's absolutely no doubt about the fact that this is a most important topic. But I personally feel a little left out, because the subject of our panel is the U.S. Foreign Claims Settlement Commission (FCSC). And as most of you know, claims that get to the Commission are almost always filed long after the confrontation between the two countries has been resolved, they have already patched up their differences, and they have signed an agreement that allows the U.S. Government then to let its nationals file and receive compensation for the claims they legitimately have against the other government.

In other words, as you can all appreciate, the foreign policy problems or confrontations have all preceded and have been worked out between the two countries when the claims are filed with, and pending before, the Commission. While I will have no hesitation discussing one of the major problems currently pending in connection with the Libyan claims settlement agreement and the Commissions' work in this area, I want to first alert you to an example of foreign affairs litigation that is right now a very real confrontation between two major governments—in this instance the United States and France. I would like very briefly to discuss this confrontation not only because it has not been considered in this successful Colloquium, but also because it is a confrontation for which there does not appear to be an easy solution like, for example, a claims settlement agreement. Moreover, the confrontation that I will be discussing revolves around what all of

[1] Allan I. Mendelsohn is of counsel to Cozen O'Connor where he represents companies involved in transportation industry matters before the courts, federal agencies and departments, and the Congress. The views expressed in this speech/article are those only of the author and do not necessarily reflect those of any client or participant in any of the matters discussed.

John Norton Moore (ed.) Foreign Affairs Litigation in United States Courts, pp. 165–174
 ISBN 978-90-04-25727-6

my colleagues know just happens to involve my favorite subject in international law, namely *forum non conveniens* and international air crash litigation in the U.S. Courts.

II. Confrontation between the United States and France

On December 7, 2011, the High Court of France, its Cour de Cassation, issued a decision in what is now quickly becoming the all-important *West Caribbean Airlines* case. As some of you know, this case involved an airline that was registered in Colombia, that did no business in the United States, and that was carrying some 152 Martinique citizens on a charter flight between Martinique and Panama when, en route back to Martinique, it crashed in Venezuela with no survivors. Suit was brought on behalf of the 152 Martinique citizens in the U.S. District Court in Miami and, without going into further details about the facts, I was retained as defense counsel and immediately filed a motion to dismiss the case under the doctrine of *forum non conveniens*. After extensive briefing on the *travaux preparatoire* of the Montreal Convention of 1999 and specifically on the issue of whether U.S. courts could apply the *forum non* doctrine in cases brought under that Convention, District Court Judge Ursula Ungaro issued a multi-page, comprehensive and very well-reasoned decision holding that the legislative history of Article 33(4) clearly established that U.S. courts could use and apply the doctrine in cases brought in the U.S. under the Montreal Convention. Judge Ungaro's decision was appealed to the 11th Circuit Court of Appeals, which itself issued another very well-reasoned decision affirming in all respects Judge Ungaro's decision.[2]

Meanwhile, counsel for plaintiffs, in a collateral attack on the U.S. decisions, brought an action in the French lower court in Martinique seeking to prevail on that court to hold that *forum non conveniens* could not be used by a U.S. court under the Montreal Convention and that the case, therefore, had to be returned to the United States. A three-judge court heard that case in Martinique and in a lengthy opinion fully agreed with Judge Ungaro's decision. That three-judge court decision was affirmed shortly thereafter by a French appellate court.

Despite all of these four decisions, and without even once alluding to them—much less discussing either their reasoning or the doctrine of international comity—the French Cour de Cassation accepted the case for review, and held that a plaintiff's choice of forum under the Montreal Convention is inviolable and cannot be defeated by a U.S. court applying the *forum non conveniens* doctrine. The plaintiffs have since re-filed in Miami, and we are all awaiting to see what happens next. In the meantime, however, I would like to emphasize two points: first, this is a major and direct confrontation between the courts of two

2 See Allan I. Mendelsohn, *Foreign Plaintiffs, Foreign Non Conveniens, and the 1999 Montreal Convention*, 36 J. Air & Space L. 293 (Aug/Sept 2011).

very significant countries, and there does not appear to be a simple solution. And second, I have no hesitation, as I have publicly done once before, characterizing the French high court's decision as one of the most judicially irresponsible and judicially unprofessional decisions I have seen in my many years of practicing law.[3]

III. The Relationship of *Forum Non Conveniens* to ATS Litigation

Now that you can appreciate the significance of this very direct confrontation, I'd like to add a few words about the real purpose that U.S. courts have in using the doctrine of *forum non conveniens*. It is, in a word, to save U.S. courts, and the U.S. public, from the enormous expense, time and effort involved in litigating cases that involve primarily foreign citizens and events (in this instance aviation crashes) that have occurred outside the United States. The *forum non* doctrine has become an extremely important tool that has been used in the past 10 to 15 years by literally dozens of U.S. federal courts to rid themselves mainly of international air crash litigation that, like the case I just described to you, should never have been brought in a U.S. Court in the first place and that, despite the French Court's decision, should not be allowed to be brought back.

But what is even more interesting about the precedent of *forum non conveniens* in aviation litigation is the precedent it may well be setting in an area that has been widely discussed by other panels in this colloquium, namely, the area of claims that are brought under the Alien Tort Statute (ATS). You have all heard the reports and discussion about Judge Alito's now famous question in the *Kiobel* case: why that case—which involved Nigerian plaintiffs suing foreign oil companies for human rights violations in Nigeria—should even be in a U.S. court. And if we discuss that question in the context of the *forum non conveniens* doctrine, we can have no question but that cases involving foreign citizens suing under the ATS for events that occurred abroad and have little or no relevance to the United States should no more be able to take up the time, effort and expense of

[3] See Allan I. Mendelsohn, *International Aviation Today, What's Wrong?* 11 Issues in Aviation L. & Pol'y 327, 335 (Spring 2012). Following the decision of the Cour de Cassation, the plaintiffs refiled their cases in the U.S. District Court in Miami requesting reinstatement and judgment in accordance with the Cour de Cassation's decision. On May 16, 2012, in an extraordinarily persuasive and well-reasoned decision, Judge Ungaro again dismissed their cases on *forum non conveniens* grounds. *In re West Caribbean Airways*, No. 06-22748-CIV, 2012 WL 1884684 (S.D. Fla May 16, 2012). The plaintiffs have since appealed to the 11th Circuit where their cases are presently pending. See Allan I. Mendelsohn and Carlos J. Ruiz, *The United States vs. France: Article 33 of the Montreal Convention and the Doctrine of Forum Non Conveniens*, 77 J. Air Law and Com. 467 (Summer 3012).

U.S. courts and U.S. citizens than the multitudes of air accident cases that U.S. courts have regularly *"forum non'd"* in the past 10 years.[4]

In other words, whether achieved by way of *"forum non'ing"* ATS cases or by limiting the scope of the ATS only to suits involving private citizens as well as events that occur in the United States, I am one of those who would be overjoyed if future ATS litigation follows the precedent of aviation litigation. In short, cases like *Rio Tinto*, *Talisman Energy*, and more recently the case brought by *Turkell* and involving corporate skullduggery in South Africa—all of which involve foreigners suing over events that occur abroad—should simply not be heard in our courts, no matter how that result is achieved. I have much the same view about cases like *Chevron v. Ecuador* that are not necessarily brought under the ATS but under general law to recover for alleged pollution and other similar damage.

IV. The Foreign Claims Settlement Commission (FCSC) and U.S. Nationality

But now to the very different issue facing us and the U.S. Government's Foreign Claims Settlement Commission (FCSC)—an agency whose functions and responsibilities are described to you in such excellent terms in this volume by its very esteemed and highly regarded Chairman. In this instance, the issue is not about keeping foreigners out of our courts so much as it is about acknowledging what is American and what rights Americans should have before the Commission. The claim that is currently pending before the Commission and that is creating what many view as a very major problem involves the issue of whether that once famous airline that for so many years quintessentially represented the United States at home and abroad—and I am speaking now of Pan American World Airways—should be treated before the Commission as a U.S. citizen. As many of you know, it was Pan American World Airways, simply because it was so representative of America, that was chosen by Muammar Gaddafi and the Libyan government to be the victim of the infamous airline sabotage event now known as the Lockerbie disaster. As many of you also recall, all the 259 passengers and crew aboard that Pan American flight—about 200 Americans and others of differing

[4] In June 2012, the Solicitor General of the United States filed in the *Kiobel* Supreme Court litigation "A Supplementary Brief for the United States as Amicus Curiae in Partial Support of Affirmance." That brief took precisely the position espoused above, namely, that:

> "Other doctrines [in addition to the doctrine of exhaustion], such as forum non conveniens, should also be applied with special vigor in ATS cases. If the parties and the conduct have little connection to the US, and an adequate alternative forum exists, courts should presumptively dismiss", adding further that "[i]n the ATS context... dismissal on forum non conveniens grounds should not be the rare exception." (Brief at p. 24).

nationalities—died, as did eleven people on the ground at Lockerbie. The families of all the victims brought suit against Pan American in New York and, when the litigation was ultimately concluded, Pan American was required to and did pay some $485 million in full compensation to the families and survivors of all the victims.

The question right now before the Commission is whether Libya should be required to reimburse Pan American for that $485 million. As background, you should be aware that within two years of the Lockerbie disaster and at least in part, if not very largely, because of that disaster, Pan American filed in bankruptcy, terminated its services and was ultimately some years later dissolved as a corporate entity. Fortunately, however, and because the U.S. Government requires that all U.S. flag airlines maintain substantial insurance coverage for disasters of this and other types, Pan Am, through its insurers, was able to pay out some $485 million to the Lockerbie victims.

Several years later, in 1998, after Libya was designated as a terrorist nation under the Foreign Sovereign Immunities Act (FSIA), the underwriters or insurers that had insured Pan American brought suit against Libya under that Act. The suit was brought by and in the names of the underwriters (*i.e.*, Hartford Fire Insurance Company, etc.) at least partly because Pan American had filed in bankruptcy and would shortly be liquidated as a corporate entity. In any event, that FSIA suit pended before Judge Hogan on the U.S. District Court in the District of Columbia for the better part of ten years during which time Libya, through its U.S. counsel, raised any number of defenses—including the very important defense that, because the suit was brought by the underwriters and because many of the underwriters were foreign, the suit could not properly be brought under the FSIA which limited suits and recoveries only to U.S. nationals. Before discussing Judge Hogan's decision in that case, it would be useful to focus on some background into the extraordinary world of international aviation and aviation insurance.

V. The Globalization of Aviation Insurance Underwriting

Way back in 1966, instead of denouncing the 1929 Warsaw Convention and its very low limits of liability for personal injury and death, the U.S. Government succeeded in getting the airlines of the world voluntarily to very substantially raise their limits of liability and to adopt absolute liability as the basis for liability.[5] But for airlines to be able to obtain insurance to cover this very expanded exposure to liability, it became necessary for aviation accident insurance to become a globally multi-lateralized market. As time went forward and limits of liability began to disappear altogether (which is the prevailing and established system

[5] Andreas F. Lowenfeld and Allan I. Mendelsohn, *The United States and the Warsaw Convention*, 80 Harv. Law Rev. 497 (1967).

today under the 1999 Montreal Convention), and as more and more new airlines entered into service with larger and larger jet aircraft, it became essential for the aviation insurance market to partner together on a globally multi-lateralized basis in order to be able to provide the coverage necessary to insure the huge and ever growing risks that confronted the international airline industry. That is why, even by the time of Lockerbie in 1988, 48% of Pan American's insurance coverage was provided by foreign insurance companies or, like Lloyd's, foreign insurance markets.

Today, some 25 years later, the insurance coverage of all the world's airlines is even more multi-lateralized, as the ever increasing coverage requirements have inevitably led to the steadily evolving practice that is known today as reinsurance coverage and even retrocession insurance coverage. But, and this is the critically important point that must be made: no one in the world pays much if any attention to the nationality of the underwriters or the reinsurers. The important question is, and has always been, what is the nationality of the airline—in other words, what flag does that airline fly? In the case of Pan American and Lockerbie, everyone knew that it was a U.S. flag airline and, indeed, that was the sole and only reason Libya picked it to be the victim of its despicable terrorist act.

VI. The Inquiries from the Staff of the FCSC

But what I should have said is that, while no one anywhere in the world pays much if any attention to the nationality of those who help to fully insure airlines operating internationally, that very issue of nationality seems to have become the major issue for the staff of the Foreign Claims Settlement Commission in handling the $485 million claim that is pending before the commission. This is the claim: (1) that Pan American had against Libya; and (2) that, on Pan Am's bankruptcy, was brought by the underwriters as a claim against Libya under the FSIA (*i.e.*, the *Hartford Fire Insurance Company* litigation); and that (3) has since been forcibly dismissed by the Department of Justice and referred to the Commission in accordance with the 2008 agreement reached between the United States and Libya. To date, the Commission has yet to issue a proposed decision on the claim, but the inquiries received for additional information from the Commission's staff are very troubling.

Operating under U.S. citizenship requirements almost identical to those in the FSIA, the inquiries from the FCSC's staff clearly imply that because 48% of the $485 million that was paid to the Lockerbie victims came not directly from Pan American as the insured but rather from the foreign underwriters who provided that portion of the insurance, the Commission may well not be able to pay that portion of the $485 million claim. Even as to the 52% of the coverage provided by U.S. underwriters, there is some fear—due to other inquiries from the Commission's staff—that the Commission may ultimately take the extreme position that, because some of that 52% may have been reinsured and some of the reinsurers may have been foreign, that percentage is likewise tainted so that there may well be no recovery at all.

If I can sum up the irony of this situation: Libya maliciously destroys a U.S. flag airliner; largely because of that act of terrorism, the U.S. airline company goes bankrupt and disappears; because it disappears the insurers of the airline directly pay the victims and bring suit against Libya under the FSIA and now before the FCSC—only to be told by the Commission's staff that, because the aviation insurance industry is necessarily multi-lateralized and globalized, Libya's bill for the enormous damage it caused may well be substantially reduced if not eliminated. I cannot help but say that there is something terribly wrong with this approach to making Libya fully responsible for its terrorist act of sabotage that destroyed a U.S. flag airline and killed all of its passengers. To be sure, the Commission may well say that, after paying all the other claims, the $1.5 billion that the U.S. Government negotiated for and received from Libya was not enough to pay the Pan Am 103 claim in its entirety or at all. But if the $485 million could and would have been recovered under the FSIA, it should be equally recoverable before the FCSC, especially given that the Department of Justice forced the dismissal of the FSIA suit and then had it referred to the FCSC.

VII. Prevailing Law to the Contrary

Moreover, it is not only the facts and international circumstances that militate against this approach of totally ignoring the nationality of the airline and focusing instead only on the nationality of the underwriters, it is also prevailing law and directly applicable precedent. Initially, I do not believe I need refer to, much less cite cases to support, the basic and long established principle of subrogation law that insurers, as subrogees, when bringing suit to recover from the actual tort feasor, generally sue in the name of the insured (or the subrogor). They may add a reference to themselves as subrogees suing in the name of the insured-subrogor, but it was the policy holder (the subrogor) to whom the suit originally belonged, as he/it was the injured party. Let me add at this point that if our only precedent was this well-established principle of subrogation law, I could probably conclude my discussion right now. But it is even more important for you to all appreciate that the very U.S. District Court that I referred to earlier (that was handling the FSIA case brought by *Hartford Fire Insurance Company* and its partner-underwriters), reached precisely the same conclusion.

VIII. Judge Hogan's Decision in *Hartford Fire Insurance Co. v. Libya*

In the course of the litigation before Judge Hogan, and as I mentioned earlier, Libya brought a motion to dismiss based on several grounds but principally on the ground that the FSIA allowed suits only by "natural persons who are nationals of the United States" and that the plaintiffs here were corporate insurers many of whom were foreign. The plaintiff insurers countered that the then Section 1605(a)(7) of the FSIA must be read "more broadly, so as to encompass third-party claims for indemnity and contribution." Judge Hogan had no hesitation holding against Libya and doing so in words that clearly deserve repetition:

> Although the [legislative history] does not contain a discussion of contribution or indemnity, it does state the principal statutory purpose of the FSIA, which is to deter foreign States from sponsoring terrorist activities. The failure to permit insurance companies to sue for contribution would undermine this goal, as victims of a plane crash can usually obtain compensation more easily from an airline and its insurers for not providing proper safety than against a sponsoring state. Only if the airline and, in turn, its insurers can step into the shoes of the victims does FSIA fulfill its statutory purpose of providing 'an important economic and financial weapon against . . . outlaw states.

Hartford Fire Insurance Co. v. Socialist People's Libyan Arab Jamahiriya, 1999 WL 33589331 at p. 3 (D.D.C. Sept. 23, 1999).

There are two very salient conclusions that one can and should draw from this decision: First, if the underwriters would have been able, as Judge Hogan specifically concluded, to obtain full compensation under the FSIA had their suit been allowed to continue forward under the FSIA, it would be totally unfair and unjust for the U.S. Government, having forced the dismissal of that FSIA suit, to now conclude via the FCSC that underwriters, whether foreign or U.S., are not permitted to sue or collect under the precedent and procedures of the FCSC.

And second, when Judge Hogan framed the issue as "[o]nly if the airline and, in turn, its insurers can step into the shoes of the victims," there is no suggestion that, by using the terms "shoes of the victims," he had any intention of limiting the recovery of those who had insured a U.S. flag airline only to the amounts they paid to the U.S. victims. Pan American World Airways was as much a victim of Libya's terrorism as were the 259 passengers aboard that flight. Indeed, and as I shall discuss very shortly, the FSIA's then Section 1605(a)(7) was amended in 2008 with at least one purpose being to make it clear that suits by insurers, whether U.S. or foreign, were perfectly appropriate under the FSIA as were the payments they made to foreign as well as to U.S. victims.

IX. The Court of Appeals Decision in *La Reunion Aerienne* (LRA)

Before getting to that amendment, however, I would like to mention that Judge Hogan's decision was not the only decision holding that insurers, no matter their nationality, had rights to sue under the FSIA. A similar decision was reached by the U.S. Court of Appeals for the District of Columbia in *La Reunion Aerienne v. Libya*, 533 F.3d 837 (D.C. Cir. 2008). In that case, a French partnership, representing interests of insurance companies, brought suit against Libya for $2 million paid to the families of seven U.S. nationals who were among the victims of a Libyan act of terrorism that destroyed a French airliner over Niger, Africa. The Court of Appeals had no difficulty in concluding that "claims may be brought by assignees/subrogees [even if foreign] of the victims' families and their estates . . . against a subrogation defendant such as Libya, under the FSIA."

X. The Amended FSIA and Certain Underwriters

I should finally like to mention the latest case that has been decided in the federal courts and that bears directly on these issues. Brought under the FSIA's new Section 1605A—which is the 2008 amendment to Section 1605(a)(7)—and specifically its subsection (d), this decision not only holds that foreign underwriters can sue and recover under the FSIA, but that they can do so for terrorism-related damage done to a foreign flag airline, in this instance Egypt Air. See *Certain Underwriters at Lloyd's London, et al. v. Libya*, 811 F. Supp. 2d 53 (D.C.D.C., Sept. 2, 2011). In the face of these established precedents, it would be the ultimate of unfairness if the U.S. Government, having forced the dismissal of the insurers' *Hartford Fire Insurance* suit under the FSIA, were now, via the FCSC, to ignore all the FSIA precedent and hold that when making a claim before the FCSC, the insurers (even if tainted with foreign characteristics) cannot recover at all against Libya or can only recover for U.S. victims.

XI. Conclusion

Two conclusions become very apparent from this discussion. First, if the suit brought by the underwriters before Judge Hogan had been allowed to proceed to judgment—instead of being forcibly dismissed by the Department of Justice—there can be almost no question, given recently established precedent under the FSIA, but that the underwriters would have received a judgment for the full amount of $485 million. If an award of such a judgment would have been proper under the FSIA—which has a nationality requirement almost identical to that imposed by the FCSC—it should be equally as proper an award before and by the FCSC. Moreover, it would be uniquely unfair for the FCSC not to render such an award when it was the U.S. Department of Justice that preemptively forced the dismissal of the suit before Judge Hogan.

And second, we cannot help but note the difference between, on the one hand, the solicitousness with which foreign plaintiffs have so far been so welcomed, indeed encouraged, to use U.S. courts when suing under the Alien Tort Statute (ATS) and, on the other hand, the possible unwillingness of the FCSC to provide full reimbursement to a U.S. flag airline for the damages it and its underwriters paid out following Libya's act of terrorism against that airline. Indeed, and from a different perspective, it borders on the incredulous that the ATS is viewed as so concerned about foreign plaintiffs obtaining justice in U.S. tribunals while the

FCSC may be denying justice to foreign underwriters without whose presence and active participation Pan American World Airways may well not have been able to have been fully insured in 1988, and the international aviation insurance marketplace might well not be able to function nearly as successfully and as effectively as it does today.[6]

---

[6] On January 30, 2013, the Foreign Claims Settlement Commission (FCSC) issued its final decision holding, *inter alia*, that because so much of the insurance was provided by foreign insurance interests—whether acting as primary insurers, reinsurers, retrocessionaires or otherwise—there would be no recovery allowed on any portion of the $485 million claim for any of the insurers, US or foreign. The decision is right now under careful study by all participants in the international aviation insurance industry. In accordance with established procedure, however, the FCSC's decision is unreviewable.

INTERNATIONAL CLAIMS AND THE FOREIGN CLAIMS SETTLEMENT COMMISSION*

David E. Bradley**

I. Introduction

The Foreign Claims Settlement Commission of the United States ("FCSC") came into being in 1954, under the President's Reorganization Plan No. 1 of 1954.[1] It exists today as the successor of both the War Claims Commission, an independent body created pursuant to the War Claims Act of 1948,[2] and the International Claims Commission, which had been set up in the Department of State in 1950 pursuant to the International Claims Settlement Act of 1949,[3] as amended (hereinafter "ICSA").

The War Claims Commission's first task had been to study the various issues associated with the maltreatment of U.S. service members and civilians held as prisoners of war and civilian internees by the Axis powers during the recently ended world war and to report its findings and recommendations to the President. Concurrent with this, Congress enacted amendments to the Act[4] directing the Commission to receive and evaluate claims of former prisoners of war and internees for inhumane treatment during World War II (claims for inadequate rations had already been covered in the original legislation), and also to receive and evaluate claims of service members and civilians captured or interned during the Korean Conflict. Compensation for the World War II prisoners of war and

* Based on an oral presentation given by the author at the 25th Sokol Colloquium, University of Virginia School of Law, April 19, 2012.

** Member, District of Columbia Bar and the Florida Bar; Chief Counsel, Foreign Claims Settlement Commission, U.S. Department of Justice, 1988–2008.

1 19 F.R. 3985, 68 Stat. 1279, effective July 1, 1954 (22 U.S.C. 1622 note).

2 Pub. L. 896, 80th Cong., approved July 3, 1948, 62 Stat. 1240 (50 U.S.C. App. § 2001 *et seq.*).

3 Pub. L. 455, 81st Cong., approved March 10, 1950, 64 Stat. 12 (22 U.S.C. § 1621 *et seq.*).

4 Pub. L. 303, 82d Cong., approved April 9, 1952, 66 Stat. 47 (50 U.S.C.App. 2005(d)); Pub. L. 615, 83d Cong., approved August 21, 1954, 68 Stat. 759 (50 U.S.C.App. 2005(e)).

John Norton Moore (ed.) Foreign Affairs Litigation in United States Courts, pp. 175–186
 ISBN 978-90-04-25727-6

civilian internees was paid out of funds derived from German and Japanese government assets in the United States that had been frozen by the Alien Property Custodian in the Department of Justice at the beginning of the war and eventually liquidated, as authorized under the Trading with the Enemy Act of 1917, as amended.[5] Compensation for those held in Korea was paid from appropriated funds.

After it came into existence in 1954 the FCSC continued this claims evaluation process. In addition, it received and evaluated several further categories of claims under succeeding amendments to the War Claims Act, including claims of captured U.S. merchant seamen,[6] American servicemen captured while fighting with the forces of other Allied nations,[7] and Guamanian workers captured on Wake Island,[8] among others.

In the 1960s, Congress enacted a major amendment to the Act,[9] directing the Commission to evaluate claims of U.S. citizens and corporations for damage to and loss of property as the result of World War II military operations in the European and Pacific theaters, and to award compensation out of the proceeds from the liquidation of enemy assets, which was still ongoing. Some of the last enemy assets liquidated were shares of stock in the General Aniline & Film Corporation worth some $340 million.[10]

The Commission's awards in this program, which it called the General War Claims (GWC) Program, ultimately amounted to a total of over $335 million.[11] However, there were not enough remaining liquidation proceeds to allow full payment of those awards.[12] The GWC Program authorizing statute provided for payment priority according to a formula that favored individuals and small businesses ahead of corporations and other larger entities and interests.[13]

The last amendment to the War Claims Act, enacted in the early 1970s,[14] authorized the Commission to evaluate and award compensation in the claims of U.S. service members and civilians who had suffered maltreatment while held as prisoners of war and civilian internees by the Vietnamese Communist regime. In addition, the amendment covered the claims of the crew of the *USS Pueblo* for the maltreatment they had endured following the ship's capture and detention

---

5 Act Oct. 6, 1917, Ch. 106, 40 Stat. 411 (50 U.S.C. App. 1 *et seq.*).
6 Pub. L. 744, 83d Cong., approved August 31, 1954 , 68 Stat. 1034 (50 U.S.C. App. 2015).
7 *Id.*
8 Pub. L. 87-617, approved August 31, 1962, 76 Stat. 413 (50 U.S.C. App. 2004(h)).
9 Pub. L. 87-846, approved October 22, 1962, 76 Stat. 1107 (50 U.S.C. App. 2017 *et seq.*).
10 *The Crime and Punishment of I.G. Farben*, by Joseph Borkin, The Free Press, New York, NY, 1979, at 221.
11 FCSC Annual Report to Congress for 2011 at 52, http://www.justice.gov/fcsc/annrep11.pdf, at 60.
12 *Id.*
13 *Id.*
14 Pub. L. 91-289, approved June 24, 1970, 84 Stat. 323 (50 U.S.C. App. 2005).

by North Korean forces in 1968. This grant of authority technically is still in place and was last used in 1993, when the Commission received and evaluated a claim by the survivors of a service member whose remains had recently been repatriated by the Vietnamese government and who, according to that government, had been held as a prisoner of war before he died.[15]

II. Claims under the ICSA

Turning to the international-claims side of the Commission's operations, the creation of its predecessor, the International Claims Commission, had been carried out in order to deal with the mass of claims covered by the $17 million settlement agreement concluded with Yugoslavia in 1948.[16] Those, of course, were the early days of the Cold War and the Iron Curtain. As many will recall, Marshal Tito maintained over the years that Yugoslavia was not in fact behind the Iron Curtain, though he called the country the "Federal People's Republic of Yugoslavia" and expropriated many U.S.-owned properties and other assets, following the example of the Soviet Union in purporting to implement the tenets of Marxism regarding the ownership of property. But unlike in other cases that came later, the Yugoslav government allowed representatives of the U.S. government to enter the country and take depositions regarding the facts of individual claims.[17] In addition, the Commission took into account briefs and other submissions made by the Yugoslav government in its evaluation of some of the claims.

The Cold War and the continued existence of the Iron Curtain kept the Foreign Claims Settlement Commission in business from its 1954 inception until well into the 1990s. First, it took on the adjudication of expropriation and war damage claims against Romania, Bulgaria and Hungary,[18] as well as expropriation claims against the Soviet Union itself[19] that had arisen before the 1933 "Litvinov Assignment" given to President Roosevelt. This last later led to the famous Supreme

---

[15] Claim of ERNA MCKINNEY, et al., Claim No. SPN-1870, *reprinted in* FCSC Annual Report to Congress for 1993 at 61.

[16] *Agreement Between the Governments of the United States of America and the Federal People's Republic of Yugoslavia Regarding Pecuniary Claims of the United States and its Nationals*, July 19, 1948, TIAS. 1803.

[17] *Id.*, Art. 5.

[18] Pub. L. 285, 84th Congress, Title III, approved August 9, 1955, 69 Stat. 570 (22 U.S.C. 1641b). This legislation was required because the ICSA barred the FCSC from exercising its self-executing authority under the Act to conduct property expropriation claims programs pursuant to government-to-government claims settlement agreements—such as the 1960 agreement with Poland, discussed *infra*—in the case of countries such as Romania, Bulgaria and Hungary, with which the United States had been at war during World War II.

[19] *Id.* In the case of the Soviet Union, the legislation was necessary because there had been no government-to-government en bloc settlement agreement between the U.S.

Court cases, *U.S. v. Belmont*[20] and *U.S. v. Pink*,[21] which are—or used to be, anyway—central to the study of international law in law school.

As mentioned above, the International Claims Commission had been allowed to verify the facts of claims within Yugoslavia, and also had had the benefit of input from the Yugoslav government in individual claims. This was not the case, however, with Romania, Bulgaria, Hungary, or the Soviet Union, nor with Czechoslovakia,[22] and it brings into focus a disadvantage the President and Department of State have had to take into account in relying on the Commission to serve as evaluator of claims. That is, the Commission's proceedings are essentially *ex parte*, and because these just-mentioned Communist bloc governments—as well as others to be discussed *infra*—Cuba, China, the German Democratic Republic, and Vietnam—would not give the Commission access to or provide information that would support or refute the claimants' submissions as to the facts of their claims. Rather, their more usual stance was that they did not recognize the legitimacy of such claims, based on their Marxist-Leninist ideology regarding the ownership of property. Consequently, the Commission had to make its determinations based on its assessment of the credibility of the claimants' affidavits and documentation, combined with whatever corroborative information it could obtain from sources outside those countries. This, in turn, meant that the Commission's determinations inevitably were open to challenge to some degree when the U.S. Government eventually persuaded those countries' governments to sit down to negotiate claims settlement agreements. Partly because of this—though also for practical, political reasons (half a loaf being considered better than none, for one)—the settlement amounts eventually obtained were sufficient in most cases to allow only pro rata payments of the Commission's awards.[23]

Concerning this question of access, however, the Government of Poland was an exception. Following the completion of a registration of potential U.S. claims against Poland which the Commission carried out in the late 1950s, the United

---

and the U.S.S.R. for the FCSC to implement. To the contrary, the Assignment expressly stipulated that it was

> *preparatory to a final settlement* of the claims and counter claims of the Governments of the Union of Soviet Socialist Republics and the United States of America and the claims of their nationals[.] (emphasis added).

In addition, the legislation served to authorize the distribution of the proceeds from the Litvinov Assignment by the Executive Branch. (As a footnote to the footnote, this final settlement still remains to be concluded, as 2012 ends and 2013 begins.)

20 301 U.S. 324 (1937).

21 315 U.S. 203 (1942).

22 Authorized in 1958 by Pub. L. 85–604, approved August 8, 1958, 72 Stat. 527 (22 U.S.C. 1642).

23 FCSC Annual Report to Congress for 2011 at 50, http://www.justice.gov/fcsc/annrep11.pdf at 58.

States and Poland agreed to a settlement of the claims for $40 million,[24] and shortly thereafter, as provided for in the agreement,[25] the Commission established a field office in Warsaw staffed with Polish-speaking attorneys who were able to check the facts of many claims.

Referring back to the General War Claims program, another means some claimants used to try to substantiate their claims was to ask contacts—often local officials—back in their countries of origin to give sworn statements regarding the facts of their claims. In one set of claims, however, where the property involved was located in Albania, the Commission decided it could not rely on the submitted statements, standing alone, because there was suspicion that bribes were being paid to mayors of Albanian villages and other local officials for statements helpful to some claimants. In fact, rumor had it the FBI even looked into the matter at one point—although it ultimately concluded, apparently, that an investigation was not warranted.

Continuing on through the 1960s, Congress enacted further amendments to the International Claims Settlement Act authorizing the Commission to evaluate further U.S. claims against Romania and Bulgaria,[26] and to prospectively evaluate U.S. claims against Cuba[27] and China.[28] Given Cuba's geographical proximity and the extensive U.S. involvement in its economy, the claimants in the Cuba program—which were for the most part corporations and other commercial entities—were able to document their claims fairly easily. And almost all of the value of the Commission's certifications of loss lay in the claims of corporations—almost $1.6 billion out of a total of just under $1.8 billion.[29] With 6 percent simple interest, the total value of the claims in 2012 is over $7.5 billion.

Similarly, approximately two thirds of the value of the Commission's certifications of loss in the claims filed in the China Claims Program related to property

---

[24] *Agreement Between the Government of the United States of America and the Government of the Polish People's Republic Regarding Claims of Nationals of the United States*, July 16, 1960, TIAS 4545.

[25] *Id.*, Art. 5.

[26] Pub. L. 90-421, approved July 24, 1968, 82 Stat. 420 (22 U.S.C. § 1641b); *Agreement Between the Government of the United States of America and the Government of the People's Republic of Bulgaria Regarding Claims of United States Nationals and Related Financial Matters*, entered into force July 2, 1963, TIAS 1650; *Agreement Between the United States of America and the Rumanian People's Republic Relating to Financial Matter Between the Two Countries*, entered into force March 30, 1960, TIAS 1649. See also fn. 17, *supra*.

[27] Pub. L. 88-666, approved October 16, 1964, 73 Stat. 1110 (22 U.S.C. 1643 *et seq.*).

[28] Pub. L. 89-780, approved November 6, 1966, 80 Stat. 1365 (22 U.S.C. 1643 *et seq.*).

[29] FCSC Report on Completion of the Cuban Claims Program Under Title V of the International Claims Settlement Act of 1949, Exhibit 15, available at http://www.justice.gov/fcsc/final-report-cuba-1972.pdf, at 345.

owned by American corporations and other businesses.[30] Notably, however, most of the remaining one third related to claims for property owned by American religious and other non-profit organizations and their employees, including Christian missionaries proselytizing in China. The total value of those claims was certified by the Commission to have been approximately $196.68 million, plus interest.[31]

In the 1970s the Commission was given authority to receive further claims against Hungary,[32] following the 1973 U.S.-Hungary claims settlement agreement[33] which was part of the Hungarian government's economic opening to the West, as it found itself able to move increasingly toward "Goulash Communism"—i.e., adhering to less strict interpretations of Marxist-Leninist economic ideology in the first years of the Détente era. A notable feature of that agreement was its provision for acceleration of the rate of the installment payments which the Hungarian government had obligated itself to make, depending on the value of the goods that Hungary was able to export to the United States.[34]

Later in the 1970s, and also as a Détente-related development, the Commission received authorization from Congress to evaluate claims against the German Democratic Republic ("GDR" or "East Germany").[35] It was notable at that time that the GDR regime seemed conflicted as to how to deal with this initiative by the United States, which occurred in tandem with the signing of an "Agreed Minute" by the United States and the GDR affirming the two countries' intent to establish full diplomatic relations. The German Communist Party's history and experience before and during World War II, together with their rigid Marxist-Leninist orthodoxy, seemed to make the issue of property expropriation claims a sensitive subject. But at the same time, the East Germans insisted adamantly that their country was entitled to be treated as the political and economic equal of the Federal Republic of Germany (West Germany) which, as part of its conduct of diplomatic relations with the United States had long before resolved practically all outstanding private property ownership issues with the United States—including, most particularly, the restitution of property of victims of religious and racial persecution during the National Socialist era. At one point, soon after

---

30 Relevant to the discussion in today's Colloquium, one of those corporations was the Shanghai Power Company, another claimant that later brought a Fifth Amendment taking claim against the United States for allegedly settling its claim for less than "full" value. Shanghai Power Co. v. U.S., 4 Cl. Ct. 237 (1983), *aff'd mem.*, 765 F.2d 159 (Fed. Cir.), *cert. denied*, 474 U.S. 909 (1985).

31 FCSC Annual Report to Congress for 2011 at 50, http://www.justice.gov/fcsc/annrep11.pdf at 58.

32 Pub. L. 93-460, approved October 20, 1974, 88 Stat. 1386 (22 U.S.C. 1641b).

33 *Agreement Between the Government of the United States of America and the Government of the Hungarian People's Republic Regarding the Settlement of Claims*, entered into force March 6, 1973, TIAS 7569.

34 *Id.*, Art. 4.

35 Pub. L. 94-542, approved Oct. 18, 1976, 90 Stat. 2509 (22 U.S.C. 1644 *et seq.*).

the Commission's completion of the claims adjudication program in 1981, there was a rumor that the GDR government had tried to finesse the entire matter by asserting that the property at issue was not worth much anyway, and had proffered a settlement figure of approximately $11 million—as against a total value of $77.88 million plus interest determined by the Commission. Needless to say, this offer was rejected.

Nor would the GDR authorities consider the idea of allowing the Commission to establish a field office within their territory. Fortunately, however, there were many real property and other legal records from before World War II and from the immediate post-war occupation period that were located in West Germany and which the Commission's staff attorneys could draw upon to verify the facts of many of the claims. So it did the next-best thing and established a field office at the U.S. Consulate in Munich (which had been the headquarters of the U.S. military occupation zone) to which it assigned German-speaking staff attorneys for varying lengths of time.

At about the same time, the United States and China concluded a claims settlement agreement,[36] based on the determinations that the Commission had made and certified to the Secretary of State in its China claims program in the 1960s (discussed above). The percentage of the value of the claims determined by the Commission which the Chinese were persuaded to pay was within the range of percentages that several other Communist regimes had agreed to, suggesting that the Chinese had hired lawyers to research past settlement agreements or had done so themselves.

Moving into the 1980s, the Commission took on, at almost the same time, separate programs for U.S. nationals' claims against Vietnam, for property in South Vietnam expropriated or otherwise taken in and after 1975, the year of the takeover of South Vietnam by the Vietnamese Communist regime, and a program for further U.S. claims against Czechoslovakia, following the 1982 U.S.-Czechoslovak settlement agreement and gold release. In both cases, legislation was required to authorize the Commission to proceed.

In the case of Vietnam, legislation was necessary because there was no government-to-government en bloc settlement agreement in place to trigger the Commission's contingent standing jurisdiction to adjudicate claims—nor, for that matter, any imminent likelihood of one, since at that time the United States and Vietnam did not even maintain diplomatic relations. But at the same time there was a need to compile a timely record of the claims, so Congress enacted another

36 *Agreement Between the Government of the United States and the Government of the People's Republic of China Concerning the Settlement of Claims*, entered into force May 11, 1979, TIAS 9306.

amendment[37] to the ICSA providing for a pre-settlement adjudication program, as it had done with respect to Cuba and others, discussed above.

In the case of Czechoslovakia, legislation was required to enable the Commission to proceed because in 1974 Congress had enacted a statute[38] barring the President from entering into a claims settlement agreement with that country without its prior review and approval, following a previous attempt at a settlement that it considered inadequate. The enabling legislation eventually enacted was the Czechoslovakian Claims Settlement Act of 1981,[39] granting approval to the President to enter into a claims settlement agreement that had been tentatively concluded with the Czech Government earlier in 1981 and specifying how the settlement amount received under the agreement should be apportioned. That agreement, signed in early 1982, provided for settlement of U.S. nationals' claims in exchange for payments from the Czech Government to the United States Government totaling $81.5 million.[40] In addition, the Act authorized the United States Government's assent to the release of hundreds of millions of dollars' worth of gold belonging to Czechoslovakia which had been held by the Tripartite Commission on Monetary Gold since the end of World War II.

The return of its gold was of course a strong inducement to the Czech government to enter into a settlement agreement more acceptable to the United States. However, even in that case the settlement amount was not sufficient to allow payment of all of the Commission's awards in full. After completion of second Czech claims program authorized as part of the 1981 Act, covering expropriation claims that had arisen after the authorization of the first Czech claims program in 1958, the funds received under the 1982 agreement proved sufficient to pay the awards in the pre-1958 and post-1958 claims to the extent of approximately 76 percent and 29 percent, respectively (approximately $113.6 million and $5.3 million, respectively).[41]

In the case of the claims against Vietnam adjudicated by the Commission, the inducement for the Vietnamese government to conclude a settlement agreement was the prospect of taking possession of the several hundred million dollars' worth of frozen assets of the former South Vietnamese government that the United States Government had held since 1975. Though it was nine years in coming,

---

37 Pub. L. 96-606, approved December 28, 1980, Stat. 3534 (22 U.S.C. 1645 *et seq.*).

38 Trade Act of 1974, Pub. L. 96-318, approved Jan. 3, 1975, 88 Stat. 1978 (19 U.S.C. 2901 *et seq.*).

39 Pub. L. 97-127, approved December 29, 1981, 95 Stat. 1675 (22 U.S.C. note prec. 1642).

40 *Agreement Between the United States of America and the Government of the Czechoslovak Socialist Republic on the Settlement of Certain Outstanding Claims and Financial Issues*, entered into force Feb. 2, 1982, TIAS 11264.

41 Annual Report to Congress for 2011 at 42, 50; http://www.justice.gov/fcsc/annrep11.pdf at 50, 58.

the Vietnamese government eventually agreed in 1995 to a claims settlement[42] which, despite the *ex parte* nature of the Commission's determinations and the possibly weak suppositions underpinning some of those determinations, allowed for payment of 100 percent of the principal amounts of the Commission's awards (approximately $99.472 million) plus over 80 percent of the interest to which the Commission had found the claimants entitled. Even the GDR claims settlement did not quite attain that level: In 1992 the government of the newly unified Germany paid 100 percent of the principal value of the claims which the Commission had determined (approximately $77.88 million) but only about 40 percent of the interest awarded.[43]

Concurrent with the completion of the Vietnam claims program in early 1986, the Commission turned to consideration of U.S. claims against Ethiopia, exercising its authority under Title I of the ICSA to implement claims agreements providing for lump-sum settlements of property expropriation claims—in this case, the U.S.-Ethiopian agreement of December 19, 1985.[44] That agreement provided for payment by the Provisional Military Government of Socialist Ethiopia of a total of $7 million in settlement of all outstanding U.S. nationals' claims, consisting of an initial payment of $1.5 million and ten semiannual installment payments of $500,000 each.

Compared with most of its other programs, the Commission's Ethiopia claims program was small. The Commission received a total of 45 claims, and of those it found 27 to be compensable. Despite this small number, however, some of the claims presented notable sets of facts and novel issues of international claims law. One of the largest claims was based on the cancellation of a government-granted regional concession for the purchase and export of gum Arabic and sesame seeds.[45]

In the periods of time leading up to Department of State's negotiation of the claims settlements with both Czechoslovakia and Ethiopia, representatives of the Commission were able to emphasize informally to the Department the importance of obtaining provisions in the agreements obligating the Czechoslovak and Ethiopian Governments to supply corroborating information to assist the Commission in accurately evaluating the claims it received under the agreements.

---

[42] *Agreement Between the Government of the United States of America and the Government of the Socialist Republic of Vietnam Concerning the Settlement of Certain Property Claims*, entered into force January 28, 1995, TIAS 12602.

[43] *Agreement between the Government of the United States and the Government of the Federal Republic of Germany Concerning the Settlement of Certain Property Claims*, entered into force May 13, 1992, TIAS 11959.

[44] *Compensation Agreement between the Government of the United States of America and the Provisional Military Government of Socialist Ethiopia*, entered into force December 19, 1985, TIAS 11193.

[45] Claim of Ethio-Gum Program and James E. Maxwell, Claim No. E-019, Decision No. E-034 (1987).

In both instances the Department succeeding in doing so,[46] and as a result the Commission received numerous responses from both governments to requests transmitted through diplomatic channels for details on specific cases.

The last Communist country with which the United States reached a claims settlement agreement, and under which the Commission then conducted a claims adjudication program, was Albania.[47] It is a small country, and the settlement amount was small—only $2 million. Despite the small size of the settlement, however, as of 2012 a portion of those monies still remains in the United States Treasury—mainly because a number of Albanian-Americans who had initially indicated interest in pursuing compensation claims through the Commission later decided instead to seek to resume possession of their families' former properties under the Albanian restitution laws passed by the newly democratic government. On the issue of claim verification, it is worth noting that in the case of Albania, unlike in other, earlier programs previously discussed, the transition to a democratic government in Albania in 1990 produced circumstances that allowed representatives of the Commission to travel relatively freely around the country to investigate and verify the facts of virtually all of the claims the Commission received.

The arrival of the 1990s also took the Commission off in new directions, first with the so-called "small claims" (valued at less than $250,000 each) against Iran arising out of the 1979 Islamic revolution that were settled under an agreement concluded at The Hague, Netherlands, in June 1990. Though they included a number of property expropriation claims, there were other types of claims that the Commission had never previously addressed, such as breach of contract claims and claims for wrongful expulsion. In fact, it was a breach of contract claim that gave rise to the Youri case, first before the U.S. Court of Federal Claims and later (unsuccessfully) before the Supreme Court, asserting a Fifth Amendment taking claim against the United States.[48]

In the mid-1990s the Commission took on one of its most challenging programs, the Holocaust Claims Program, in which it evaluated claims of Americans who had been held in German concentration camps during World War II. The program grew out of long years of effort by one of the participants in today's Colloquium, Steve Perles, on behalf of his client Hugo Princz to persuade the German government to give his case the recognition it deserved because of his having been detained in the Dachau concentration camp in disregard of his

46 U.S.-Czech Agreement (fn. 35 *supra*), Art. 4; U.S.-Ethiopian Agreement (fn. 37 *supra*), Art. VII sec. 2.

47 *Agreement Between the Government of the United States of America and the Government of the Republic of Albania on the Settlement of Certain Outstanding Claims*, entered into force April 18, 1995, TIAS 12611.

48 *Walter-Abrahim Youri et al. v. United States*, 36 Fed. Cl. 482 (1996)), aff'd 139 F.3d 1462 (Fed. Cir. 1997), *cert. denied sub nom. Gurney v. United States*, 524 U.S.951 (1998).

American citizenship. The claims were for deprivation of liberty and damage to health, and over 200 claimants received awards.

III. Nearing the End?

In the early 1990s, not long after the collapse of the Iron Curtain and the dismantling of the Berlin Wall, Francis Fukiyama published a book advancing the hypothesis that the world had "reached the end of history."[49] At about that same time, it seemed that maybe the Commission was also going to reach the end of its history: There were no U.S. claims against Communist countries remaining to be evaluated, once the Albanian program was completed, and the Iran and Holocaust programs both were based on foreign governments' actions from far in the past. However, as the 2000 decade progressed, that proved not to be true. In 2002, under a statute entitled the "Guam War Claims Review Commission Act,"[50] the Secretary of the Interior asked the Commission's Chairman to accept appointment as Chairman of the "Guam War Claims Review Commission," which she had been authorized to constitute pursuant to the Federal Advisory Committee Act, as amended.[51] The author of this paper served as Executive Director of the Review Commission's staff, and over the course of nine months the members of that staff conducted an extensive investigation and review to determine whether the people of Guam had been accorded parity of treatment compared with other U.S. nationals who had lived under Japanese military occupation during World War II. The Commission issued a comprehensive report of its findings in June 2004[52] and was then dissolved. The next year, in 2005, the Secretary of State used for the first time the referral-of-claims authority, spoken of earlier by Chairman Feighery, to refer to the Commission certain U.S. nationals' claims against Cuba arising after May 1, 1967, to be evaluated for future settlement negotiations with Cuba.[53] And after that, following the author's retirement in June 2008, the Secretary of State referred the terrorism-victim claims against Libya to the Commission for adjudication—a process which as of October 2012 remains ongoing.[54]

---

49 *The End of History and the Last Man,* by Francis Fukiyama, Free Press, New York, NY, 1992.

50 Pub. L. 107-333, approved December 16, 2002, 116 Stat. 2875 (50 U.S.C. App. 2061 note).

51 Pub. L. 92-463, Sec. 1, approved October 6, 1972, 86 Stat. 770 (5 U.S.C. App. 2).

52 *Report of the Guam War Claims Review Commission,* June 2004, http://www.doi.gov/archive/oia/Stories/warclaim/guamwcrcreport.doc.

53 FCSC Annual Report to Congress for 2005 at 15, http://www.justice.gov/fcsc/annrep05.htm#section2b; FCSC Annual Report to Congress for 2006 at 11, http://www.justice.gov/fcsc/06rpt/annrep06.htm#section2b.

54 Reports on the progress of the program are included in the FCSC Annual Reports to Congress for 2008, 2009, 2010, and 2011:

To conclude, a couple of final points would seem worth mentioning with regard to the advantages and disadvantages of having the Commission serve as the evaluator of blocks of U.S. nationals' claims. First, the exemption of the Commission's determinations from review by any court or government official[55] is important, as it helps to ensure that in the instances where a settlement fund has been established, payment of the Commission's awards is not hindered by demands for judicial or administrative review by dissatisfied claimants or others wishing to challenge its determinations.

Secondly, the Commission performs an important function by serving as a buffer to insulate the President and the Department of State from political pressures exerted by competing groups of claimants. Instead, the responsibility of determining the standards and criteria defining who is entitled to compensation, and how much, is assigned and reserved to the Commission. Of course, this requires the Commission to take great care in ensuring that those standards and criteria are clearly and rationally delineated and consistently applied. The author believes the Commission will continue to do all of that; during his tenure as Chief Counsel, he did his level best to ensure that it did so.

---

http://www.justice.gov/fcsc/annrep08.pdf, at 14; http://www.justice.gov/fcsc/annrep09.pdf, at 16;
http://www.justice.gov/fcsc/annrep10.pdf, at 13; http://www.justice.gov/fcsc/annrep11.pdf, at 15.

55 22 U.S.C. 1623(h); 50 U.S.C. App. 2010.

THE FUTURE OF THE FOREIGN CLAIMS SETTLEMENT COMMISSION RESTS WITH THE MODERNIZATION OF ITS JURISPRUDENCE: THE REGRETTABLE RESULTS ARISING FROM AN INTERSECTION BETWEEN THE FOREIGN CLAIMS SETTLEMENT COMMISSION AND THE U.S. INSURANCE INDUSTRY, A CASE STUDY

Steven R. Perles and Edward B. MacAllister[1]

A recent decision by the Foreign Claims Settlement Commission to deny compensation to a U.S. insurance company flouts the language found in applicable governing documents and effectively means that a U.S. insurance company will rarely, if ever, be able to win compensation at the Commission.

The Perles Law Firm, PC has represented victims of terrorism for over two decades, including several groups of victims of Libyan terrorism. One of these matters was a case called *Certain Underwriters at Lloyd's London v. Great Socialist People's Libyan Arab Jamahiriya*, Civil Action No. 06-731, which was filed in the United States District Court for the District of Columbia on April 4, 2006. The *Certain Underwriters* plaintiffs, which were a consortium of insurance companies acting as reinsurers for an Egyptian airline, brought that action against the governments of Libya and Syria pursuant to the provisions of the Foreign Sovereign Immunities Act, ("FSIA"), codified at 28 U.S.C. § 1602, *et seq.* seeking judgment and an award of damages for acts of state-sponsored terrorism that resulted in the hijacking of EgyptAir Flight 648 on November 23, 1985, while the aircraft was bound for Cairo, Egypt from Athens, Greece. The hijacking subsequently spiraled out-of-control and culminated in the complete destruction of the EgyptAir Flight 648 aircraft when Egyptian commandos stormed the plane. Despite the availability of a valid cause-of-action under US federal law for the reinsurers, the Foreign Claims Settlement Commission ("the Commission") has refused to compensate any of the reinsurers, a group that includes a U.S. company as defined by the Commission's own precedent.

EgyptAir the owner of the hijacked airplane, originally contracted with MISR, an Egyptian insurance company, which then sought to reinsure its risk by

---

[1] Perles Law Firm, PC, Washington, DC. This paper was the foundation of the oral presentation and comments by Mr. Perles at the 2012 Sokol Colloquium on the topic of "Jurisprudence of the Foreign Claims Settlement Commission: A look to the Future."

John Norton Moore (ed.) Foreign Affairs Litigation in United States Courts, pp. 187–199
 ISBN 978-90-04-25727-6

contracting with several insurance underwriters through the London insurance market. A London broker facilitated this complex transaction by contracting the reinsurance of MISR with many syndicate underwriters at Lloyd's of London and surrounding insurance companies, as is commonly done in modern commerce when the placement of the asset in question into the stream of commerce could create large scale exposure for its owner. The insurance companies who contracted to reinsure the aircraft for MISR are the *Certain Underwriters* Plaintiffs. The risk insured by the reinsurers was for the damage faced by MISR should the airplane be destroyed or damaged within the terms of the aviation hull war policy. The single U.S. reinsurer is a company called New York Marine and General Insurance Company ("New York Marine").

We represented not only the foreign and U.S. insurance companies, but the U.S. personal injury victims as well. The representation included the advocacy of the clients' interests in court and with the U.S. government, in an effort to force the Libyan government to settle the claims. This effort ultimately succeeded as the U.S. and Libyan governments signed the Claims Settlement Agreement ("CSA").[2] The court case was dismissed against Libya as a result of the application of the Libyan Claims Resolution Act ("LCRA"), Pub. L. No. 110-301 (2008), passed by Congress on July 31, 2008. On August 14, 2008, the United States and Libya entered into the CSA. Then on October 31, 2008, the Secretary of State provided her certification of receipt of funds in accordance with the Claims Settlement Agreement and with Section 5(a)(2) of the LCRA. In Executive Order 13,477, President George W. Bush espoused the claims of "United States nationals within the terms of Article I" of the CSA. Article I of the CSA refers to settlement of property loss claims brought by "nationals (including natural and juridical persons)" of the parties to the agreement.

The object of the CSA and the LCRA was to settle the claims of U.S. citizens against Libya for acts of international terrorism, and in return to restore Libya's sovereign immunity for its sponsorship of acts of terrorism. The LCRA contemplates a "comprehensive settlement... pursuant to an international agreement between the United States and Libya as a part of the process of restoring normal relations between Libya and the United States."[3] Eligible claimants would have the opportunity to seek compensation through a claims-settlement mechanism to be administered by the U.S. government.[4] Section 4(a) of the LCRA requires that the Department of State "designate 1 or more entities to assist in providing compensation to nationals of the United States, pursuant to a claims agreement."[5]

2 Claims Settlement Agreement between the United States of America and the Great Socialist People's Libyan Arab Jamahiriya, Aug. 14, 2008.

3 Act at § 3.

4 *Id.* at § 5(a)(2)(B)(ii).

5 Pub. L. No. 110-301, 122 Stat. 2999 (2008).

The cases, including the *Certain Underwriters* case, were referred to the Commission, which describes itself as follows:

> The Foreign Claims Settlement Commission of the United States (FCSC) is a quasi-judicial, independent agency within the Department of Justice which adjudicates claims of U.S. nationals against foreign governments, under specific jurisdiction conferred by Congress, pursuant to international claims settlement agreements, or at the request of the Secretary of State.[6]

The *Certain Underwriters* case continued against Syria in the district court however and the court later confirmed in its final judgment that all the reinsurers, including New York Marine, possess a valid cause of action against a state sponsor of terrorism under US law.[7] "[A]ctions may also be brought for reasonably foreseeable property loss, whether insured or uninsured, third party liability, and loss claims under life and property insurance policies, by reason of the same acts on which the action under subsection (c) is based."[8] Thus the Commission's refusal to award compensation to any of the reinsurers stands at odds with U.S. law.

Having a clear valid claim and cause of action, as confirmed by the recent *Certain Underwriters* decision, it is only reasonable to believe that Congress intended that the LCRA would provide an alternative source for compensating those with such valid claims under the FSIA.[9] Denial of recovery for New York Marine would contravene the expressed language of Executive Order 13,477, the Claims Settlement Agreement, the LCRA and raises the specter of a takings claim against the United States.

Despite the fact that New York Marine been a U.S. national under the Commission's guidelines[10] at all relevant times, the Commission has indicated that it intends to deny New York Marine's claim on the basis that its claim does not meet the "continuous nationality" requirement.[11] More specifically, the Commission argues that "in order for a claim to be compensable; the claim must have been held by a 'national of the United States' from the date it arose until the

---

6 http://www.justice.gov/fcsc/about-comm.html.

7 *Certain Underwriters at Lloyd's London v. Great Socialist People's Libyan Arab Jamahiriya*, 811 F. Supp. 2d 53, 71 (D.D.C. 2011).

8 *Id.* (*quoting* 28 U.S.C. § 1605(d)).

9 *Cf. Dames & Moore v. Regan*, 453 U.S. 654, 687 (1980) (stating in upholding the Iran-U.S. Settlement that the "fact that the President has provided such [an alternative] forum here means that the claimants are receiving something in return for the suspension of their claims, namely, access to an international tribunal before which they may well recover something on their claims.").

10 Both at the time of the underlying terrorist attack and the time of the filing of the claim at the Commission, natural persons who are nationals of the U.S. held, directly or indirectly, an interest in New York Marine equivalent to at least 50 percent of its capital stock.

11 *Claim of New York Marine and General Insurance Company*, Claim No. LIB-II-170, Decision No. LIB-II-165, at pp. 4–5, 7 (2012).

date of the Claims Settlement Agreement."[12] The Commission based its proposed denial upon these facts:

> a commercial loss that was first suffered by an Egyptian entity, EgyptAir. Through its insurance contract, this loss was then passed on to MISR, another Egyptian company. MISR, in turn, passed part of the loss, through an English broker, Leslie & Godwin, to a syndicate of underwriters at an English entity, Lloyd's, which included the claimant.[13]

Whether New York Marine has a cognizable claim before the Commission should be settled by the language found in the CSA, as required by the FCSC's enabling statute[14]—and widely accepted canons of statutory construction, in addition to a recognition of common place business practices. The Commission must "apply in the following order" first the "[t]he provisions of the applicable claims agreement as provided in this subsection."[15] The CSA states specifically that the objective of the agreement is to settle the claims of the parties' nationals and defines a claim by describing existing lawsuits brought under the Foreign Sovereign Immunities Act ("FSIA"). Thus the CSA explicitly settled the claim of New York Marine, a U.S. national with a valid claim under the FSIA.[16] And it is New York Marine's satisfaction of this two-step test that should qualify it for compensation from the Commission.

The CSA, related implementing statute, Executive Order and the referral itself all contain the same language to describe whose claim was settled by the CSA, a U.S. national with a claim under the FSIA. All these documents describe the settlement of existing claims brought by U.S. nationals in the present tense.[17] Thus, there is no need to resort to "[t]he applicable principles of international law, justice, and equity"[18] to define who qualifies as a "U.S. national." All of the pertinent documents speak of the U.S. nationals and their pending claims, which they *presently* possess against Libya.

To recognize and compensate the claim of New York Marine avoids the taking claim issue—as discussed in *Dames v. Moore*—that would result from construing

---

12 *Id.* at 4.

13 *Id.* at 7.

14 22 U.S.C. § 1623.

15 22 U.S.C. § 1623(a)(1)(C)(2)(A).

16 *See Certain Underwriters at Lloyd's London v. Great Socialist People's Libyan Arab Jamahiriya*, 811 F. Supp. 2d 53, 73 (D.D.C. 2011) (finding a cause of action for reinsurers against a state sponsor of terrorism that caused them "reasonably foreseeable property loss" under 28 U.S.C. § 1605A).

17 This issue was raised in the appeal of a denial of the claim of Francesco Zerilli. The Commission disagreed that the status of U.S. nationality in the CSA, LCRA, referral letters and Executive Order is stated in the present tense. Decision No.-I-019 at p. 4 n. 6. The Commission's views expressed in the denial of the Zerilli appeal are addressed below at pp. 10–12.

18 22 U.S.C. § 1623(a)(1)(C)(2)(B).

the Commission's jurisdiction to exclude U.S. nationals holding valid claims under the FSIA at the signing of the CSA. The DC district court in fact dismissed New York Marine's claim against Libya because it found that the CSA, LCRA and Executive Order terminated ongoing litigation by U.S. nationals with current claims against Libya. If a US federal court, reading the CSA, LCRA and Executive Order, dismissed New York Marine's claim on the basis that those documents required its dismissal,[19] which only could be true if New York Marine was a member of the class of U.S. nationals settled by the CSA, then the Commission must find New York Marine qualifies as a U.S. national in the January 15, 2009 referral letter because its usage of "U.S. national" is borrowed from the CSA, LCRA and Executive Order.

I. The Commission's Enabling Statute, 22 U.S.C. § 1623(A)(1)(C), Requires the Commission to Look First to the Claims Settlement Agreement in the Commission's "Decision of Claims"

Article I of the Claims Settlement Agreement ("CSA") settled the existing claims of U.S. nationals for claims under the Foreign Sovereign Immunities Act ("FSIA"). New York Marine is a U.S. national that had such a claim against Libya. The Commission's enabling statute requires that in its "decision of claims" the Commission "*shall* apply in the following order" first the "[t]he provisions of the applicable claims agreement as provided in this subsection." 22 U.S.C. § 1623(a)(1)(C)(2) (emphasis added). In interpreting a federal statute such as 22 U.S.C. § 1623, one must first look to the plain meaning of the wording of the statute; "[t]he first (and most basic) step on any interpretive path is the language of the statute itself."[20] The Commission failed to restrict itself to the "applicable claims agreement" as required by 22 U.S.C. § 1623(a)(1)(C)(2)(A), instead dropping down to 22 U.S.C. § 1623(a)(1)(C)(2)(B) in order to draw from "[t]he applicable principles of international law, justice, and equity" to define "U.S. national." However it is clear from the text of the CSA, and associated documents, that it settled the claim of any U.S. national with an existing, valid claim under the FSIA.

By signing the CSA, the United States and Libya intended to settle all valid FSIA claims held by U.S. nationals at the time of the signing of CSA and thereby immunize Libya against those claims. To restrict the settlement of claims held by U.S. nationals under the CSA to a smaller subset of claims held by U.S. nationals who were U.S. nationals at the time of their terrorism related injury would be to deny the intent of the CSA, which was to wipe the slate clean and end all U.S.

---

19 *See Certain Underwriters at Lloyds London v. Great Socialist People's Libyan Arab Jamahiriya*, 677 F. Supp. 2d 270, 275 (D.D.C. 2010).

20 *See, e.g., U.S. v. McGoff*, 831 F.2d 1071, 1077 (D.C. Cir. 1987).

litigation against Libya.[21] Libya sought closure as to *all* claims which were pending against it but the Commission's above-construction of the CSA leaves a small gap, perhaps no larger than New York Marine, in the coverage provided by the CSA. The Commission has no authority to ignore or override the mutual agreement of the parties to the Claims Settlement Agreement.

The Commission counters that the usage of "[t]he applicable principles of international law, justice, and equity" via 22 U.S.C. § 1623(a)(1)(C)(2)(B) is required to define terms in the CSA. However, in ascertaining the meaning of a treaty, the words used are to be given their natural and ordinary significance, and a sensible and reasonable effect must be given unless the words forbid it.[22] In other words, "the text of a treaty must be 'interpreted in good faith in accordance with the ordinary meaning to be given to the terms of the treaty in their context and in light of its object and purpose.' "[23]

The plain words of the CSA explicitly settled New York Marine's lawsuit. In the CSA, we find the following text:

- "the objective of this Agreement is to reach a final settlement of the Parties' claims, and *those of their nationals* (including natural and juridical persons);"
- "if such claim or suit *is against* the other Party... and such claim or suit *is brought* by or on behalf of a Party's nationals (including natural and juridical persons)...."[24]

This text refers to nationals of a party to the agreement and their claims and "pending suits."[25] This is language in the present tense. This is confirmed by the CSA's separate reference to the preclusion of any "future suits."[26] Article III states that "each party shall accept the resources for distribution as a full and final settlement of its claims and suits and those of its nationals as specified in Article I."[27] The compensation is explicitly intended for the claims settled by the CSA.

If the Commission interprets the CSA's usage of U.S. national to exclude New York Marine, then its claim was not settled. Then the question arises, where is New York Marine's claim? The Commission's interpretation would deny the

21 Although, "wiping the slate clean" and ending pending litigation against Libya under the FSIA must occur within constitutional limits by also creating an alternate forum to compensate U.S. nationals with valid claims under the FSIA. *See Dames v. Moore*, 453 U.S. 654, 686–87 (1981).

22 *See, e.g., Kreimerman v. Casa Veerkamp, S.A. de C.V.*, 22 F.3d 634, 638 (5th Cir. 1994).

23 *Id.*

24 Claims Settlement Agreement between the United States of America and the Great Socialist People's Libyan Arab Jamahiriya, Aug. 14, 2008, art. 1 (emphasis added).

25 *Id.*

26 *Id.*

27 *Id.* at art. 3.

intent of the contracting parties—to wipe the slate clean and end all U.S. FSIA litigation against Libya.

As described below, if the CSA was not referring to New York Marine's claim, then it could not have been espoused by the President under Executive Order 13,477 which raises the issue of a takings claim based upon the Commission's interpretation of the referral letter. Importantly, as discussed below the description of the class of persons whose claims are settled by the CSA—U.S. nationals with valid claims under the FSIA—matches the class described in the Libyan Claims Resolution Act ("LCRA")[28] and the implementing Executive Order 13,477,[29] and the January 15, 2009 referral letter could not have deviated from that class. As the letter itself noted, it was a response to Executive Order 13,477's command to the State Department to "establish procedures governing applications by United States nationals with claims coming within the terms of the Claims Settlement Agreement. . . ." The consistency of the usage regarding the class of claims settled by the CSA among these documents leads to only one conclusion: that the CSA settled New York Marine's claim, which was explicitly contemplated by the text of the LCRA, for the compensation mechanism it devised, and then the President espoused the claim in Executive Order 13,477.

Under 22 U.S.C. § 1623(a)(1)(C)(2), the plain meaning of the CSA must control and its lack of ambiguity precludes the imposition of "[t]he applicable principles of international law, justice, and equity" to determine when one must be a "U.S. national" via 22 U.S.C. § 1623(a)(1)(C)(2)(B).

II. The Libyan Claims Resolution Act, the Underlying Statutory Authority for the Libya Claims Program, May Be Used to Interpret the Claims Settlement Agreement

If the text of the CSA does not dispositively settle the question of whether New York Marine, a U.S. national with valid claims under the FSIA as described by the CSA, may be compensated by the Libya Claims Program, the Commission must be governed by the LCRA, the statutory authority for the Libya Claims Program. The Restatement (Third) of Foreign Relations Law of the United is quite clear: "[a] court *or agency* of the United States *is required to take into account* United States materials relating to the formation of an international agreement that might not be considered by an international body such as the International Court of Justice."[30]

The LCRA states in many different places that it and the CSA address *current* FSIA lawsuits brought by U.S. nationals, a group that New York Marine

[28] Libyan Claims Resolution Act, Pub. L. No. 110-301, 122 Stat. 2999 (2008).
[29] Executive Order No. 13,477, 73 Fed. Reg. 65,965 (Oct. 31, 2008).
[30] Reporters' Note 5 to § 325, at 201 (emphasis added).

indisputably fell within. The LCRA states its purpose is "[t]o resolve pending claims against Libya by United States nationals, and for other purposes."[31] The LCRA defines the CSA "as an international agreement between the United States and Libya, binding under international law, that provides for the settlement of terrorism related claims of nationals of the United States against Libya through fair compensation;" which once again confirms, also in the present tense, that the purpose of the CSA was to settle the claims of U.S. nationals with pending claims, which included New York Marine.[32] The LCRA defines a "national of the United States" by statutory cross-reference to 8 U.S.C. § 1101(a)(22).[33, 34] Finally, the "Sense of Congress" confirms the intent of the CSA:

> Congress supports the President in his efforts to provide *fair compensation to all nationals of the United States* who have terrorism-related claims against Libya through a comprehensive settlement of claims by such nationals against Libya pursuant to an international agreement between the United States and Libya as a part of the process of restoring normal relations between Libya and the United States.[35]

All claimants who were U.S. nationals at the time of the enactment of the CSA were to be included in and compensated through the Libya Claims Program.

A material section of the LCRA conditions the restoration of Libya's immunities from lawsuit on the receipt of funds to compensate U.S. nationals with pending FSIA cases.[36] Its subsection 2 required the Secretary of State to certify "that the United States Government has received funds pursuant to the claims agreement that are sufficient to ensure":

> fair compensation of claims of nationals of the United States for wrongful death or physical injury in cases *pending* on the date of enactment of this Act against Libya arising under section 1605A of title 28, United States Code[37]

This confirms the CSA's intent that the money funding the Libya Claims Program was meant to provide compensation to U.S. nationals *with lawsuits "pending on the date of enactment of this Act."* This is further language of the present tense—the lawsuits must exist at the time of the passage of the act. Just as with the CSA, the term "U.S. national" is only modified by the limitation to those possessing a valid claim under the FSIA. This match in description between the CSA and the LCRA to describe which U.S. national's claim had been settled is also carried over into the Executive Order 13,477, so that there can be no confusion as to what the

---

31 Pub. L. No. 110-301.

32 Pub. L. No. 110-301, sec. 2(2).

33 Notably, as explained below, the definition of a U.S. national under the LCRA matches that found in Executive Order 13,477.

34 Pub. L. No. 110-301, sec. 2(3).

35 Pub. L. No. 110-301, sec. 3 (emphasis added).

36 Pub. L. No. 110-301 sec. 5.

37 Pub. L. No. 110-301 sec 5(2) (emphasis added).

State Department meant by "U.S. national" in its January 15, 2009 referral letter, where it referenced both the CSA and LCRA.

Furthermore, statements in the Congressional record demonstrate yet further proof of the legislative intent behind the LCRA—that U.S. nationals with current valid claims under the FSIA lawsuits should be compensated through the Libya Claims Program. For example, then-Senator Joseph Biden stated in the Congressional Record that:

> If this bill [the LCRA] is approved... Congress will have joined with the President to solve an issue of national and international importance, while protecting the interests of *its nationals who have valid claims against Libya.* Under the Constitution, there is no question the executive and the legislative branches have the authority to work together to settle claims so as to help the hundreds of American claimants who will benefit from this initiative.[38]

Senator Biden also noted that it is his understanding the CSA will have "enough funds to ensure that *every* American claimant in these cases involving Libyan terrorism will receive financial compensation comparable to the Pan Am 103 and LaBelle settlements... *[a]nd [the LCRA] assures the American claimants that their lawsuits will not be extinguished unless the funding promised under the agreement is provided.*"[39] Senator Biden was commenting on the effect of the LCRA mandated certification of the arrival of funds for "fair compensation of claims of nationals of the United States... in cases pending on the date of enactment of this Act," which would also trigger the termination of those claims.[40]

In sum, the LCRA set the groundwork for the President to implement a bargained- for-exchange; to settle *all* valid claims held by claimants who were U.S. citizens at the time of the enactment of the LCRA, *in return for restoring Libya's sovereign immunity.* As Congress clearly expressed an intention to settle claims held by those claimants who were U.S. nationals at the time of the enactment of the LCRA, the Commission cannot undermine that intent by later unilaterally narrowing the universe of eligible claimants.

III. To Deny New York Marine Compensation Raises the Issue of a Takings Claim

Executive Order 13,477 could not have espoused New York Marine's claim unless it was a U.S. national with a proper claim under the FSIA, which matches the CSA's description of which claims it settled. Section 1(a) of Executive Order 13,477 states that the claims of U.S. nationals are espoused and settled and "according to the terms of the Claims Settlement Agreement." New York Marine's claim could

38 154 Cong. Rec. S7979 (daily ed. July 31, 2008) (emphasis added).
39 *Id.* (emphasis added).
40 Pub. L. No. 110-301 sec 5.

not have been espoused and settled by this Executive Order unless it was a claim of a U.S. national. Nor could its claim have been "settled" under Section(1)(b) as it does not qualify as a claim of a "foreign national."

As mentioned elsewhere, both the Executive Order and the LCRA define a U.S. national in the same way, which demonstrates the consistency of the intent of the relevant documents, which the January 15, 2009 referral references. The Executive Order defines a U.S. national this way:

> (a) The term "United States national" has the same meaning as "national of the United States" in section 101(a)(22) of the Immigration and Nationality Act (8 U.S.C. 1101(a)(22)), but also includes any entity organized under the laws of the United States or any jurisdiction within the United States (including foreign branches).[41]

And the LCRA defines U.S. national in the same manner:

> (3) the term "national of the United States" has the meaning given that term in section 101(a)(22) of the Immigration and Nationality Act (8 U.S.C. 1101(a)(22));[42]

If the LCRA and the Executive Order both define "U.S. national" in the same way, if one document speaks of a U.S. national in the present tense, so must the other. As demonstrated above,[43] the LCRA speaks in the present tense. The LCRA operated to restore Libya's immunity *in exchange* for the settlement of *all* valid claims held by U.S. nationals *at the time of enactment*. The Executive Order also speaks in the present tense, in Section 1(a) stating that the: "Claims of United States nationals within the terms of Article I are espoused by the United States and are settled according to the terms of the Claims Settlement Agreement."

As demonstrated immediately above, the Executive Order does speak in the present tense using the verb "are." Furthermore, to describe a U.S. national with an existing claim, where the U.S. national is defined as in 8 U.S.C. § 1101(a)(22), is to describe a person existing in the present tense. The modifier is the U.S. national *with* an existing claim.

The CSA, LCRA and the Executive Order are replete with verbiage indicating the CSA concerned the treatment of U.S. nationals currently holding claims against Libya. Article I of the CSA requires the Parties to "terminate permanently all pending suits," "if such claim or suit is against the other Party or its agencies or instrumentalities" "and such claim or suit is brought by or on behalf of a Party's nationals." Section 3 of the LCRA states: "Congress supports the President in his efforts to provide fair compensation to all nationals of the United States who *have* terrorism-related claims against Libya." (Emphasis added). And Section 1 of Executive Order 13,477 states that the claims of U.S. nationals are espoused and settled and that "[n]o United States national may assert or maintain any

---

41 Executive Order No. 13,477.

42 Pub. L. No. 110-301.

43 *Supra*, at 11–12.

claim. . . ." These three statements, by using the present tense, all speak to U.S. Nationals who had existing terrorism claims against Libya.

IV. The Commission's Denial of Claims for New York Marine Effectively Means that Insurance Companies Are not Welcome at the Commission

If the Commission denies New York Marine's claim, it has no other forum in which to press its claim. The Commission's application of a continuous nationality principle in this case would work a particularly pernicious result in the context of a claim by any of the several parties to a reinsurance claim:

> Indeed, the Commission has consistently required U.S. nationality for all of the relevant parties in the chain of insurance: the party that suffered the loss, the insurance company that directly insured the loss, and the reinsurer that paid the insurer.[44]

An aviation reinsurance contract will involve several parties, most likely from many different countries. Thus a claim for compensation for the loss suffered by the original party and subrogated to the reinsurer will be orphaned if every country were to apply the continuous nationality principle.

In this case, an Egyptian airline company suffered the original loss which was passed successively to an Egyptian insurance company that sold the risk through the London aviation insurance market to a group of reinsurance companies, including one U.S. reinsurance company. Thus the continuous nationality principle effectively means that this claim can not be compensated by an espousal in any of the three countries because the claim was never fully owned by a set of nationals from the same country.

As discussed, if the Commission denies that the CSA settled New York Marine's claim; it would have no alternative forum to press its claim. The CSA, LCRA and the implementing Executive Order 13,477 terminated ongoing litigation by U.S. nationals against Libya.[45] This deprivation of rights is constitutional only if the Commission was meant to be a forum to address the claims of all U.S. nationals with valid claims under the FSIA.

This interpretation is buttressed by an analysis of the circumstances surrounding another U.S. executive agreement which impacted the claims of U.S. nationals against a foreign country, the Algiers Accords. In Executive Order 12,294, President Reagan suspended ongoing litigation by U.S. nationals against Iran but only

---

[44] *Claim of New York Marine and General Insurance Company*, Claim No. LIB-II-170, Decision No. LIB-II-165, at p. 6 (2012).

[45] *See Certain Underwriters at Lloyds London v. Great Socialist People's Libyan Arab Jamahiriya*, 677 F. Supp. 2d 270, 275 (D.D.C. 2010).

in the cases where the claims would be cognizable by the alternative forum—the U.S.-Iran claims tribunal set up by the Algiers Accords:

> In the first place, we do not believe that the President has attempted to divest the federal courts of jurisdiction. Executive Order No. 12294 purports only to "suspend" the claims, not divest the federal court of "jurisdiction." As we read the Executive Order, those claims not within the jurisdiction of the Claims Tribunal will "revive" and become judicially enforceable in United States courts.[46]

In *Dames*, the Supreme Court upheld the President's suspension of claims in part because the claimants' property rights were protected by the provision of an alternative forum.[47] If the claims did not qualify for the Claims Tribunal, the alternative forum, then they would be "revived" in U.S. court.[48] Such is not the case in relation to the Libya claims, as there is no alternate forum for United States nationals, such as New York Marine, to permit a revival of their claim should the Commission deny jurisdiction.

New York Marine is a distinct category of claimant, a U.S. national both at the time of the terrorist incident and the time of the filing of the claim with the Commission and with a valid claim at law. In the *Certain Underwriters* case,[49] New York Marine is the single U.S. reinsurer among several groups of reinsurers, every other claimant is a foreign entity. Counsel for Certain Underwriters therefore filed a claim *only* for New York Marine with the Commission, in view of the CSA, LCRA and Executive Order 13,477, which only settled the claims of U.S. nationals who had pending claims under the FSIA. If New York Marine is not eligible for compensation, it is difficult to understand how a U.S. insurance company will ever be able to recover at the Commission, unless the insured was a U.S. person or entity, and a foreign insurer did not subsequently participate in reinsurance of the policy. Because of the catastrophic exposures associated with insuring an airplane or any other large, valuable asset, no single insurer or group of insurers is financially able to insure the entire risk and the pooling and division of risk among insurers and multiple reinsurers is a common place practice in modern commerce.

This reality is reflected by the amendments to the FSIA, which provides a cause of action to foreign and U.S. insurers alike.[50] Considering the Commission's

---

46 *Dames v. Moore*, 453 U.S. 654, 686–85 (1981).

47 *Id.* at 686–87 ("Our conclusion is buttressed by the fact that the means chosen by the President to settle the claims of American nationals provided an alternative forum, the Claims Tribunal, which is capable of providing meaningful relief.").

48 Executive Order No. 12,294, sec. 4, 46 Fed. Reg. 14,111 (Feb. 26, 1981); *see Foremost-McKesson, Inc. v. Islamic Republic of Iran*, 905 F.2d 438, 442 (D.C. Cir. 1990) (where a claim for expropriation did not qualify for the U.S.-Iran Claims Tribunal jurisdiction under the Algiers Accord, the claim was "revived" in US federal court).

49 *Certain Underwriters v. Syrian Arab Republic*, CA No. 06-731 (GK) (JMF) (D.D.C.).

50 28 U.S.C. § 1605A(d).

investment of time and resources in the Libya claims program, it is a likely venue for future claims programs if and when rogue states such as Libya, *e.g.*, the Syrian Arab Republic, or the Islamic Republic of Iran, resolve outstanding claims against their governments by U.S. citizens. For the Commission to play a useful role in that task, it must update its jurisprudence to match the jurisdictional scope of the FSIA.

V. Conclusion

The Commission's jurisprudence, which mostly predates the FSIA that created jurisdiction and causes of action against foreign sovereigns, is in sore need of an update to reflect both the jurisprudence of the FSIA and modern commercial practices. Otherwise, the Commission will not be able to play a useful role in the settlement of claims by U.S. citizens against Syria or Iran, and will continue to be an unfriendly forum for insurance companies.

THE HAGUE CONVENTION ON CHOICE OF COURT AGREEMENTS

THE 2005 HAGUE CHOICE OF COURT AGREEMENTS CONVENTION: A USEFUL TOOL FOR THE TRANSNATIONAL LITIGATOR

David P. Stewart*

I. Introduction

Despite the increasingly globalized reach of modern commercial dealings, the transactional lawyer today continues to face serious challenges in finding reliable and effective dispute settlement mechanisms. Most contracting parties to a cross-border business deal will instinctively resist agreeing to litigate disputes in the other's domestic courts. Seeking to resolve those disputes before the national courts (and under the national laws) of unrelated third countries clearly carries its own risks. Over the past several decades, international commercial arbitration has gained in popularity, partly because of its "delocalized" nature and the control it offers over *situs*, rules and governing law, but also because the reliability and enforceability of the resulting arbitral awards has increased. But for many, the increasing costs, complexities and time commitments of international commercial arbitration have become daunting. From the business as well as legal perspectives, there is a perceived need for a faster, simpler, more efficient alternative with at least as strong an enforcement guarantee as international commercial arbitration has seemed to offer.

This is the job for which the 2005 Hague Convention on Choice of Court Agreements was designed.[1] By its terms, the Convention will require Contracting States

* Visiting Professor of Law, Georgetown University Law Center. The author is retired from the Office of the Legal Adviser in the U.S. Department of State, where his last position was Assistant Legal Adviser for Private International Law.

[1] The Convention on the Choice of Court Agreements was adopted by The Hague Conference on Private International Law in June 30, 2005. The text and the report of the Diplomatic Conference are available at http://www.hcch.net/index_en.php?act=conventions.text&cid=98, reprinted at 44 I.L.M. 1294 (2005) and 6 J. Priv. Int'l L. 270 (2006). Under Art. 31(1), the Convention will enter into force on the first day of the following the expiration of three months from that date when then the second instrument of ratification, acceptance, approval or accession has been filed. To date, Mexico is the only

John Norton Moore (ed.) Foreign Affairs Litigation in United States Courts, pp. 203–226
 ISBN 978-90-04-25727-6

to give effect to exclusive "choice of forum" agreements in certain international commercial contracts. Not only will the chosen domestic courts in Contracting States be obligated to resolve disputes under those clauses, but the courts in all other Contracting States will be required to enforce the judgments which are rendered by those chosen courts.

By providing an internationally agreed basis for the recognition and enforcement of exclusive choice of court agreements as well as the resulting judicial judgments, the Convention aims to increase the certainty and effectiveness of such clauses, making them more attractive to contracting parties and more generally promoting transnational litigation as a reliable alternative to international commercial arbitration.

The Convention's origins lie in a more ambitious but ultimately unsuccessful effort to reach agreement on a broader convention covering both agreed principles of jurisdiction in civil and commercial disputes as well as the recognition and enforcement of the resulting judgments. Concluding such a treaty (generally termed a "double" convention because it would address both jurisdiction and judgments) was for many years a stated goal of the United States, in order to increase the recognition and enforcement of U.S. judgments abroad. Several early efforts had failed, including one convention agreed at The Hague Conference on Private International Law in the early 1970s and a proposed bilateral treaty with the United Kingdom. The third and most sustained effort began at The Hague in 1992. Despite intense negotiations and the preliminary adoption of a draft in 1999, the effort ultimately collapsed in 2002, due mainly to European concerns about certain expansive U.S. jurisdictional principles (such as "doing business"), extensive rules on damages (such as punitive and treble damages), and challenges raised by new forms of electronic commerce, which undercut confidence even in existing rules of jurisdiction.[2]

Building on the progress that had been made, negotiators then sought to craft a narrower agreement limited to international business-to-business agreements between contracting parties concerning civil/commercial matters that designate a single court, or the courts of a single country, for resolution of their contractual

State to have ratified the Convention, although the United States and the European Union signed it in 2009. *See Status Table: 37: Convention of 30 June 2005 on Choice of Court Agreements*, Hague Conference on Private International Law, http://www.hcch.net/index_en.php?act=conventions.status&cid=98 (last visited Dec. 15, 2012).

[2] For an elaboration of this background, see Louise Ellen Teitz, "The Hague Choice of Court Convention: Validating Party Autonomy and Providing an Alternative to Arbitration," 53 Am. J. Comp. L. 901 (2005); Andrea Schulz, "The Hague Convention of 30 June 2005 on Choice of Court Agreements," 2 J. Priv. Int'l L. 243 (2006); Matthew Adler and Michele Crimaldi Zarychta, "The Hague Convention on Choice of Court Agreements: The United States Joins the Judgment Enforcement Band," 27 Northwestern J. Int'l Law & Bus. 1 (2006).

disputes. Thus, the 2005 Convention focuses on *choice of court agreements* (or forum selection clauses, as they are often termed in U.S. practice).[3]

Assuming that it eventually gains widespread ratification, the Choice of Court Agreements Convention could potentially have significant and positive effects on the litigation prospects for transnational civil and commercial disputes. For one thing, it begins to fill a lamentable gap in the international legal structure. Some countries have entered into bilateral treaties providing *inter alia* for mutual recognition and enforcement of civil judgments, and a few regional arrangements do exist for this purpose (*e.g.*, within the European Community and the OAS).[4] But there is at present no broad international agreement on the conditions for the recognition and enforcement of civil and commercial judgments rendered by domestic courts, and the United States is party to no bilateral treaty with such provisions.

In some respects, the 2005 Convention is analogous to the 1958 New York Convention on the Recognition and Enforcement of Arbitral Awards.[5] Unlike agreements to arbitrate transnational business disputes, agreements to litigate disputes in specified courts remain subject to the vagaries of differing domestic laws in different countries. Because it is based on the principle of party autonomy, the Convention has obvious potential for increasing certainty and predictability for dispute settlement in trans-border civil and commercial contexts, based on forum selection clauses.

The following discussion describes the main provisions of the Convention, its scope and exclusions, and the ways in which (if ratified) it would affect U.S. law and the interests of U.S. parties to international transactions and litigation.[6] It concludes, in line with most other analyses of the Convention, that ratification would be in the interests of those parties and more broadly of the United States itself.

---

3 *See* Carolyn Dubay, "From Forum Non Conveniens to Open Forum: Implementing the Hague Convention on Choice of Court Agreements in the United States," 3 Geo. Mason J. Int'l Com. L. 1 (2011).

4 Within the European Union, enforcement of judgments is addressed by Council Regulation (EC) No. 44/2001 on Jurisdiction and the Recognition and Enforcement of Judgments in Civil and Commercial Matters, OJ 2001 L 12. Within the Organization of American States, *see* the 1984 Inter-American Convention on the Jurisdiction in the International Sphere for the Extraterritorial Validity of Foreign Judgments, available at http://www.oas.org/juridico/english/treaties/b-50.html.

5 The 1958 United Nations Convention on the Recognition and Enforcement of Arbitral Awards United Nations Convention on the Recognition and Enforcement of Foreign Arbitral Awards, June 10, 1958, 21 U.S.T. 2517, 330 U.N.T.S. 38 [the New York Convention].

6 For a practitioners' view of how the Convention might affect the drafting of choice of court clauses, see operate in practice, *see* Guy S. Lipe and Timothy J. Tyler, "The Hague Convention on Choice of Court Agreements: Creating Room for Choice in International Cases," 33 Houst. J. Int'l L. 1 (2010).

Although the United States signed the Convention in 2009, the Executive Branch has not yet submitted it to the Senate for advice and consent to ratification, pending a decision on how the treaty might be implemented domestically. The modalities of implementation pose a number of difficult questions. Because the Convention's requirements would necessarily apply in state as well as federal court, and because it would be the first treaty to regulate the enforcement of foreign judgments, how it is to be implemented raises sensitive issues of federalism.[7] For some years, the U.S. Government has been in consultation with interested parties about how the treaty might be given effect in domestic law—as a self-executing treaty or with implementing legislation—and if the latter whether the legislation should be solely federal or a joint federal-state effort (the latter is sometimes referred to as "cooperative federalism" approach). As of this writing, these discussions continue and no resolution has been achieved. The issues are briefly noted at the end of this chapter and will be explored more thoroughly in a separate and subsequent analysis.

II. The Convention's Main Provisions

As befits its origins, the Convention has a limited scope. It applies only to international business-to-business agreements between two or more contracting parties which involve "civil and commercial" matters, and only if they have agreed thereby to resolve disputes under those contracts by submission to a designated court (or courts) of a Contracting State.[8] Moreover, the Convention applies by its terms to "exclusive" choice of court agreements.[9] These agreements "must be concluded or documented: (1) in writing; or (2) by other means of communication which renders information accessible so as to be usable for subsequent reference."[10]

---

7 These concerns are not, of course, unique to the 2005 Convention but arise more generally (if in different ways) with other private international law treaties. *See, e.g.*, Peter H. Pfund, "Federalism and U.S. Participation In Intergovernmental Efforts to Unify Private Law," 56 Vill. L. Rev. 559 (2011).

8 An essential companion to the text of the Convention itself is the analysis prepared following its conclusion, with participation from the various states, by Trevor Hartley & Masato Dogauchi, Explanatory Report on the 2005 Hague Choice of Court Agreements Convention (2007) (hereafter "Explanatory Report") (text available at http://www.hcch.net/index_en.php?act=publications.details&pid=3959&dtid=3). A thorough textual analysis is provided by Ronald Brand and Paul Herrup, The 2005 Hague Convention on Choice of Court Agreements: Commentary and Documents (Cambridge Univ. Press 2008).

9 Article 1(1) states that "[t]his Convention shall apply in international cases to exclusive choice of court agreements concluded in civil or commercial matters."

10 Art. 3(c).

Forum selection clauses that do not satisfy all of these criteria—in particular, those that do not designate one or more courts in a Contracting State to the exclusion of all other courts for the purpose of deciding disputes which have arisen or may arise in connection with a particular legal relationship—do not fall within the scope of the Convention.

At the core of the Convention are three basic rules with respect to exclusive choice of court agreements:

(1) a court which has been designated by the parties in an exclusive forum selection clause has, and must exercise, jurisdiction to decide a covered dispute;[11]
(2) other courts—those that have not been designated by the parties—do not have jurisdiction over such disputes and are required to dismiss (or suspend) proceedings involving such disputes;[12] and
(3) judgments rendered by a chosen court in a covered dispute must be recognized and enforced in the courts of other Contracting States.[13]

An optional fourth rule, available by declaration, allows Contracting States to permit their courts to recognize and enforce judgments under non-exclusive choice of court agreements.[14]

This core structure begs a number of important questions regarding the Convention's scope of application.

What, for example, is encompassed by the term "*civil and commercial*"? The Convention provides no specific textual answer, but as used in private international law (particularly among the European countries), it means essentially a business-to-business context. Clearly it excludes criminal matters; some issues which are considered "civil" in U.S. practice (such as matters governed by labor, family or tort law or involving consumers) will also be excluded. In general, the "public law" activities of the government will not be considered "civil or commercial" but a government's commercial contracts are covered; application of the Convention is not prevented simply because one party to the contract is a "state" or a governmental agency or instrumentality.[15]

---

11 Art. 5(1).

12 Art. 6.

13 Articles 8 and 9.

14 Article 22(1) provides: "A Contracting State may declare that its courts will recognize and enforce judgments given by other courts of other Contracting States designated in a choice of court agreement concluded by two or more parties that meets the requirements of Article 3, paragraph (c), and designates, for purposes of deciding disputes which have arisen or may arise in connection with a particular legal relationship, a court or courts of one or more Contracting States (a nonexclusive choice of court agreement)."

15 Art. 2(5) provides that "[p]roceedings are not excluded from the scope of this Convention by the mere fact that a State, including a government, governmental agency or any person acting for a State, is a party thereto." *See also* Explanatory Report at paras. 49 and 85.

What is the meaning of the word "*international*"? Because the Convention applies only to international contracts, the question is important. The answer, however, depends on the context. Article 1 states that—for purposes of court jurisdiction—a case is international "unless the parties to the dispute are resident in the same Contracting State and the relationship of the parties and all other elements relevant to the dispute, regardless of the location of the chosen court, are connected only with that State."[16] Judgments are covered if rendered by a foreign court (*i.e.*, one in another Contracting State).[17]

What is an "*exclusive*" choice of court agreement? The answer is somewhat complicated. Under Article 3(a), an agreement is considered "exclusive" if it designates the courts of a Contracting State, or one or more specific courts of such a State, to the exclusion of the jurisdiction of any other state. Thus, the Convention would not apply if the parties to an international commercial contract provide that the courts of *both* of their respective countries will have jurisdiction over disputes arising from their agreement. But it would apply if the parties specify only one court, or designate two or more, or refer their dispute to "the courts" in a particular Contracting State. It would not apply to "asymmetric" clauses, such as those often found in bank loan agreements providing that the borrower may sue lender only in one court, but the lender may sue borrower anywhere he or his assets may be found. However, under Article 3(b), it is clear that agreements are to be deemed exclusive unless they expressly say otherwise.

The term "*court*" is not defined but is presumably intended to be interpreted broadly, regardless of the technical terminology applied by the relevant domestic legal system, so as to include public adjudicatory bodies capable of rendering final and binding decisions on the merits.[18] There is no indication that the term was intended to encompass decisions or awards, however denominated, of privately-appointed arbitral bodies whether domestic or international.[19]

A "*judgment*" means a decision on the merits, not a provisional order or an interim measure of protection.[20] In accordance with relevant international practice, the term "*enforcement*" should be understood to refer to the measures by which national authorities ensure that the amount which has been awarded to the prevailing party by the judgment is in fact paid by the losing party. It should

16 Art. 1(2). *See also* Explanatory Report at para. 11.

17 Art. 1(3) states that with regard to enforcement, "a case is international where recognition or enforcement of a foreign judgment is sought."

18 Article 2(1) states: "This Convention shall not apply to exclusive choice of court agreements (a) to which a natural person acting primarily for personal, family or household purposes (a consumer) is a party; (b) relating to contracts of employment, including collective bargaining agreements."

19 In fact, under Article 2(4), the Convention does not apply to "arbitration and related proceedings." *See infra* at n. 28.

20 Art. 4(1). As Article 7 states, "[i]nterim measures of protection are not governed by this Convention."

thus be distinguished from "*recognition*" (meaning giving effect to the judgment in other ways, such as in the context of *res judicata*) and from other ways in which a court might determine the rights and obligations of the parties).

III. Exclusions

Article 2 of the Convention specifies a number of exclusions which might be considered civil or commercial in the U.S. legal system but which are frequently governed in foreign legal systems by specialized legal regimes reflecting protective public policies.[21]

Among other listed exclusions are consumer contracts, contracts of employment (including collective agreements), family law matters (status and capacity, maintenance, matrimonial property), wills and succession, bankruptcy and insolvency proceedings, nuclear damage, and personal injury and property claims arising out of tort. antitrust (competition) matters, rights in rem in immovable property, marine pollution, and carriage of passengers and goods.

The Convention specifically excludes disputes over the validity of intellectual property rights with the exception of copyright and related rights.[22] Neither will it apply to proceedings involving claims of infringement of these excluded rights *unless* those proceedings are brought or could have been brought for breach of a contract between the parties related to such rights.[23] Moreover, such matters are not excluded if they arise merely as "preliminary questions" and not as an object

[21] Article 2(2) states that the Convention does not apply to the status and legal capacity of natural persons; maintenance obligations; other family law matters, including matrimonial property regimes and other rights or obligations arising out of marriage or similar relationships; wills and succession; insolvency, composition and analogous matters; the carriage of passengers and goods; marine pollution, limitation of liability for maritime claims, general average, and emergency towage and salvage; anti-trust (competition) matters; liability for nuclear damage; claims for personal injury brought by or on behalf of natural persons; tort or delict claims for damage to tangible property that do not arise from a contractual relationship; rights in rem in immovable property, and tenancies of immovable property; the validity, nullity, or dissolution of legal persons, and the validity of decisions of their organs; n) the validity of intellectual property rights other than copyright and related rights; infringement of intellectual property rights other than copyright and related rights, except where infringement proceedings are brought for breach of a contract between the parties relating to such rights, or could have been brought for breach of that contract; the validity of entries in public registers. Generally *see* Explanatory Report, paras. 50–92.

[22] Art. 2(2)(n).

[23] Art. 2(2)(o).

of the proceedings.[24] Contractual litigation over the scope of license/payment of royalties is covered.[25]

The treatment of preliminary questions is addressed by Articles 2(3) and 10. Under the former, if any matters mentioned above arises as a preliminary question rather than as "an object of the proceedings," they are not excluded from the scope of the Convention.[26] The same rule applies if the matter arises by way of defense.[27] Thus, one party to a dispute over an alleged breach of contract regarding royalties could not, merely by raising the alleged invalidity of the intellectual property right, displace the Convention.

By virtue of Article 10(1), a preliminary ruling given by a **court** on a matter excluded by virtue of Article 2(2) cannot be recognized or enforced under the Convention in other Contracting States.[28] Moreover, paragraph 2 of Article 10 provides that recognition or enforcement of a judgment "may be refused if, and to the extent that, the judgment was based on a [preliminary] ruling on [an excluded] matter." Article 10(3) adds that the recognition or enforcement authorized under paragraphs 2 and 4 of Article 10 (for payment of royalties in the example used above regarding the dispute between the licensor and the licensee) may be refused only where the ruling on which the judgment was based, namely the validity of the intellectual property rights (other than a copyright or a related right) is inconsistent with the judgment or decision of the competent authority in the requested State or another State where that intellectual property right is granted. This means that the State where the intellectual property right is granted finds it invalid.

Arbitration and related proceedings are also excluded.[29] The parties to an international commercial contract otherwise within the terms of the Convention may therefore decide to resolve their disputes by way of arbitration rather than litigation pursuant to their contractual choice of court clause.

By contrast, contracts of insurance generally fall within the scope of the Convention even where the subject of the coverage concerns a matter excluded from the scope of the Convention.[30] By way of example, although the carriage of passengers and goods is excluded under Article 2(2)(f), proceedings under a contract of insurance for such carriage would fall within the Convention's coverage.

---

[24] Art. 2(3). *See* Ved P. Nanda, "The Landmark 2005 Hague Convention on Choice of Court Agreements," 42 Tex. Int'l L.J. 773, 783–784 (Summer 2007).

[25] Explanatory Report para. 76.

[26] Art. 2(3).

[27] *Id.*

[28] The same is true, under Art. 10(4), for matters otherwise excluded because of an Article 21 declaration, which is discussed below. *See* n. 46.

[29] Art. 2(4).

[30] Article 17(1) provides that "[p]roceedings under a contract of insurance or reinsurance are not excluded from the scope of this Convention on the ground that the contract of insurance or reinsurance relates to a matter to which the Convention does not apply."

Moreover, recognition and enforcement of a judgment resulting from such litigation could not be refused on the ground that the liability arose from an excluded matter.[31]

Specifically not excluded are proceedings involving a government, a government agency, or any person acting on behalf of a government.[32]

Even with these exclusions, the reach of the Convention remains broad and able to encompass the most prevalent types of transnational commercial dealings, such as most contracts for the sale of goods and many types of non-employment contracts for the provision of services.

IV. The Convention in Operation

A convenient way to consider how the Convention is intended to operate in practice is to approach its application at the three critical events to which it is addressed: (1) what happens when the dispute is taken to the chosen court in accordance with the contractual choice of court agreement; (2) what happens if the dispute is taken to a non-chosen court in another Contracting State; and (3) what happens when the prevailing party seeks to enforce the chosen court's judgment in the courts of another Contracting State.

A. *Duties of the Chosen Court*

As indicated above, the heart of the Convention lies in Article 5, which provides in paragraph 1 simply that "[t]he court or courts of a Contracting State designated in an exclusive choice of court agreement shall have jurisdiction to decide a dispute to which the agreement applies, unless the agreement is null and void under the law of that State." Article 5(2) adds that such a court "shall not decline to exercise jurisdiction on the ground that the dispute should be decided in a court of another State." The clear thrust of the Convention is to provide contracting parties with the assurance that their choice of court agreement will in fact be accepted and respected by the court they have freely chosen—in other words, that the court they have selected will adjudicate their dispute.

Six aspects of these provisions bear emphasis. The first three are clear from the text: (1) Article 5 requires the chosen court to exercise jurisdiction over the dispute (meaning that, at the least, it must forego any discretion it might have to decline to do so) unless (2) the agreement is "null and void" under the law of that court, and (3) it may not do so in deference to any other court (clearly intended to rule out reliance on *forum non conveniens* or *lis pendens*).[33]

---

[31] Art. 17(2).

[32] Art. 2(5); Explanatory Report, para. 85.

[33] It seems clear that the exclusive choice of court agreement need not provide the exclusive jurisdictional basis for the chosen court to adjudicate the dispute. In other words,

The second three arise by implication and are best posed as questions: (4) if the chosen court would not otherwise have had jurisdiction over the dispute, is the necessary effect of ratification of the Convention to require the Contracting State to provide such jurisdiction; (5) is the exception for agreements which are "null and void" the exclusive ground on which the vested court may decline to exercise jurisdiction; and (6) what law governs the validity of the agreement itself?

The answers to some of these questions are clearer than others. Under Article 5(3), a Contracting State's rules regarding "jurisdiction related to subject matter or to the value of the claim" are not affected, and neither are rules on "the internal allocation of jurisdiction among the courts of a Contracting State."

By contrast, the Convention itself says nothing about the substantive validity of choice of court clauses, except to permit the chosen court not to decide a dispute when the agreement is "null and void" under its law. It appears that the law of the chosen court will govern the substantive validity of the choice of court agreement more broadly, so that such courts retain the ability to decline to enforce the agreement on other grounds as well, including for example public policy.

B. *Duties of the Non-Chosen Court*

In the event that a proceeding is brought in a non-chosen court within a Contracting State (which for convenience we will label the "seized court"), Article 6 of the Convention requires that **court** to suspend or dismiss the proceedings unless one of five exceptions applies:

(a) the choice-of-forum agreement is void under the law of the chosen court;
(b) one of the parties lacked the capacity to conclude it under the law applicable in the seized court;
(c) giving effect to the agreement would lead to "manifest injustice" or would be "manifestly contrary to public policy" of the seized court;
(d) the choice-of-court agreement cannot reasonably be performed because of exceptional circumstances beyond the control of the parties; or
(e) the chosen court has declined to hear the case.[34]

It may seem paradoxical that there are more exceptions to the seized court's obligation to refuse jurisdiction than there are to the chosen court's obligation to accept jurisdiction. They are, of course, more expansive than the grounds on which the chosen court may decline to exercise its jurisdiction. Nonetheless, they

---

the chosen court need not base its jurisdiction solely on the exclusive choice of court agreement, so long as the exclusive choice of court agreement chose the chosen court. *See* Explanatory Report, paras. 132 and 133.

[34] Art. 6. These rules will also apply if the chosen court transfers the case to another court in the same State as permitted under the Convention. Generally, *see* Explanatory Report paras. 141–159.

are still relatively narrow and unlikely to be satisfied in practice, and the general rule remains that, unless at least one of those exceptions applies, a seized court must suspend or dismiss proceedings brought before it in favor of the chosen court's jurisdiction, even though it would otherwise have jurisdiction to hear the case.

C. *Enforcement of Judgments*

From the practitioner's perspective, what might happen in the chosen or seized courts may not be important if the Convention is not effective when it comes to recognition and enforcement of the resulting judgment. In this respect, Articles 8 and 9 provide the "business end" of the Convention scheme.

The main rule, provided in Article 8(1) and (2), requires the recognition and enforcement of the judgment of a chosen court in the courts of other Contracting States, subject *only* to the exceptions specified in the treaty.[35] No review of the merits of the judgment is permitted, and the enforcing court is bound by the chosen court's findings of fact (unless it is a default judgment).[36]

This rule is tempered slightly by the requirement that the judgment must have "effect" and be enforceable in the State of origin.[37] If the judgment is under review in the State of origin or if the time limit for seeking "ordinary review" there has not expired, recognition or enforcement may be postponed or refused.[38]

Article 9 also incorporates a list of defenses that includes the invalidity of the agreement under the law of the chosen State (unless the chosen court determines it to be valid); lack of capacity to agree under the law of the requested State; untimely or improper notice; the judgment was obtained by fraud in connection with a matter of procedure; enforcement violates fundamental policies of the requested State include principles of procedural fairness; the judgment conflicts with a judgment rendered in the requested State; or the judgment conflicts with an earlier judgment in another State and the earlier judgment fulfills the prerequisites for enforcement in the requested State.

---

35 Article 8(1) says that "[a] judgment given by a court of a Contracting State designated in an exclusive choice of court agreement shall be recognized and enforced in other Contracting States in accordance with this Chapter. Recognition or enforcement may be refused only on the ground specified in this Convention." *See* Explanatory Report, paras. 165–181.

36 Article 8(2) states: "Without prejudice to such review as is necessary for the application of the provisions of this Chapter, there shall be no review of the merits of the judgment given by the court of origin. The court addressed shall be bound by the findings of fact on which the court of origin based its jurisdiction, unless the judgment was given by default."

37 Article 8(3) states: "A judgment shall be recognized only if it has effect in the State of origin, and shall be enforced only if it is enforceable in the State of origin."

38 Art. 8(4).

In Article 9, however, the Convention lists a number of grounds on which the requested court of a Contracting State may (but is not compelled to) refuse recognition or enforcement. Foreign judgments need not be enforced if:

(1) the relevant choice of court agreement was null and void under the law of the chosen court, unless that court has determined that the agreement was valid;
(2) one of the parties lacked the capacity to agree under the law of the requested State;
(3) the defendant (judgment debtor) was not notified in sufficient time to enable him to defend the proceeding (unless he appeared and defended the action without contesting the lack of proper notice) or was notified in a manner "incompatible with fundamental principles of the requested State concerning service of documents;"
(4) the judgment was obtained by "fraud in connection with a matter of procedure;"
(6) recognition or enforcement would be "manifestly incompatible with the public policy of the requested State" (including judgments obtained by manifestly unfair procedures);
(7) the judgment is inconsistent with a judgment of the requested State between the same parties; and finally
(8) the judgment is inconsistent with an earlier judgment from a third state that (a) is between the same parties, (b) is on the same cause of action, and (c) is otherwise enforceable in the requested state.[39]

The recognition and enforcement provisions of the Convention also apply to certain (but not all) transfers of cases. Thus, Article 8(5) states: "This Article shall

---

[39] Article 9 provides that recognition or enforcement may be refused if:
(a) the agreement was null and void under the law of the State of the chosen court, unless the chosen court has determined that the agreement was valid;
(b) a party lacked the capacity to conclude the agreement under the law of the requested State;
(c) the document which instituted the proceedings or an equivalent document, including the essential elements of the claim, i) was not notified to the defendant in sufficient time and such a way as to enable him to arrange for his defence, unless the defendant entered an appearance and presented his case without contesting notification in the court of origin, provided that the law of the State of origin, provided that the law of the State of origin permitted notification to be contested; or ii) was notified to the defendant in the requested State in a manner that is incompatible with fundamental principles of the requested State concerning service of documents;
(d) the judgment was obtained by fraud in connection with a matter of procedure;
(e) recognition or enforcement would be manifestly incompatible with the public policy of the requested State, including situations where the specific proceedings leading to the judgment were incompatible with fundamental principles of procedural fairness of that State;
(f) the judgment is inconsistent with a judgment given in the requested State in a dispute between the same parties; or, the judgment is inconsistent with an earlier judgment given in another State between the same parties on the same cause of action, provided that the earlier judgment fulfills the conditions necessary for its recognition in the requested State.

also apply to a judgment given by a court of a Contracting State pursuant to a transfer of the case from the chosen court in that Contracting State as permitted by Article 5, paragraph 3. However, where the chosen court had discretion as to whether to transfer the case to another court, recognition or enforcement of the judgment may be refused against a party who objected to the transfer in a timely manner in the State of origin."

Additional rules related to the recognition and enforcement of judgments are found in Articles 11–15. While the amount of an award or judgment is not reviewable in the enforcing jurisdiction, refusal of recognition or enforcement is permitted under Article 11(1) "if, and to the extent that, the judgment awards damages, including exemplary or punitive damages, that do not compensate a party for actual loss or harm suffered."[40] The evident purpose of this provision was to permit an enforcing court to decline to give effect to awards of exemplary or punitive damages (which are disfavored or even impermissible in some legal systems), not to permit it to review the quantum of damages or to consider whether it would or could have arrived at the same valuation as the chosen court did.

Article 12 addresses "judicial settlements" (also referred to as *transactions judicaires*). These are a form of supervised dispute resolution techniques used in civil law systems and similar to, but not the same as, agreements between disputing parties to settle their litigation. The rule adopted by the Convention is simply that such settlements are to be enforced in the same manner as judgments when they are enforceable in the State of origin in the same manner as judgments.[41]

The documents which a requesting party must present to the recognizing or enforcing court are specified by Article 13, including *inter alia* a complete and certified copy of the judgment; a certified copy (or other proof of) the exclusive choice of court agreement, and documents necessary to establish that the judgment has effect or, where applicable, is enforceable in the State of origin.[42]

The procedures for enforcing judgments will generally be determined by the law of the requested State. Article 14 states simply that "[t]he procedure for recognition, declaration of enforceability or registration for enforcement, and the enforcement of the judgment, are governed by the law of the requested State unless this Convention provides otherwise. The court addressed shall act expeditiously."

---

40 *See also* Paragraph 205 of the Explanation to the Convention (exemplary and punitive damages mean essentially the same thing: damages that are intended to punish and deter rather than to compensate for loss).

41 *See* the useful analysis of the Convention in light of U.S. law and practice contained in the Report of the Committee on International Commercial Disputes of the Association of the Bar of the City of New York on "The Hague Convention on Choice of Court Agreements," Sept. 8, 2006, available at http://www.nycbar.org/pdf/report/DOC182.pdf. (hereafter ABCNY Committee Report) at pp. 13–14.

42 Article 18 of the Convention states that "[a]ll documents forwarded or delivered under this Convention shall be exempt from legalisation or any analogous formality, including an Apostille."

Finally, the Convention expressly adopts a principle of severability with regard to enforcement of judgments, so that under Article 15, the enforcing court is obligated to give effect to part of a judgment if (i) recognition is being sought only for that part or (ii) if only part is capable of being recognized or enforcement.[43]

D. *Optional Declarations*

To a limited extent, Contracting States can limit or expand the scope of application of the Convention by means of certain optional provisions allowing specific declarations, as described below. These declarations incorporate a bit of flexibility into the scope of the Convention's application, in an effort to attract the adherence of States which, for particular reasons rooted in their national laws and policies, might otherwise have difficulty in ratifying. For the United States, the decision on whether to take advantage of any of these provisions is being considered by the Executive Branch in the context of implementation modalities.

Jurisdictional Limits. Article 19 of the Convention provides that a Contracting State may declare that "its courts may refuse to determine disputes to which an exclusive choice of court agreement applies if, except for the location of the chosen court, there is no connection between that State and the parties or the dispute." The evident purpose is to allow particular States to preserve fundamental jurisdictional requirements of a connection or nexus with the dispute or the parties thereto.

In the United States, such a requirement does exist under the laws of several states. By contrast, a few other U.S. jurisdictions, such as New York, have already declared themselves willing to resolve essentially foreign disputes where the parties have chosen New York law to govern those disputes despite the lack of connections.

Some advocates who support joining the Convention argue against adoption of an Article 19 declaration by the United States, contending for example that it would permit U.S. courts to decline to exercise jurisdiction over disputes having no connection with the United States and thereby undermine the principle of party autonomy on which the Convention is based. They further argue that an Article 19 declaration by the United States would encourage other potential Contracting States similarly to restrict their and its broadest application possible.[44]

Limits on Recognition and Enforcement. Under Article 20, a Contracting State may declare "that its courts may refuse to recognize or enforce a judgment given by a court of another Contracting State if the parties were resident in the requested State, and the relationship of the parties and all other elements relevant to the

---

[43] Article 15 provides that "[r]ecognition or enforcement of a severable part of a judgment shall be granted where recognition or enforcement of that part is applied for, or only part of the judgment is capable of being recognised or enforced under this Convention."

[44] *See* ABCNY Committee Report at pp. 13–14.

dispute, other than the location of the chosen court, were connected only with the requested State." Here again, the objective is to permit Contracting States to limit the application of the Convention in respect of judgments in cases considered essentially domestic under their own laws, thereby encouraging more States to become party to the Convention.[45]

In the United States, it appears that there is little need of or support for an Article 20 declaration. As in the case of the jurisdictional limitations under Article 19, this provision might attract a few more Contracting States but at the cost of limiting the application of the Convention in a manner inconsistent with the goal of promoting use of and respect for choice of court agreements in international commerce. Some contend that sufficient protection against risks of undue application of the Convention is provided by Article 9(e), which permits courts to refuse enforcement of a foreign judgment where the "proceedings leading to the judgment were incompatible with fundamental principles of procedural fairness of that State."

Exclusion of Specific Matters. Article 21 allows a Contracting State to expand the Article 2 list of excluded matters by declaring that it that it has a "strong interest" in not applying the Convention to a "specific matter."[46] Once again, the obvious purpose is to permit potential Contracting States to accommodate fundamental concerns about substantive issues as to which they have compelling reasons for retaining domestic jurisdiction.

Some consider the option unnecessary in light of the savings clauses under Articles 2, 6 and 9, which respectively allow a chosen court to take such interests into account under the rubric of "public policy" and similarly empower an enforcing court to do likewise.[47]

Inclusion of Non-Exclusive Choice-of-Court Agreements. Perhaps the most important optional provision is found in Article 22, which permits Contracting States to declare that their courts will recognize and enforce judgments given by courts of other Contracting States pursuant to *non-exclusive* choice of court agreements.[48]

---

45 *See* Explanatory Report, paras. 2311–233; ABCNY Committee Report at p. 14.

46 Article 21(1): "Where a State has a strong interest in not applying this Convention to a specific matter, that State may declare that it will not apply the Convention to that matter. The State making such a declaration shall ensure that the declaration is no broader than necessary and that the specific matter excluded is clearly and precisely defined." Article 21(2) provides that, when such a Declaration has been made, the Convention shall not apply either in that Contracting State or in others when an exclusive choice of court agreement designates the court(s) of the declaring State as the chosen court.

47 ABCNY Committee Report at p. 14. For an argument in favor of an Article 21 declaration for franchise contracts, see William Woodward, "Saving the Hague Choice of Court Convention," 29 U. Pa. J. Int'l L. 657 (2008).

48 Specifically, Art. 22(1) provides that "[a] Contracting State may declare that its courts will recognise and enforce judgments given by courts of other Contracting States

It appears that strong support exists within the U.S. litigating community for such a declaration.[49] Expanding the scope of the Convention to non-exclusive choice of court agreements would not only provide contracting parties with additional flexibility but would also encourage other countries to consider making such a declaration, thereby enhancing the enforceability of judgments rendered by U.S. courts designated in a non-exclusive choice-of-court agreements.[50]

Relationship with Other International Instruments. Article 26(5) permits Contracting States to address potential conflicts between the Convention and other treaties which might affect jurisdiction or the recognition or enforcement of judgments in regard to specific matters—in effect, allowing States to determine which should take priority in a given case. Because the United States is not a party to any other treaty addressing those issues, the provision has only potential future importance.

Non-Unified Legal Systems. The Convention makes an important concession to Contracting States with federal ("non-unified") governmental structures in which more than one legal system applies. Article 28 permits such States, by declaration, to specify whether the Convention will extend to "all its territorial units or only to one or more of them."

Along with Canada, Australia and various others, the United States is of course one of those "non-unified" States. Our federal structure, and the fact that much of the Convention deals with matters which are (and have been for a substantial period) within the purview of the individual states rather than the federal government, poses some difficulties with respect to implementation of the Convention. The problems are exacerbated by differences in the laws and procedures of our states, territories and possessions with respect to jurisdiction and enforcement of judgments.

However, unlike other common law jurisdictions with federal systems, it has never been U.S. practice to apply treaties only to a portion of the United States. It therefore seems unlikely that serious consideration would be given to an Article 28 declaration by the United States.

---

designated in a choice of court agreement concluded by two or more parties that meets the requirements of Article 3, paragraph c), and designates, for the purpose of deciding disputes which have arisen or may arise in connection with a particular legal relationship, a court or courts of one or more Contracting States (a non-exclusive choice of court agreement)."

49 *See* ABCNY Committee Report at p. 15.

50 Article 22(2) requires other Contracting States to recognize and enforce judgments made in a Contracting State that has made such a declaration if "(a) the court of origin was designated in a non-exclusive choice of court agreement; (b) there exists neither a judgment given by any other court before which proceedings could be brought in accordance with the non-exclusive choice of court agreement, nor a proceeding pending between the same parties in any other such court on the same cause of action; and (c) the court of origin was the first seized."

E. *Consistency with U.S. Law*

Current U.S. law is generally consistent with the fundamental thrust of the Convention, in that it supports party autonomy and gives effect to contractual forum selection clauses, including both choice of court agreements and those that submit existing or future disputes to arbitration.[51] Under the U.S. Supreme Court's decision in *M/S Bremen v. Zapata Offshore*, forum selection agreements in sophisticated international contexts are to be honored absent compelling considerations of forum state public policy.[52] Indeed, U.S. courts often refer to a "strong presumption" in favor of a plaintiff's choice of forum.

Moreover, the principle that the forum selection clause is separable from the underlying contract, explicitly adopted in the Convention and widely accepted in the context of international commercial arbitration, is consistent with current U.S. case law, which generally treats forum selection clauses in a contract as independent ("separable") from the underlying contract.[53] The consequence of this principle is that the validity of the forum selection clause is a different question from the validity of the underlying contract.[54]

At the same time, the Convention in its details poses some challenges. It is clear, for example, that private parties cannot agree on their own to override domestic law or to confer jurisdiction on a U.S. court that it would not otherwise have or be able to exercise. In addition, U.S. courts generally may refuse to honor choice-of-court clauses when giving them effect would contravene fundamental (constitutionally-based) concepts of fairness and due process. These requirements cannot be waived or overridden by individual contracting parties. Moreover, the common law doctrine of *forum non conveniens* operates as a discretionary basis on which U.S. courts may decline to exercise jurisdiction (including when it results from a choice by one or both parties to the contract).

Exclusivity of Choice of Court Agreements. Article 3(b) of the Convention provides that a choice-of-court agreement "shall be deemed to be exclusive unless the parties have expressly provided otherwise." For clauses falling within the scope of the Convention, this provision would effectively overrule current U.S. law, under

---

51 *See also* the ABCNY Committee Report, *supra* note 41.

52 *M/S Bremen v. Zapata Off-Shore Co.*, 407 U.S. 1 (1972).

53 Generally, *see Prima Paint Corp. v. Flood & Conklin Mfg. Co.*, 388 U.S. 395, 402 (1967), holding as a matter of federal law that arbitration clauses are separable from the underlying contracts in which they are embedded. Cf. ABCNY Committee Report at pp. 3–4.

54 The Committee's comments suggest that in regard to the scope of separability, Article 3(d) may go "too far in some respects and not far enough in others"—in particular, that separability may be read to encompass only challenges to the validity (rather than the very existence) of the underlying contract and by extending separability to challenges to the validity of the underlying contract that necessarily also call into question the validity of the choice-of-court clause. *Id.* at p. 4.

which forum selection clauses are generally presumed to be non-exclusive in the absence of clear and express language making them exclusive.[55]

The presumption is one found in U.S. decisional law rather than statute, and the determination is typically made case-by-case on the basis of the specific language adopted by the parties to the contract. In general, forum selection clauses are considered "mandatory" when they contain clear language showing that jurisdiction is appropriate only in the designated forum; in contrast, those that merely authorize jurisdiction in a designated forum, but do not prohibit litigation elsewhere, are considered permissive.[56]

Ensuring the enforceability of exclusive choice of court agreements is at the heart of the Convention. Because the choice remains with the contracting parties, and the change would only apply to clauses falling within the scope of the Convention, this change would seem to be beneficial.[57]

Forum Non Conveniens. A second way in which the Convention would alter existing U.S. law is by effectively eliminating the opportunity for U.S. courts to rely on the doctrine of *forum non conveniens* to dismiss cases falling within the scope of the Convention.[58]

As indicated above, Article 5(2) provides explicitly that a chosen court cannot decline to exercise jurisdiction on grounds that another court has jurisdiction. Under the *forum non conveniens* doctrine, a U.S. federal or state court has discretion to decline to exercise its jurisdiction where it concludes that an adequate and effective foreign forum exists and that adjudicating the dispute in that alterative forum would be fairer and more convenient.[59] Dismissal is not mandatory, however, and courts may decide not to do so in the face of an explicit choice of court provision.[60]

---

[55] *See, e.g.*, Montoya v. Financial Federal Credit Inc., 2012 WL 1965751 (D. New Mexico May 30, 2012).

[56] *See, e.g.*, K & V Scientific Co., Inc., v. Bayerische Motoren Werke Aktiengesellschaft, 314 F.3d 494 (10th Cir. 2002); Thompson v. Titus Transportation, LP, 2012 WL 5933075 (D. Kansas, Nov. 27, 2012).

[57] The risk that some parties may be caught "unaware" and thus inadvertently subject to the Convention's rules is inherent in all amendments and improvements to existing law. Cf. Committee report at p. 3.

[58] The Convention would also preclude the *lis pendens* (or "first filed") rule applied in many civil law jurisdictions. Explanatory Report at para. 133.

[59] Cf. Gulf Oil Corp. v. Gilbert, 330 U.S. 501 (1947); Piper Aircraft Co. v. Reyno, 454 U.S. 235 (1981). Generally, see Christopher A. Whytock and Cassandra Burke Robertson, "*Forum Non Conveniens* and the Enforcement of Foreign Judgments," 111 Colum. L. Rev. 1444 (2011).

[60] Cf. The Bremen v. Zapata Off-Shore Co., 407 U.S. 1 (1972). A plaintiff's choice of forum is typically given great weight in a *forum non conveniens* analysis, especially if the plaintiff is a U.S. national. *See, e.g.*, In Re Banco Santander Securities—Optimal Litigation, 732 F.Supp.2d 1305 (S.D. Fla. 2010); LaSala v. UBS, AG, 510 F.Supp.2d 213 (S.D.N.Y. 2010).

Precluding application of the *forum non conveniens* doctrine in cases where jurisdiction is based on a freely-negotiated choice of court clause is an essential element of the Convention, and would seem unlikely to work any hardship on the parties who have made that agreement.

Jurisdictional Issues. The Convention raises some important jurisdictional issues with respect to adjudication of the dispute as well as enforcement of the resultant judgment. These concern the court's duty (i) to exercise jurisdiction to adjudicate the underlying dispute when it is the chosen court and (ii) to enforce foreign judgments rendered by courts of another Contracting State.[61]

In particular, recall that Article 5(1) provides that a court designated by the parties in an exclusive choice of forum clause has and must exercise jurisdiction to decide a covered dispute, and Article 8(1) restricts refusal to enforce a resultant judgment to certain specified grounds, which do not include the enforcing court's lack of jurisdiction over the matter. In both instances, adherence to the Convention would require U.S. courts to have and exercise jurisdiction in circumstances where they might not otherwise be able or compelled to do so.

As a general matter, U.S. law and practice require some measure of connection with the forum as a prerequisite to the exercise of jurisdiction. This is true whether the issue is one of adjudicating the substantive dispute or enforcing a judgment from a foreign court. The requirement of an adequate jurisdictional basis is fundamentally a matter of due process; depending on the specific circumstances, it may be grounded textually in the federal Constitution or in the relevant state constitutions and legislation. The same is generally true with respect to enforcement of foreign judgments; the lack of jurisdictional connections can be a threshold defense in an action in U.S. court to enforce a foreign judgment.[62]

The problems are most likely to arise first, when parties with no other connection to the United States seek to adjudicate their dispute solely on the basis of their choice of court agreement and second, when a party which has obtained a judgment in a foreign court attempts to enforce in a U.S. court again despite the lack of any connecting factors. The second situation may well be less likely than

61 The requirements that the non-chosen court decline to exercise jurisdiction does not seem to present much of a jurisdictional issue under U.S. law. *See* ABCNY Committee Report pp. 6–7.

62 The precise jurisdictional nexus required for enforcement actions remains opaque. *See e.g.*, Lenchyshyn v. Pelko Electic, Inc., 281 A.D.2d 42, 723 N.Y.S.2d 285 (2001). Cf. Milliken v. Meyer, 311 U.S. 457 (1940); International Shoe v. Washington, 326 U.S. 310 (1940). The issue also arises in connection with awards under the New York Convention. *See e.g.*, Frontera Resources Azerbaijan Corp. v. State Oil Company of the Azerbaijan Republic, 582 F.3d 393, 397 (2d Cir. 2009). On this issue see Caroline Edsall, "Implementing The Hague Convention on Choice of Court Agreements in the United States: An Opportunity to Clarify Recognition and Enforcement Practice," 120 Yale L.J. 397 (2010).

the first (since enforcement actions are typically brought where assets can be found). But both are possible and central to compliance with the Convention.

Whether the acceptance of the Convention obligations (through ratification) would in and of itself be sufficient to overcome the problems is questionable, given the constitutional foundation of the nexus requirements. Another issue concerns the authority (or lack of authority) of the federal government to impose jurisdictional requirements upon state judicial systems, particularly if they would be contrary to state constitutional or statutory law.[63] It is possible that insistence on a sufficient jurisdictional nexus might be excused on grounds that it does not conflict with any specific provision in the Convention. With regard to enforcement issues, it is also possible to look to Article 14, which permits Contracting States to condition enforcement on local procedures.[64] It is also possible that an Article 19 declaration will be deemed necessary to resolve the issue.

Enforcement of Judgments. Other questions arise in connection with enforcement responsibilities under the Convention. U.S. law is generally quite favorable to the recognition and enforcement of foreign judgments and (with some variations among the several states) poses relatively few obstacles to implementation of the Convention's obligations. However, the Convention would narrow the grounds on which the resisting party could challenge the validity of the choice of court agreement.

In particular, Article 9(a) appears to provide that the only ground for doing so is that the [choice-of-court] agreement was null and void under the law of the State of the chosen court (unless the chosen court has determined that the agreement is valid). However, U.S. courts may decline to enforce foreign judgments if they determine that the jurisdiction exercised by the foreign court violated fundamental U.S. concepts of due process. It might well be sufficient in such a situation to rely on the grounds specified in Article 9(e), that enforcement would be "manifestly incompatible with the public policy of the requested State including situations where the specific proceedings leading to the judgment were incompatible with fundamental principles of procedural fairness of the State."

63 For an argument that resolving personal jurisdiction issue is appropriately dealt with in implementing legislation, *see* Peter Trooboff, "Proposed Principles for United States Implementation of the New Hague Convention on Choice of Court Agreements," 42 N.Y.U. J. Int'l L. & Pol. 237, 248–249 (Fall 2009).

64 Article 14 of the Convention provides in relevant part: "The procedure for recognition, declaration of enforceability or registration for enforcement, and the enforcement of the judgment, are governed by the law of the requested State unless this Convention provides otherwise."

V. Implementation Issues

In considering the implications of ratification, the Executive Branch will need to make a number of important decisions about the manner in which the Convention is to be given effect. Presumably it will continue to do so in broad consultation with the various interested parties, including among others the practitioners and private parties most likely to use and benefit from the Convention's provisions, the organizations representing the most affected industries (for example, those representing the insurance and intellectual property sectors), the federal and state court judges who will be obliged to apply the Convention in resolving cases, the institutional representatives of the states and their legislatures, etc. The following simply highlights some of the issues that will need to be considered.[65]

Self-Execution vs. Implementing Legislation. The United States will have to decide whether the Convention should be self-executing (*i.e.*, directly applicable as federal law without the aid of implementing legislation) or whether it should be implemented by means of legislation. The former is procedurally much simpler and would defer to the courts on resolution of the many difficult questions of interpretation as they arise in the context of specific litigation. By contrast, implementing legislation would give the political branches the opportunity to address and resolve issues such as those raised above in a broader (non-case-specific) context, providing guidance to the courts and thus contributing to a more uniform interpretation and application of the Convention.[66]

Federal or Cooperative (Federal/State) Implementation. Assuming that legislative implementation is pursued, the question then arises whether that legislation should be federal or state legislation or a combination of the two. The obvious reason this issue arises is that the Convention inevitably implicates questions of state law, not simply because parties to choice of court agreements may designate state as well as federal courts but also because questions relating to (i) the validity and enforceability of forum selection clauses and (ii) the enforcement of judgments rest primarily on state law.

In one sense, this presents a unique situation. The United States is not at present party to any treaty or convention specifically addressing the recognition and enforcement of foreign judgments or choice of forum clauses. Nor is there any general federal legislation in either area.[67] The effect of ratification of the

---

65 A useful analysis of these implementation issues can be found in the ABCNY Committee Report at pp. 9–13.

66 Notably, Art. 23 of the Convention states: "In the interpretation of this Convention, regard shall be had to its international character and to the need to promote uniformity in its application." *See* Explanatory Report, para. 256.

67 In 2005, the American Law Institute proposed a federal statute on the recognition and enforcement of foreign judgments. ALI, Recognition and Enforcement of Foreign Judgments: Analysis and Proposed Federal Statute (2006), available at www.ali.org.

Convention, however, will inevitably be to federalize both areas, by virtue of the Supremacy Clause in Article VI of the U.S. Constitution. The interests of the States are thereby directly implicated.

Given the expansive constitutional authority of the federal legislature in the field of foreign commerce, it does not appear that implementation of the Convention by federal legislation would in principle present the same type of federalism concerns that have been occasionally been raised with regard to treaties.[68] Moreover, a strong precedent is provided by the implementation of the New York Convention and the Inter-American Convention on International Commercial Arbitration through federal legislation.[69] Some argue strongly that, in an increasingly globalized world, enforcement of forum selections agreements and foreign judgments (whether or not based on choice-of-foreign-court clauses) should be governed only by federal law.[70] Others counter that federalizing the topics covered by the treaty is unnecessary, that the existing allocation of authority within the federal structure, as well as the substantive provisions of existing law, should be preserved, and that (for example) a uniform state law would be entirely adequate to the purposes of the Convention. A third approach ("cooperative federalism") would blend the two, by adopting federal legislation but allowing states to enact some form of uniform act which would be sufficient to satisfy the Convention's requirements at the state level.

Federal or State Jurisdiction. However the Convention is eventually implemented (directly or by legislation), a related and equally difficult question will need to be decided: whether federal courts should have exclusive subject matter jurisdiction to enforce choice-of-court agreements and foreign judgments falling under the Convention, or whether state court jurisdiction should be preserved.

If the latter, the Convention would have to be implemented consistently in both court systems. That presents an issue of supervision and control. The federal government has the obligation, and therefore the responsibility, to ensure

---

68 *See, e.g.*, Nicholas Quinn Rosenkranz, "Executing the Treaty Power," 118 Harv. L. Rev. 1867 (2005); Missouri v. Holland, 252 U.S. 416 (1920). Cf. United States v. Bond, 681 F.3d 149 (3rd Cir, 2012), cert. granted 133 S.Ct. 978 (Jan. 18, 2013); John Eastman, Will Mrs. Bond Topple Missouri v. Holland?, 2011 Cato Sup. Ct. Rev. 185.

69 The 1958 New York Convention, *supra* n. 4, is implemented through Chapter II of the Federal Arbitration Act, 9 U.S.C. §§ 201–208. The 1975 Inter-American Convention on International Commercial Arbitration (the "Panama Convention") (text available at http://www.oas.org/juridico/english/treaties/b-35.html) is implemented through Chapter III, 9 U.S.C. §§ 301–307.

70 For a particularly critical assessment of state interests in the Convention's implementation, *see* Stephen B. Burbank, "A Tea Party at The Hague?," 18 Southwestern J. Int'l Law 101 (2012). *See also* Burbank, "Saving the Hague Choice of Court Convention," 29 U. Pa. J. Int'l L. 657 (2008). A different view is provided by Tess deLiefde, "Filling in the Gaps: A New Approach to Treaty Implementation Reconciling The Supremacy Clause and Federalism Concerns," 66 U. Miami L. Rev. 267 (2012).

that the United States complies with its international responsibilities under the treaty. Because the treaty addresses issues that will almost exclusively arise in the context of litigation, the ultimate interpreter of its provisions will likely be the U.S. Supreme Court. But if (as seems likely) some parties choose state courts in their forum selection clauses, the Supreme Court's supervisory role will be at some distance. Accordingly, an argument has been made in favor of giving the lower federal courts a direct role in supervising the state judiciary, for example by providing a right of removal (particularly with respect to the enforcement of foreign judgments).[71] Whether such a rule would be consonant with the Convention is open to question. Permitting removal of cases initially filed in state court under choice-of-court agreements would seem even more problematic.[72]

VI. Conclusion

Despite the challenges posed by implementation, the benefits of United States' adherence to the Convention seem clear. It would provide private parties to international transactions a viable alternative to arbitration by making their choice of court agreements more reliable and enforceable. It would promote the long-standing U.S. goal of enhancing recognition and enforcement of U.S. judgments by foreign courts. It could encourage foreign parties to choose U.S. *fora* for their disputes and to seek enforcement of their judgments in U.S. courts.

More generally, it could contribute to increased certainty and predictability for dispute settlement in trans-border civil and commercial contexts based on party autonomy. As one has writer put it, "[t]he Convention has the potential to enhance world trade by creating the necessary legal certainty for parties to commercial contracts to control the risks they are exposed to in court litigation."[73]

---

71 The argument rests in part on such a provision in 9 U.S.C. §205, which allows removal of an action pending in state court related to an arbitration agreement or award falling under the New York Convention.

72 The main rule, of course, is that the parties' choice of court should be respected, so an explicit choice of state court presumably would not include a federal court. However, Article 5(3) does provide that the main rule "shall not affect rules (a) on jurisdiction related to subject matter or to the value of the claim or (b) on the internal allocation of jurisdiction among the courts of a Contracting State. However, where the chosen court has discretion as to whether to transfer a case, due consideration should be given to the choice of the parties." In addition, Article 25(c) states that "any reference to a court of courts of a State shall be construed as referring, where appropriate, to the court or courts in the relevant territorial unit."

73 Paul Beaumont, "Hague Choice of Court Agreements Convention 2005: Background, Negotiations, Analysis and Current Status," 5 J. Priv. Int'l L. 125 at 126.

At the same time, others caution against characterizing the Convention "as a great achievement in the history of multilateral reform of private international law."[74]

Overall, the Convention appears to enjoy broad support within the affected U.S. legal and business communities. Of course, as a multilateral treaty, the impact and success of the Convention will depend on widespread ratification. With only one ratification and two signatures to date, it appears the international community is waiting for the United States to act.

74 Richard Garnett, "The Hague Choice of Court Convention: Magnum Opus or Much Ado About Nothing?", 5 J. Priv. Int'l L. 161, 180 (2009).